DIVE THE RED SEA

GUY BUCKLES

Series Consultant: Nick Hanna

Interlink Books

An imprint of Interlink Publishing Group, Inc.
Northampton, Massachusetts

Guy Buckles ran a highly successful dive operation in Southeast Asia for many years. He is also the author of *Dive Guide Indonesia.*

This edition first published in 2008 by
INTERLINK BOOKS
An imprint of Interlink Publishing Group, Inc.
46 Crosby Street, Northampton, Massachusetts 01060
www.interlinkbooks.com

10 9 8 7 6 5 4 3 2 1

ISBN 978-1-56656-708-4

Publishing Manager: Jo Hemmings
Senior Editor: Kate Michell
Assistant Editors: Kate Parker, Rose Hudson
Design concept: Philip Mann, ACE Ltd
Design/cartography: ML Design
Cover design: Peter Bosman
Index: Alex Corrin
Production: Joan Woodroffe

Typeset by ML Design, London
Reproduction by Hirt & Carter, South Africa
Printed and bound in Singapore by Tien Wah Press (Pte) Ltd

Photographic Acknowledgements:
All photographs by Alex Misiewicz except: Guy Buckles 21; Footprints 50; Gunnar Bemert 137.
Front cover: *A diver explores a sponge on one of the Red Sea's many walls.*
Spine: *Grouper and anthias.*
Back cover: *A dive boat in the Egyptian Red Sea (top); coral trout outlined against the clear waters of the Red Sea (bottom).*
Title page: *A Spanish Dancer.*
Contents page: *Diver exploring a wreck, with sweepers and soft corals.*

Author's Acknowledgements

Many thanks to all the people who helped me to complete *Dive Guide The Red Sea*. Their time, energy and insight have made this a far better book than I could ever have managed on my own.

In particular, I'd like to extend special appreciation to the following:

Hesham Gabr, Jonathan Shawyer, Martin, Rajan, Robert, Barbara and the rest of the crew at Camel Divers in Sharm el Sheikh – too many to name, but all deserve a round of applause; Umbarak & Maria from Shark Bay – thanks for your generosity and enthusiasm; Sherif & Arman from Nesima Diving in Dahab; Mark Maurice and Marc Cornelissen at Subex in Quseir; Siag Travel for rescuing my car; Adly Al Mestikawy at Sanafir; Martin De Banks for excellent info on the south; Khaled for being a great landlord; Raffi & Rachel Shayngesicht in Israel – for years of friendship & unending information; Allan Colclough, Hussein M. Aimarh and the crew at Royal Diving Centre in Aqaba; The Red Sea Hotel, a home from home; Chris Hillman, Dania Avallone, Tesfamichael Basilius (Jerrican), Maria & Sabrina, Ato Tewolde Kelati & Eritrean Shipping Lines; David Wright at Dive & Sail; Alex Misiewicz, photographer extraordinaire and guide to south Sinai; and finally a huge thank you to my wife, Samira Abbassy, for following me to the desert when she had better things to do.

As well as those listed by name, my thanks go out to the hundreds of others who helped me along the way – there's not enough space in the book to thank each of you, but you know who you are!

Publishers' Acknowledgements

The publishers gratefully acknowledge the generous assistance during the compilation of this book of the following: Nick Hanna for his involvement in developing the series and consulting throughout and Dr Elizabeth M Wood for acting as Marine Biological Consultant and contributing to The Marine Environment.

Special thanks to **Gunnar Bemert** for contributing the dive site entries and the regional directory for the Saudi Arabia section. Many thanks also to **Jack Jackson** for his invaluable assistance.

Sixth edition updated by Jack Jackson, who has spent over three decades diving the entire Red Sea, including 12 years running a Dive Operation in the Sudanese Red Sea.

CONTENTS

How to Use this Book

THE REGIONS

The dive site areas included in the book are divided into six regions: Israel, Jordan, Saudi Arabia, Egypt, Sudan and Eritrea (including Djibouti and Yemen). Regional introductions describe the key characteristics and features of these areas and provide background information on climate, the environment, points of interest, and advantages and disadvantages of diving in the locality.

THE MAPS

A map is included near the front of each regional or subregional section. The prime purpose of the maps is to identify the location of the dive sites described and to provide other useful information for divers and snorkellers. Although certain reefs are indicated, the maps do not set out to provide detailed nautical information, such as exact reef contours or water depths. In general the maps show: the locations of the dive sites, indicated by white numbers in red boxes corresponding to those placed at the start of each dive site description; the locations of key access points to the sites (ports, marinas, beach resorts and so on); reefs and wrecks. Each site description gives details of how to access the dive site. (Note: the border round the maps is not a scale bar.)

MAP LEGEND

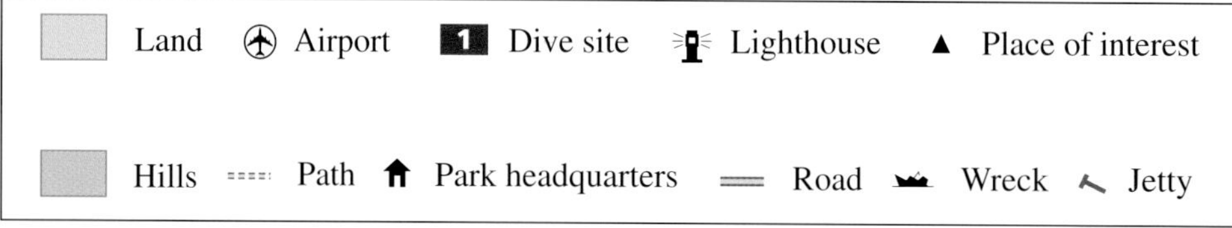

THE DIVE SITE DESCRIPTIONS

Within the geographical sections are the descriptions of each region's premier dive sites. Each site description starts with a number (to enable the site to be located on the corresponding map), a star-rating (see opposite), and a selection of key symbols (see opposite). Crucial practical details (on location, access, conditions, typical visibility and minimum and maximum depths) precede the description of the site, its marine life, and special points of interest. In these entries, 'typical visibility' assumes good conditions.

THE STAR-RATING SYSTEM

Each site has been awarded a star-rating, with a maximum of five red stars for diving and five blue stars for snorkelling.

Diving

★★★★★ **first class**
★★★★ **highly recommended**
★★★ **good**
★★ **average**
★ **poor**

Snorkelling

★★★★★ **first class**
★★★★ **highly recommended**
★★★ **good**
★★ **average**
★ **poor**

THE SYMBOLS

The symbols placed at the start of each site description provide a quick reference to crucial information pertinent to individual sites.

 Can be done by diving (applies to all sites except those that are good purely for snorkelling)

 Can be reached by swimming from the nearest shore (even if, in order to get to the shore, you need to take a boat)

 Can be reached by local boat

 Can be done by snorkelling

 Can be reached by live-aboard boat

 Suitable for all levels of diver

THE REGIONAL DIRECTORIES

A regional directory, which will help you plan and make the most of your trip, is included at the end of each regional section. Here you will find, where relevant, practical information on how to get to an area, where to stay and eat, and available dive facilities. Local non-diving highlights are also described, with suggestions for sightseeing and excursions.

OTHER FEATURES

At the start of the book you will find practical details and tips about travelling to and in the area, as well as a general introduction to the region. Also provided is a wealth of information about the general principles and conditions of diving in the area. Throughout the book there are features and small fact panels on topics of interest to divers and snorkellers. At the end of the book are sections on the marine environment (including coverage of marine life, conservation and codes of practice) and underwater photography and video. Also to be found here is information on health, safety and first aid, and a guide to marine creatures to look out for when diving in the Red Sea.

INTRODUCTION TO THE RED SEA

The Red Sea is the stuff of legend for most divers. It is the epitome of all that is enticing and fascinating about tropical reefs, with fabulous coral walls and gardens stocked with mythically beautiful sea life. Its exploration was pioneered by the giants of diving's early history: Hans Hass and Jacques Cousteau – Hass's films and Cousteau's maiden voyage here in *Calypso* were both influential in bringing diving, and the Red Sea, to the hearts and minds of a whole generation.

But diving is not the whole story. Away from the aquatic realm, the Red Sea region is a rich and varied patchwork of peoples, cultures and landscapes. Made up of eight separate nations, each with a distinct blend of ethnic and religious groups, but the same stark geography, the Red Sea is as fascinating above the waves as below them.

The Land

Formed along the massive fault line that separates the African tectonic plate from the Arabian plate to the east, the Red Sea lies along a northern section of this huge geological cleft – called the Great Rift Valley – which runs from the Jordan Valley in the north, down through the Dead Sea and all the way to Mozambique, thousands of kilometres away in southeast Africa. The sea is a 2235-km (1400-mile) section of this huge depression, which is flooded by the waters of the Indian Ocean entering through a shallow opening at its southern end.

Most of the Red Sea coastline is shared between Saudi Arabia and Egypt. To the north of these two giants, Jordan and Israel each has a tiny toehold on the northern Gulf of Aqaba, while Sudan, Eritrea and Yemen all have reasonable slices of shoreline, and Djibouti has a tiny piece of the coast at the Bab el Mandeb, the sea's southern gateway.

On all sides, the Red Sea is surrounded by remarkably similar terrain – a narrow band of lowland desert backed by rugged mountain ranges. This harsh but devastatingly beautiful landscape forms the perfect background for the deep blue jewel of the Red Sea. Dry rivers (wadis) run back from the coast to reach isolated green oases, while lofty mountain peaks are the remnants of active volcanoes.

Opposite: *Snorkellers enjoying the crystal waters off Gezîret Zabargad, Deep South, Egypt.*
Above: *Taking things easy in the bar while a diving group begins a shore dive at Blue Hole, Dahab.*

THE PEOPLE

The vast majority of the people living around the Red Sea are Arabs, though they practise different factions of the Islamic religion. Many other groups bring their own unique heritage and culture to the greater Arab identity, including Coptic Christians, Animists, Christians and Jews. Linguistically, while each of the region's Arab tribes speaks the Arabic language, each speaks it with its own distinct regional dialect, so there are considerable variations in spelling, pronunciation and vocabulary from group to group. Sudanese Arabic is quite bastardized while Yemeni Arabic is very pure.

As the southern Red Sea stretches down toward East Africa, a distinctly different mix of peoples begins to emerge. Southern Sudan and Eritrea each boasts a range of decidedly non-Arab ethnic and cultural groupings. Many languages are spoken along the southwest Red Sea coast, including Afar, Tigre and Tigrinya in Eritrea; Sudan's various tribes have more than 100 different languages and dialects, although on the coast mainly Arabic is spoken.

RELIGION

The dominant religion of the Red Sea is Islam, and Muslims make up the overwhelming majority of inhabitants of almost all the countries in the region. At one extreme, the ascetic Wahhabi sect controls Saudi Arabia, constraining all residents to follow codes of conduct laid down in the Koran and Hadith (traditions of the Prophet Muhammad); at the other, Egypt maintains a secular brand of Islam, stressing tolerance for its Christian and other minorities.

The Western media has tended, in recent years, to portray all Muslims as religious fundamentalists. This is, of course, not the case. Most of the region's Muslims are intensely proud of their religion and culture – and welcome the chance to show it to you – but they are also more than willing to tolerate your beliefs.

However, as guests in a predominantly Muslim society, there are certain taboos and restrictions that you should observe. These generally have less to do with religion than with common courtesy and cultural sensitivity. In a society that places a high value on modesty, for example, a Western woman dressed in shorts or a bikini (which is considered as outrageous as walking down the road naked) will receive stares, comments and hassle.

Aside from Islam, a number of other religious traditions coexist in the Red Sea area. Israel is the home of the region's only major Jewish community; Eritrea boasts a Christian majority, and both Sudan and Egypt have substantial Christian populations adhering to a variety of interpretations of the faith, including the Coptic and Catholic traditions. In addition, a small minority of people in Eritrea, and up to 20 per cent of the Sudanese, follow traditional animist religions.

WEATHER AND CLIMATE

Weather throughout the region is mainly hot and sunny, though in the winter months it can be cold in the wind at sea or on the coast. Some areas can have short periods of heavy monsoon rainfall. However, overall the high land temperatures and volcanic action underwater evaporate the water faster than it can be replaced by rainfall, producing a salinity level that is among the highest in the world.

Temperatures vary along the length of the Red Sea, although by the standards of most temperate countries the whole area is very hot. Northern Egypt, Israel and Jordan vary from freezing in the desert in winter to as high as 45°C (113°F) in summer, while in Southern Egypt and regions further south, winter temperatures can drop to 20°C (68°F) in the wind at sea and rise to a humid 47°C (117°F) at sea or 50°C (122°F) on land in summer.

Seasonal winds affect some regions' weather patterns. In the north, one such wind is the *Khamsin*, a blast of hot, dry air from the North Sahara desert that arrives between February and May. The name is derived from the Arabic for 'fifty' as it can last for up to fifty days. Off Sudan, torrential rain in southern Sudan and Ethiopia causes the prevailing north winds to become south winds during August. These winds cause the normally sheltered south-facing dive sites to become rough and reduce visibility to within a few metres thanks to the *Haboobs* that the winds often bring with them – violent squalls of Force 8 or more with dense sandstorms, which even well out to sea.

Because recreational Red Sea diving mainly began as land-based diving in the very north, the temperature on land made it sensible to visit the area in winter when the temperatures are not too high. More recently the northern areas have become package holiday destinations, which means that cheaper charter flights are available at this time. However, the water temperatures can be quite cold in the north in winter, and it can be cold in the wind out at sea. In summer, although hot on land it can be quite comfortable at sea and the water temperatures are more pleasant. Late spring is the time when many marine animals gather in shoals to spawn.

Craggy rock and brilliant blue water are typical of the Red Sea coasts.

TRAVELLING TO AND IN THE RED SEA AREA

Getting there

The majority of visitors to the Red Sea arrive by air. Each of the countries reviewed here has one or more international airports, served by a range of local and long-range flights. In the northern Red Sea destinations, the scheduled flights of major carriers are augmented by a range of charter flights, making access to these areas easy and inexpensive. Many countries have domestic routes linking the diving areas with the international airports. Internet-only cheaper flights are available from the UK to Sharm el Sheikh and Marsa 'Alam, see www.redseaflights.com.

In Israel, Eilat is the closest airport to the dive sites but it can only accommodate small aircraft; some divers fly to Tel Aviv and then travel to Eilat by road, but the majority fly to the military airport at Ovda, 40 minutes from Eilat by road. Some tourists will cross the border to and from the airport at Aqaba in Jordan. Egypt currently has international airports receiving charter flights at Râs el Naqb for Northern Sinai, Sharm el Sheikh (the airport is at Râs Nusrâni) for Southern Sinai, Hurghada for itself, El Gouna and Port Sâfaga, and Marsa 'Alam for deep, southern Egypt. There are also connecting flights and asphalt roads from Cairo. Sudan's air connections have deteriorated over the past years, but if you fly directly to Port Sudan (via Cairo) the local agents can sort out any problems and Customs are accustomed to diving equipment and do not request a bond, unlike the situation if you fly via Khartoum. Eritrea's Asmara airport has good international connections, but little recreational diving now occurs there. Yemen's Sana'a airport also has good international connections, but recent events have put tourism there on hold. Djibouti has international connections with France.

Arriving by land and sea is an attractive option for European residents who want to see a bit of the Middle East. Car and passenger ferries link Alexandria, in Egypt, with Greece and Italy; Haifa in Israel is linked by ferries from Greece and Cyprus. For the adventurous, there is the overland route through Turkey and Syria to Jordan. Train and bus services work well in Egypt. Opting to drive your own car is not an option for the faint-hearted. Bureaucratic obstacles begin before you leave home (you will need a *Carnet de Passages en Douane* – a sort of international customs guarantee – from an automobile association) and mount steadily as you progress.

Opposite: *Divers preparing for a shore dive, south of el Quseir, Egypt.*

Above: *In Egypt, dive centres are often situated right on the beach next to the entry points.*

GETTING AROUND

Domestic flights and short-hop international flights link most of the countries in the region. Schedules range from several daily flights between the major centres of the north, to once-a-week links between some of the southern countries.

Ferries run internally between Sharm el Sheikh and Hurghada, and internationally between Nuweiba in Egypt and Aqaba in Jordan. The Hurghada service is only for passengers, but the Aqaba-Nuweiba service takes cars.

The Egyptian/Sudanese border at Wadi Halfa is now open again, so it is possible to travel overland from Jordan to Sudan, but the route south of this border to about 160km (100 miles) north of Khartoum has no roads; it requires a good four-wheel drive vehicle and desert driving experience. The coastal route, Southern Sudan and all other Sudanese borders are still closed. It is possible to get a transit visa through Saudi Arabia into Yemen or the United Arab Emirates and then get a boat onward to Djibouti or Kenya for travel further south, avoiding Eritrea and Sudan. The route through Yemen used to be popular, but since 1999 there have been several fatal incidents involving tourists on this route. There are many restrictions on those crossing Saudi Arabia, especially women.

Car rental, on a self-drive or chauffeured basis, is an option in Egypt, Israel and Jordan. If you plan on driving yourself, you will need to be over 25 years of age and must bring the correct international driving permit (available through automobile associations) and a major credit card.

Public transport overland between and within countries comes in a number of forms. Buses of all types ply a wide variety of routes, from the air-conditioned splendour of Israeli tour buses to the rattletrap unreliability of Sudan's local bus services. Service taxis operate over most of the region. These are basically estate cars, which run on set routes for a set price, departing when all seats are filled. They are quicker and more comfortable than buses as a general rule. Minivans often fulfil the same function as service taxis.

In urban areas, local taxis sometimes operate in the same way as service taxis, running fixed routes for fixed prices. However, there are also plenty of taxis operating in the Western way, in which you charter the entire vehicle. Buses and minibuses also run in most towns, and in some tourist areas you can rent bicycles, motorcycles and even off-road quadbikes to get around on.

BATTERIES

If you intend to pack anything that requires batteries, such as personal stereos, underwater lights, camera equipment or other electronic items, you should be aware of some local difficulties in obtaining batteries.

First, some sizes of battery, such as AAA and C size cells, are unavailable or difficult to find in some areas. If you know you need them, bring a good supply of your own. You may want to bring your own supply of even the readily available AA and D cells, as locally purchased batteries have a reputation for low power and early failure. A set of Western alkalines can last two to three times longer.

A battery charger and a supply of rechargeable NiMH batteries is a sensible alternative for heavy battery users; 220-volt power is standard throughout the Red Sea, so choose your charger accordingly. Be aware, though, that power blackouts may occur, and generators on live-aboards may only work for a few hours a day, so you should have some backup alkalines with you just in case.

VISAS

Visa regulations differ from country to country, but in almost all cases you will need a visa to enter any of the countries surrounding the Red Sea. National regulations range from the draconian to the accommodating: Saudi Arabia has at last begun to allow tourists in special circumstances including diving; your local Saudi Arabian dive operator will have to act as sponsor for you to obtain a visa. Jordan, Israel and Egypt will all issue visas on arrival for most nationalities. You should check with the nearest embassy or consulate of the country you intend to visit for full details, but a few tips are listed below.

The visa issued on arrival at Sharm el Sheikh is valid for travel only within a limited portion of the Sinai, so if you intend to travel elsewhere in Egypt, get a full visa in advance.

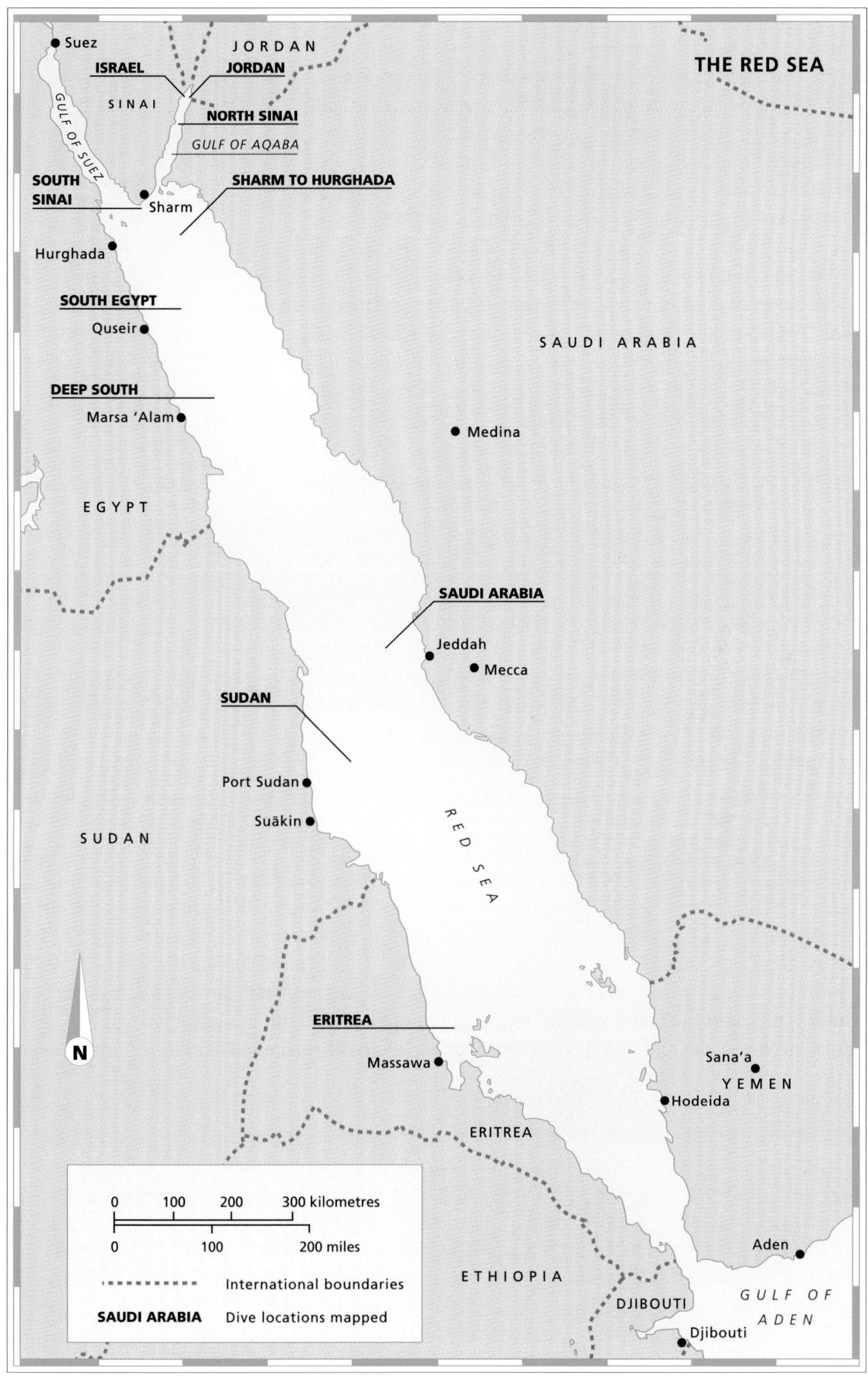
THE RED SEA
Suez
JORDAN
ISRAEL
JORDAN
SINAI
GULF OF SUEZ
NORTH SINAI
GULF OF AQABA
SOUTH SINAI
Sharm
SHARM TO HURGHADA
Hurghada
SOUTH EGYPT
Quseir
SAUDI ARABIA
DEEP SOUTH
Marsa 'Alam
Medina
EGYPT
SAUDI ARABIA
Jeddah
Mecca
SUDAN
Port Sudan
Suākin
SUDAN
RED SEA
ERITREA
Massawa
Sana'a
YEMEN
Hodeida
ERITREA
0 100 200 300 kilometres
0 100 200 miles
International boundaries
SAUDI ARABIA Dive locations mapped
ETHIOPIA
Aden
DJIBOUTI
Djibouti
GULF OF ADEN
N

If you plan to visit Sudan, apply for your visa early, as processing can take several weeks. You are well advised to apply from home rather than at an embassy in the Middle East. Under no circumstances should you apply at the Cairo consulate, as applications are invariably turned down.

The peace process has paid dividends, and it is now no problem to visit Egypt and Jordan if you have Israeli stamps in your passport. Other countries in the region are not so liberal, however. Sudan, Yemen, Saudi Arabia, and most of the world's Islamic countries maintain a ban on the entry of anyone who has been in Israel. The Israelis have responded to these restrictions by providing their visas on separate sheets of paper on request, so anti-Israeli countries now routinely check for exit stamps from neighbouring countries, Taba in Egypt and Maber/Wadi al 'Araba in Jordan being their prime targets. If there is evidence that you have crossed a border into Israel, you will be refused. If you have any such stamps in your passport it is wise to get a new one before applying.

FOOD HYGIENE

The most severe health problem most travellers are likely to encounter is diarrhoea. There are a few basic measures which will make an attack less likely:

- Never drink water (or any other drink) which does not come from a sealed container, unless you are sure it has been thoroughly boiled for at least ten minutes.
- It is advisable not to eat raw vegetables, including salads, or fruit, unless you peel them yourself.
- Cooking is the best method of killing germs. Try to eat only freshly cooked rather than pre-prepared dishes, especially for the first few days. Reheated dishes may not be heated above boiling point all the way through.
- Use boiled or bottled water even for tooth-brushing.
- Don't have ice in your drinks unless you are certain it is made from boiled water.

HEALTH AND INOCULATIONS

In Britain, MASTA (Medical Advisory Services for Travellers Abroad) are affiliated to the London School of Hygiene and Tropical Medicine and offer health briefs on specific countries for a fee – tel 0906 8224100; www.masta.org. The British Airways Travel Clinics (tel 020 7439 9584), other travel clinics, and your local GP can also arrange vaccinations and advise you on your inoculation schedule.

Vaccinations for typhoid, paratyphoid, tetanus, meningitis and polio are all recommended. If you are not immune to Hepatitis A then the HAVRIX vaccine is worth having. You will be required to show proof of vaccination for yellow fever if you have visited an infected region within one week of your arrival. An International Health Certificate, issued by the clinic that administered your inoculations and kept up to date, should be carried and presented if asked for. Malaria occurs in all countries bordering the Red Sea, and Western visitors are advised to take a course of anti-malarial prophylactics, starting at least one week before arrival, throughout your stay and continuing for six weeks after your return. Many countries now have strains of malaria that are resistant to most medication, so check with a knowledgeable doctor as to which prophylactics you should take. It is easy to think that if you are going to be on a live-aboard that you will not experience mosquitoes, but you have to travel to and from the live-aboard at the start and end of your holiday, and just one bite is enough to contract malaria or Dengue fever. (See box on page 17 for more information.) Two new Cholera vaccines, Dukoral and Mutacol, were recently licensed for use in many countries other than America. Dukoral helps protect travellers against enterotoxigenic Escherichia coli (ETEC), the most common cause of travellers' diarrhoea, and in the UK is recommended for adventurous people travelling to remote regions with limited access to medical care.

MONEY

The currencies of each of the countries discussed in this book are: Israel: the new Israeli shekel (NIS); Jordan: Jordanian dinar (JD); Saudi Arabia: Saudi riyal (SAR); Egypt:

Egyptian pound (LE); Sudan: the Sudanese dinar (SDD) replaced the Sudanese pound in 1992, though the Sudanese pound is still legal tender; Eritrea: Eritrean Nafka; Djibouti: Djibouti Franc (FD); and Yemen: Yemeni riyal (YR).

In general, banks give the best exchange rates in most countries, but may have very short opening hours, and are usually closed on every holiday. Official money-changers exist in countries with more developed tourist industries; these are open well into the evening, seven days a week in major tourist areas.

US dollars and, to a lesser extent, pounds sterling, are the favoured currencies. You can change most other major currencies at banks and money-changers in major cities and tourist destinations, but the exchange rate will often be lower. In some areas US dollars are the only foreign currency recognized, so you would be well advised to bring a supply, both in traveller's cheques and cash.

Credit cards are accepted in many shops and hotels in urban and tourist centres in Jordan, Israel and Egypt, and can even be used in some quite remote regions. Many banks and some money-changers give cash advances against credit cards. Visa and Mastercard are widely accepted, American Express to a slightly lesser degree. Other cards may be difficult to use even in the north, and you should be aware that a surcharge of up to four per cent may be levied on credit card transactions. In the south, it is a different story. Plastic is virtually useless in Sudan and Eritrea, and you should take a good supply of US dollars in both traveller's cheques and cash. In Yemen much better exchange rates are available for cash. Also be aware that many countries in the region have strict exchange restrictions: you will rarely be able to re-exchange local currency for foreign currency on your way out of the country even if you have kept official bank receipts of your original exchange.

Finally, don't assume that you will always be able to change money at airports on arrival or departure. Many airports have twenty-four-hour banking, but some airport banks close in the evenings and through the night. The bank at the airport in Asmara (Eritrea) will change hard currency into Eritrean Nafkas, but not vice versa.

MOSQUITO-BORNE DISEASES

One of the biggest health worries for travellers in the tropics is malaria, a parasitic disease spread by the Anopheles mosquito. Anti-malarial medicines exist, and short-term visitors are encouraged to take them, but there are other considerations you should be aware of:

- Many anti-malarial drugs have side effects, and the side effects of the newer ones may not yet be known. Confirm with your doctor which medicines you should take.
- There are many strains of malaria, some of which are resistant to certain drugs. You may need to take a combination of medicines for adequate protection.
- No anti-malarial drug is 100 per cent effective. It is important to avoid being bitten. Use repellent lotion, mosquito coils and mosquito netting when possible, especially between sunset and sunrise.
- Many people are unaware of dengue fever, another mosquito-borne disease endemic in much of the world. It can be as debilitating and life-threatening as malaria, and is also excruciatingly painful. No cure or preventive medicine exists for this disease, so it is doubly important to protect yourself from bites – see above. Dengue-bearing mosquitoes are active in daylight, usually in the early morning hours, so continue your mosquito protection until at least midday.

ELECTRICITY

The electric current throughout the region is 220/240 volts AC, 50 cycles, though there may be 110 volts AC on live-aboards. Plugs vary from country to country, so carry a selection of adaptors. The supply is fairly reliable in urban areas of Egypt, Israel, Jordan and Saudi Arabia, but can fail elsewhere. You should carry a torch and spare batteries. If you are charging any batteries, make sure that they are disconnected before the power comes back on as it is likely to have surges that can damage the chargers. Anyone relying on rechargeable equipment should also have a backup system that works on non-rechargeable alkaline batteries.

What to Bring

As you prepare for a dive trip to the Red Sea, whether it is for a week in Hurghada or a month on a live-aboard, it is worth packing a few of the basic necessities that can be difficult, even impossible, to find in the region. The further you travel from the main commercial and tourist areas of the northern Red Sea, the less available things become. In the south of central Egypt even batteries and film can be difficult to find, and dive equipment just plain impossible. Wherever you are, dive gear and other imported goods are likely to be very expensive even if they are available, so it makes sense to bring what you will need.

Spares kit

As every diver knows, an extra mask strap or a length of heavy-duty tape can make the difference between a memorable dive and a missed one. Aside from the basic spares you would normally take for a weekend's diving, here are a few suggestions:

- **Extra tank valve 'O' rings.**
  While most dive shops will have plenty of these in the compressor room, there is no guarantee that a supply of extras will make it on to the boat. Bringing a few spares will ensure that your tank will always be usable.
- **A scuba tool and some regulator blanking plugs.**
  A burst hose or a free-flowing octopus should not necessarily put your regulator out of service. If you have the equipment to cap off the relevant port, at least you can finish the day's diving and see to the problem once you are ashore.
- **Spare hoses – low and high pressure.**
  Hoses do wear out and the closest source for replacements is likely to be Eilat, Sharm el Sheikh or Hurghada.
- **Nylon parachute cord**
  Useful for temporarily replacing any broken strap – it can even be used to improvise a replacement for a broken tankstrap cam buckle.
- **Sewing kit.**
  Zips, Velcro patches and even whole sections of BCD have a nasty habit of coming unstitched as soon as you take them to the middle of nowhere. Some strong nylon thread and a couple of needles can be indispensable. Dental floss and a needle with a large eye are good for heavy-duty repairs.
- **Extra bulbs for underwater lights.**
  These will be impossible to find through most of the region, so take a supply.
- **Kettle descaler or similar limescale solvent.**
  When you are miles from the nearest authorized service centre, the buttons, switches, valve seats and other moving parts of your dive and underwater camera gear have a way of seizing up. A quick soak in descaling solution will often get things freed up and working again. At a pinch, overnight soaking in vinegar and water will do the same, although not nearly as effectively.

First Aid Kit

This should be better equipped than the usual scratch, cut and scrape repair kit (see pages 164–169). Some sort of treatment for tropical gastric upset is absolutely essential, and a few extras you might consider are:

- **Antihistamine cream and tablets.**
  The Red Sea has more than its share of fire corals and other marine hazards, which can cause painful reactions.
- **Broad-spectrum antibiotic ointment.**
  Small scrapes and cuts, especially coral cuts, can become infected alarmingly quickly in a tropical climate. Application of antibiotic ointment can make the difference between enjoying your dive holiday and sitting on the boat all day watching your buddy's bubbles.
- **Motion sickness treatment.**
  If you need this, bring it from home. Local equivalents can be hard to find and often have unpleasant side effects.

- **Decongestant.**
  A safe decongestant can keep a mild sinus irritation from turning into a diving disaster. Ask your doctor at home to prescribe one that will causes no adverse side effects while diving, rather than than wait until you are on holiday.
- **Sunblock.**
  The sun in the Red Sea is very, very strong. Even people who don't tend to burn should be aware of the dangers.

Reading Material

There is hardly any foreign-language reading material on sale outside the northern tourist areas. The little you can buy is limited in scope and hideously expensive. Bring as many books as you think you will need. If you rely on swapping with other travellers you may end up with a murder mystery missing the last ten pages or a three-month-old copy of *Practical Knitting Magazine*.

Cash

It is easy to forget, in our credit card society, that there are places where cold, hard cash is still the only acceptable method of payment. There are places in the Red Sea region where the only foreign currency accepted is US dollars (cash, not traveller's cheques). There are also places where no foreign currency at all is acceptable, and where there are no facilities whatsoever for changing money. Be sure to keep a variety of money on hand, including traveller's cheques, cash dollars and plenty of local currency.

The author, Guy Buckles, keeping well clear of the lionfish, which has a toxic sting.

DIVING AND SNORKELLING IN THE RED SEA

Warm water, stunning coral, colourful reef fish, crystal visibility, and tropical sun the year round is what Red Sea diving is all about. Nonetheless, for divers unfamiliar with tropical diving, there are particular concerns and some specifically local factors to consider. Aside from a few unfamiliar marine animals and some weather factors, few of these concerns are likely to be dangerous, but the information in the following pages is worth your attention. It should increase your enjoyment of diving in the Red Sea and steer you away from a few pitfalls which could otherwise ruin a dive holiday.

The climate of the Red Sea region follows the seasonal patterns familiar to northern hemisphere residents: summer falls between May and September, and the coldest months are December and January. The region is bounded on all sides by desert and has a very low annual rainfall in the north; precipitation is unlikely to affect diving in the region. However, surface winds will have an effect on dive plans: autumnal and winter storms and prevailing winds in particular can make the Red Sea very rough and choppy. Many live-aboard routes are suspended during the autumn and winter months, and even those routes still operating can be uncomfortably rough at times.

Visibility and Temperature

Visibility is also affected by seasonal considerations. With the exception of the Gulf of Suez and parts of the extreme south, the Red Sea is too deep for surface weather to cause much trouble by stirring up bottom sediment. However, seasonal temperature variations play a big part in determining visibility.

In the northern Egyptian Red Sea, algal and planktonic growth linked to temperature change can cause marked drops in visibility as sea temperatures change from cool to warm and back again in the spring and autumn months. Winter tends to be the period of best visibility, with waters too cool to support explosive growth of marine micro-organisms. South of central Egypt, conversely, it is summer that offers the best visibility. There, the blistering hot surface temperatures translate into sea temperatures too hot to support plankton or algal

Opposite: *The imposing wreck of the* Loullia *on Gordon Reef, Straits of Tiran.*

Above: *A camel dive safari is part of the attraction for visitors to the Red Sea.*

growth, while the more moderate temperatures of the winter months are perfect conditions for such growth.

No matter where you are in the Red Sea, unexpected blooms of micro-organisms can crop up at any time, bringing visibility way down. Fortunately, these occurrences are rare, and the general run of visibility in the region is really excellent.

Brochures often promise water temperatures in the Red Sea of 26°C (80°F) and above, and indeed this is true in much of the area for much of the year. Unfortunately, on individual dives conditions can be very different. In the north, water temperatures frequently fall as low as 20°C (68°F) in winter, and seasonal winds can chill you before and after dives, making it seem even colder.

The majority of divers will want at least some exposure protection, and even diehards will feel the cold after two or three dives a day with no wet suit. The best solution to the exposure protection dilemma is to bring both a 1mm (0.04in) Lycra suit and a 3mm (0.12in) neoprene wet suit. This gives you the possibility of three different levels of insulation, from the Lycra alone in warm water to the combination of both suits for cold conditions. A light vest/hood combination and gloves could also be advisable for those who chill easily. For winter trips to the northern Red Sea, a 5mm (0.20in) or even 7mm (0.28in) wet suit would not be overdoing it, and some divers use dry suits.

SALT AND BUOYANCY

Red Sea diving has many surprises in store for divers from other areas – clear visibility, astounding coral growth, colourful fishes, and much more. One surprise that few divers bargain for is the increased buoyancy of the Red Sea's highly saline water, a fact that has left many an embarrassed newcomer bobbing underweighted at the surface.

Although the Red Sea is thousands of metres deep at some points, its southern opening into the Indian Ocean, the Bab el Mandeb, is almost entirely closed by a shallow threshold that effectively blocks off the Red Sea from oceanic currents, preventing any substantial interchange between the two bodies of water.

This isolation, hot open fissures under water and the sand of the surrounding deserts absorbing the heat of the sun, all result in a high rate of water evaporation, causing the Red Sea to have the highest salinity of any open sea on Earth. For divers, this translates as a marked increase in buoyancy, and the need for added weight to compensate. Even divers familiar with tropical diving, and using familiar equipment, would be well advised to start their Red Sea dive trip with a proper weight check.

CURRENT PATTERNS

The Red Sea's long, narrow shape, north to south, minimizes tidal currents. As the moon has most effect on tidal flow, and as the moon moves east to west, the Red Sea is too narrow for the tidal stream to gather much momentum. As a result, there are often local currents around reefs but these are more affected by the wind and the sun than by the tide. Some larger reefs may not have much current in the cool of early morning, but quite a strong current in the heat of the sun by mid-afternoon.

MARINE LIFE

The spectacular variety of the Red Sea's marine life is the main attraction. At the small end of the scale, blennies, basslets and anthias form a vivid pattern of tiny, colourful flashes on virtually every reef in the Red Sea. Slightly larger damselfish, cardinals, butterflyfish and a dazzling variety of wrasse of every size and description are equally common, sometimes in uncountable quantity. Parrotfish and magnificently patterned angelfish mingle with triggerfish of several families, including the beautiful blue trigger and the bulky titan trigger. Groupers lurk in caves and crevices, while the big schooling reef fish patrol the reef – red and black snapper, surgeons and unicornfish in all shapes and sizes, as well as pelagic visitors.

The big end of the spectrum is shared between bulky bumphead parrotfish, stately Napoleon wrasse, giant grouper, and sleek

Opposite: *Schooling masked pufferfish (*Arothron diadematus*), summer mating season.*
Overleaf: *A group of Bafish (*Platax pinnatus*) sheltering in a lagoon at dusk.*

barracuda that cruise in from the open sea to feed on the rich pickings provided by the abundant species on the reef. More exotic inhabitants include the giant moray eel, trumpetfish, pufferfish, boxfish, frogfish, crocodilefish, eagle and Manta Rays, and the rare, majestic Whale Shark.

On the subject of sharks, the Red Sea is famed for the possibility of exhilarating encounters with these shadowy predators. Several species are found in these crystal clear waters, ranging from schooling Hammerhead Sharks off the point of Râs Muhammad's shark reef to Nurse and Guitar Sharks on sandy bottoms all along the coast. The Red Sea's generally excellent visibility makes it easy for enthusiasts to spot these elusive creatures.

As well as fish, marine mammals such as dolphins and the reclusive, endangered dugong make their homes in the Red Sea. Some species of whale visit the area. Reptiles such as Green and Hawksbill turtles are also common.

There is an endless diversity of corals and other reef life, from the lacy delicacy of gorgonian sea fans to the rugged solidity of *Porites* and *Favites* outcrops, and from the waving, flower-like tendrils of *Xeniid* soft corals to the thorny spikes of staghorn *Acropora*. Sponges, anemones and bright-hued algae all add to the riot of form and colour that typifies the Red Sea reef.

HAZARDS

Divers unfamiliar with tropical reefs should be aware of the few potential hazards posed by some marine species in the area. While almost no species are known to be overtly aggressive toward divers, the natural defences of several can come as a nasty and painful shock. See pages 152–3 for more detailed information.

CONSERVATION

Although the Red Sea's marine wealth may seem inexhaustible, the pressures of growing marine tourism are capable of tipping the delicate balance of fragile marine ecosystems. The Red Sea is a natural treasure mostly because of its traditional isolation; with an almost non-existent coastal population, reefs could grow without damage from human activities. With the advent of interest in the region's reefs, however, has come an increase in traffic – hundreds of anchors being dropped by dive boats every day have pulverized reefs in some areas, to say nothing of the damage done by uncaring or poorly trained divers.

In many parts of the Red Sea, marine conservation programmes have evolved to protect this fragile natural resource, combining local government lawmaking and international expertise in the establishment of marine reserves with enforceable conservation regulations.

Some of these conservation programmes include the ground-breaking Râs Muhammad National Park in Egypt, HEPCA (see page 86) in Hurghada, and the establishment of the Marine Peace Park in Israel and Jordan, whose architects hope one day to expand to cover the entire Gulf of Aqaba, transcending international borders and politics.

DIVE OPERATORS

Due to recent European Union regulations, many of the small specialist dive operators in Europe have had to cease trading, and the much larger package tour operators have taken their place. However, if you want quality or adventurous diving you would be better off paying a little more to one of the specialist diving-only operators who have survived. Most operations boast high levels of technical sophistication, large staffs of international, multilingual guides and instructors, and facilities and equipment which meet the most exacting of standards.

There have also been changes to the live-aboard scene, with local regulations and taxes in Egypt making it very difficult for Western-operated boats to work. Having removed the foreign competition, the Egyptian live-aboard scene has matured; most fleets now have luxury vessels and some are equipped to specialize in technical diving.

Due to a number of diving incidents, culminating in a serious emergency off the Brothers Islands, where a group of 12 divers, including a dive guide, got lost and drifted 42km (26 miles) in 13 hours before being found after dark by another boat, new regulations have been drawn up by the Red Sea Association for Diving and Watersports (RSADW). These cover the area of sea from El Gouna to the border with Sudan – the area where most live-aboard boats operate. Southern Sinai, covering Sharm El Sheikh, Dahab, Nuweiba and Taba, falls under a separate governing body.

ALL RED SEA LIVE-ABOARD DIVE CHARTER BOATS NEED TO PROVIDE:

- One diving guide per maximum of eight diving guests for Marine Park safaris (The Brothers, Gezîret Zabargad, Dædalus and Rocky Islet)
- One diving guide per maximum of 12 diving guests for non-Marine Park safaris
- Minimum one crew member to be responsible for surface cover. These crew members must be certified in emergency oxygen administration and medical first aid
- Valid Red Sea Association professional ID card for each dive guide.

PREREQUISITES FOR DIVING GUESTS:

- Minimum of 50 logged dives for Marine Park safaris (no minimum number of logged dives required for non-Marine Park safaris)
- Self-declaration medical form signed by the diving guest
- Valid insurance cover against diving accidents, from a reputable company.

SAFETY EQUIPMENT FOR THE SAFARI DIVE GUIDE, BOTH FOR MARINE PARK AND NON-MARINE PARK SAFARIS:

- Surface marker buoy
- Strobe and underwater light
- Heliograph or similar light-reflecting device.

SAFETY EQUIPMENT FOR THE SAFARI DIVING GUEST, BOTH FOR MARINE PARK AND NON-MARINE PARK SAFARIS:

- Surface marker buoy
- One underwater light for each buddy pair (even on daytime dives).

ADDITIONAL SAFETY EQUIPMENT FOR SAFARI BOATS:

- Minimum of two binoculars on each safari boat for surface cover
- Minimum of one inflatable or other tender/chase boat on all safari boats
- Each safari boat must have a number of life rafts that corresponds with the number of its occupants.

VARIABLE VISIBILITY

Throughout this book, figures for average visibility are given for each dive site. It is important to remember, though, that visibility in the Red Sea, like all seas, can vary markedly due to seasonal changes, surface weather and other factors (for example, algal blooms in spring and autumn and a response to annual temperature changes). In addition, the last few seasons in the northern Red Sea have seen intermittent periods of very poor visibility, sometimes less than half the average indicated in the text. The exact cause of this phenomenon is unknown, but appears to be connected to plankton growth.

You should therefore take these figures as a rough guide only; on any given day, visibility at a given site might be far better, or far worse, than the stated figure.

CHECKOUT DIVES

The Red Sea is one of the planet's great natural treasures but it is also a finite natural resource, which needs constant protection from the demands placed on it by ever-increasing dive tourism. For this reason, many diving areas now have strict rules governing diver conduct, with penalties including a complete ban on divers who damage the reef through carelessness or poor diving technique.

Divers are visiting the Red Sea in greater numbers each year. Many dive only occasionally, and are often not used to the specific conditions which apply to Red Sea diving. While the Red Sea may seem the perfect diving environment, current and weather conditions can leave the unwary diver out of control, endangering not only himself/herself but also the marine environment.

To meet the twin needs of diver safety and environmental protection, most dive centres insist that guests do a supervised checkout dive before diving on the area's delicate reefs. As a visitor to the Red Sea, you should accept this restriction with good grace; it is designed to protect you and your continued enjoyment of one of the world's great natural wonders.

Above: *The awesome sight of a spiralling barracuda shoal (*Sphyraena sp.*).*
Below: *Schooling jacks (*Caranx sp.*) are usually found in open water near drop-offs.*

Day-boat diving rules (in addition to that currently in place, such as liability release etc.):

- One dive guide for every 12 certified divers (with 25 dives or more)
- One dive guide for every eight novices (less than 25 dives)
- Dive guides must have a valid Red Sea Association professional ID card.

The Governor of the Red Sea has made membership of the RSADW, a non-governmental organisation, compulsory for centres and boat operators connected with diving or other marine-related tourism. Diving regulations will be posted on its web site, www.redseaexperience.com.

If you are looking for a live-aboard, check first with other divers as to the quality and safety record of the boat that you have in mind, particularly of any boats claiming to go to the Brothers, Dædalus Reef and the Rocky Islet, Gezîret Zabargad, Saint Johns Reef area. It is not unusual for some boats to regularly substitute a cheaper cruise, regardless of the weather.

Language problems are rarely an issue in dive planning and other important communications. Learning a few words of Arabic will certainly help throughout the region, but most dive operators have plenty of experience with visitors from all over the world – some dive guides routinely give their dive briefings in four or five languages.

In some areas off Jordan, Egypt and Israel, shore diving is prevalent; operators arrange transport to the local sites in four-wheel-drive vehicles or minivans, depending on terrain, and generally make every effort to keep your shore dive running as smoothly as any boat dive. For the adventurous diver, there are also many areas off Jordan, Egypt and Israel where you can arrange your own transport to shore dive sites, avoiding the crowds and recalling the relatively recent era when the only way to dive the Red Sea was to load a trailer with gear and camp on the beach.

Most dive operators run their diving on a two-dives-a-day, all-inclusive package basis. Included in the cost are two full tanks, boat transport to the sites and possibly transfers to and from your hotel. Equipment rental (where necessary) is extra, and lunch and soft drinks on the boat are usually charged separately – crews rely on this income to supplement their often low wages. A dive guide will almost always be provided, although buddy teams can often arrange to dive on their own if they prefer. Larger groups may be split into smaller units, each with its own guide.

Unlike the general practice at many Western diving destinations, many Red Sea dives (though certainly not all) are planned as 'drift' dives, where the boat follows your bubbles and picks you up when you surface. The generally

Checking Rental Equipment

A few points to pay special attention to when checking over and using rental equipment:

- Look for perished, split, kinked or frayed hoses – particularly the high pressure hose, where a blowout could cause the most damage.
- Check for cracks or deep scratches in the gauge faces.
- Check the tank valve/regulator seat (where the first stage seals against the tank valve 'O' -ring), on both the first stage and the tank valve, for dents, nicks or irregularities that could cause leaks.
- Always check that your tank has a tank valve 'O'-ring in place - they frequently fall out of worn tank valve seats. It is quite possible to mount your regulator mistakenly to a tank with no 'O'-ring with no apparent leakage, but the 'false seal' thus created is very fragile, and prone to blowouts at the slightest movement.
- Look carefully at all straps and fastenings on mask, fins and BCD – ask for a replacement if they show any signs of decay or weakness.
- Check all metal components carefully for corrosion - particularly the low-pressure inflator mechanism, whose moving parts may stick or jam.
- Check for sand or other debris in the second stage – particularly the octopus, which the last diver may have allowed to drag on the bottom. Sand is often the cause of persistent free-flowing.
- Smell the air directly from the tank by cracking the tank valve slightly to test for purity – this is much more effective than tasting the air through the regulator, which can impart smells of its own.
- Compare your depth gauge with that of your buddy on the first dive with new equipment – if there is a discrepancy, use the gauge which shows the deeper depth.
- Always maintain a larger reserve of air than you think you need – pressure gauges on rental gear can be very inaccurate.

calm seas and the predominance of wall reefs in much of the Red Sea make this both a safe and practical diving style, and where appropriate it is certainly more fun than covering the same ground twice and searching for the anchor line.

Medical facilities are sparse in the area. While most operators have first aid kits and oxygen equipment available, the isolation of most diving areas means that hospital facilities and recompression chambers are often many hours or days away. This leaves the burden of assuring dive safety squarely on your shoulders. You should carry a first aid kit of your own and make sure to bring it on the boat for every dive; you should review your first aid training before you begin your trip; and, most importantly, you should concentrate on diving conservatively and safely on every dive you do in the Red Sea. You are your own boss here. Dive safely and the lack of facilities need never affect you. No one is going to stop you from doing dangerous dives, but if you put yourself in danger, there is no sophisticated safety net to get you out of trouble.

Despite the widespread availability of quality rental equipment in the far north, you would be well advised to bring your own equipment if you have it. Renting gear adds a substantial amount to dive costs, and though the equipment is generally excellent, you can never be as sure of reliability and regular servicing as you can with your own. If excess baggage is a consideration, a good compromise is to bring your own regulator with you, as well as mask, fins and snorkel.

Equipment sales are confined to the resorts of the northern Red Sea, where prices are rarely as low as you will find at home; further out, there are no dive equipment shops at all, so if you have any shopping to do, you should do it before you leave home. The same is true of servicing, so get your gear checked thoroughly before you leave to avoid any problems.

NITROX AND TECHNICAL DIVING FACILITIES

Most operators can now supply Nitrox fills to suitably qualified divers, and the larger operators can provide training in Nitrox diving and technical diving.

DIVE TUITION

You can learn to dive at almost all of the Red Sea's dive centres; only the most remote destinations are unable to support some kind of dive education. The main centres are the large-scale tourist destinations, where a steady supply of customers makes running a dive school a potentially lucrative business. Eilat, Aqaba, Sharm el Sheikh and Hurghada are all major education centres. Common certification organizations include PADI, BS-AC, CMAS and SSI. Depending on where you decide to take your course, it is possible to find tuition in almost all major European languages, especially English, German, Italian and French, and most centres can provide tuition in Arabic and other local languages.

ARABIC – NORTHERN EGYPT

This brief primer won't make you fluent (there are several excellent phrasebooks for that), but a few of these diving-related words and phrases might make your dives in the Red Sea safer and more enjoyable.

Note that in Egyptian Arabic, the 'j' sound is pronounced as a 'g' – alternative pronunciations are given below. The 'gh' is pronounced like a French 'r', at the back of the throat.

- Boat = Merkab
- Harbour = Mina
- Beach = Shatt, Bilaaj
- Wave = Mooj, Moog
- Coral = Marjan, Margan
- Island = Jezira, Gazira
- Rock = Sakhra
- Fish = Samak
- Shark = Samak Qirsh/Girsh
- Whale = Hout
- Dolphin = Dolfin, Dalfin
- Turtle = Sulahfa
- Eel = Samak Kalhaya, Hankaliis
- Big wave/s = Mooj (moog) Kebir, Amwaj (amwag) Kebir
- Current = Tayyar
- There is current = Fi Tayyar
- There is no current = Ma fi Tayyar
- Strong current = Tayyar Qawi
- Which direction? (from where) = Min Wain?
- Where is the current coming from? = Tayyar Min Wain?
- Diving = Ghats
- First Dive = Ghatsa al-Awil
- Second Dive = Ghatsa at-Tani
- Where is the first dive? = Wain al Ghatsa al-awil?
- How many dives here? = Kem Ghatsa Hinak?
- What time is the second dive? = Sa'a Kem al-Ghatsa at-Tani?
- How long from X to Y? = Kem Waqt min X li Y?
- What time do we arrive? = Sa'a Kem 'Nwassal?

ISRAEL

Eilat, Israel's southernmost city and port, was for decades the unofficial capital of the Red Sea diving industry and the training centre for an entire generation of Red Sea divers. Eilat boasts warm waters, clear visibility and a wealth of marine species, and despite the emergence of newer, more exotic destinations, the town continues to hold its own as a premier venue for diver education.

Israel's Red Sea coastline is a mere 7km (4 miles), sandwiched between Egyptian Sinai and Jordan, at the top of the Gulf of Aqaba. Eilat takes up most of this shoreline, its commercial port facilities servicing the import/export industries and military docks supporting the navy. Beyond the ports and the frontage of the city itself, there remains precious little coast for divers to explore. Yet there are several distinct dive sites, some of them offering unique attractions.

The People and the Culture

The majority of the country's population is Jewish, made up of returnees from the centuries of the Jewish Diaspora, and their descendants. Broadly, the Jewish population is divided into two groups — the Ashkenazim, descended from the Jews of Europe, and the Sephardim, whose forefathers come from the countries of the Middle East and North Africa. As well as these two main groups, there are Jewish minority groups who trace their origins to countries such as India and China.

In addition to the Jewish majority, there is a sizeable minority of Arab Israeli citizens. These are the descendants of Palestinian Arab families who chose to remain in Israel after the country was founded; the majority of the Arabs are Muslim, but there are also large populations of Druze and Christian Arabs. Another piece in the cultural mosaic is provided by the Bahai, followers of one of the world's newest major religions, whose world headquarters is in Haifa on the Mediterranean coast.

There is no problem in terms of communication. Israelis are required to study English in school and it is widely spoken.

Opposite: *Almost all diving in the Eilat area is done from the shore.*
Above: *The hawksbill turtle (*Eretmochelys imbricata*) is the smallest of the marine turtles.*

Climate

Eilat is warm and dry in winter, hot and dry in summer. There is little annual rainfall, and temperatures range from 35°C (95°F) or more in summer to a reasonably cool winter average of 20°C (70°F).

Dive Highlights

The impact of decades of unregulated diving have taken a toll on Eilat's reefs, and coral growth here is not the luxuriant spectacle you will find further south. But there are hidden bonuses, such as the almost guaranteed presence of unusual fish, a selection of wrecks and a marine nature reserve. However, the real highlight of diving in Eilat is Dolphin Reef (Site 1, page 34), a unique marine habitat where divers and snorkellers have the chance to interact with semi-wild dolphins.

Marine Life

Eilat's reefs provide a home for jacks, snapper and surgeonfish, while barracuda, parrotfish and wrasse dart among the coral with grouper and sweetlips; sweepers, basslets and damsels provide scintillating points of light, while frogfish, stonefish, rays and crocodilefish lurk on the bottom. Squid and octopus are common, and colourful nudibranchs dot the reef. Moray eels inhabit cavelets and holes and there are chances to spot unusual species such as Ghost Pipefish and even the rarely sighted sunfish.

Eilat's coast is marked by sandy bottoms with moderate to dense coral patches, although

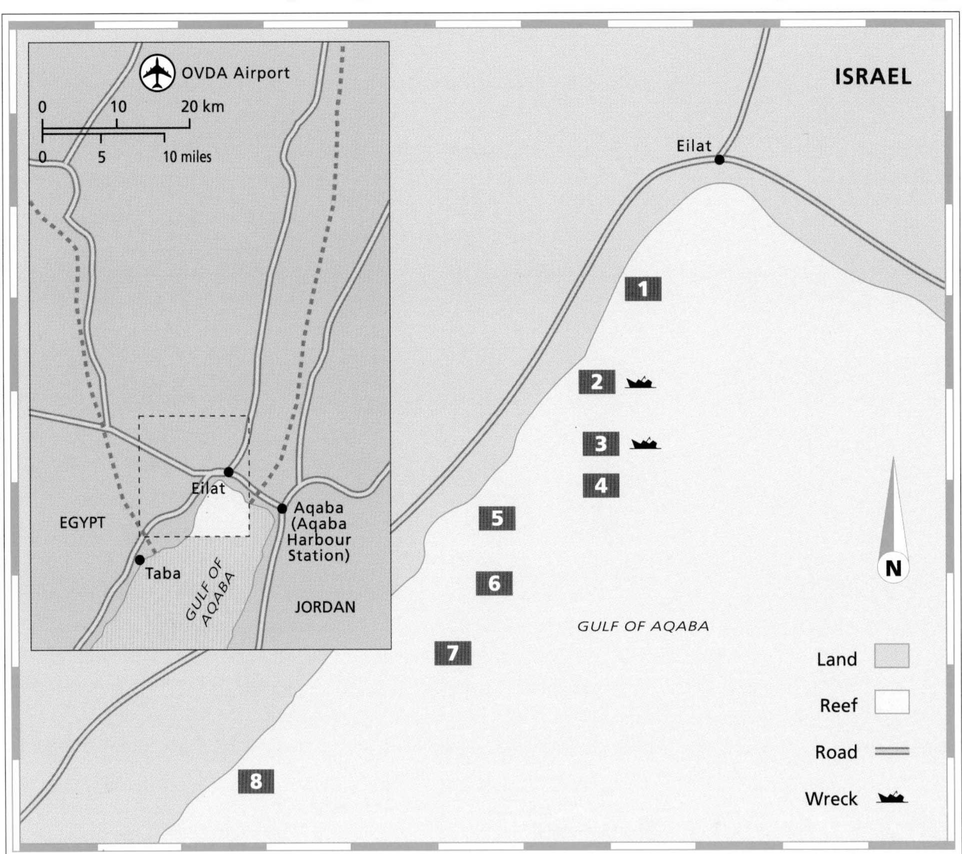

the quality of coral life is certainly less pristine than that of the Sinai. Pinnacles and distinct heads are the usual formation, and an inshore shallow reef along much of the coastline provides interest for snorkellers. A mixture of soft and stony coral species make up the area's reefs, with concentrations of such species as *Dendronephthya*, *Xeniid* soft corals, *Acropora*, cabbage and plate corals. Sponges and anemones are also common.

CONDITIONS

Eilat's location, at the northern tip of the Red Sea, gives it more seasonal variation in dive conditions than most other areas. Summer water temperatures are usually in the upper 20s°C (80s°F), while winter lows can drop to 19°C (66°F) or lower. Visibility tends to be lower on average than in other parts of the Red Sea, due in part to the heavy industrial activity along the coast.

ACCESS

Almost all diving in the Eilat area is done from shore, with the exception of a single site which is restricted to boat access only. Dive centres arrange transport, usually in minibuses, to and from the sites, but from some centres, access to the best sites is a matter of crossing the road.

DIVE OPERATORS AND FACILITIES

Eilat's long dive history has made it one of the most technically advanced dive bases in the entire region. The town's dive centres are highly professional, with the most modern, state-of-the-art-equipment, and staffed by highly trained, multilingual dive guides and instructors. A full range of quality rental equipment is usually available.

PASSPORT PROBLEMS

The political landscape of the Middle East is changing very rapidly, and the ongoing peace process is paying dividends all over the region. However, some countries in the region are less eager than others to move with the times, and there is still considerable tension between Israel and some neighbouring states.

Evidence of a visit to Israel can cause problems when travelling to certain other countries in the region. An Israeli stamp in your passport will rule out a visit to many Islamic countries all over the world. To a lesser degree, this is also true of exit stamps indicating that you have left neighbouring countries at their border with Israel. This is because Israel will, on request, stamp you in on a separate paper instead of your passport. If you have any such stamps in your passport, it is recommended that you obtain a new 'clean' passport before travelling in the Arab world.

By the same token, Israeli citizens and dual nationals may be refused entry to certain Middle Eastern countries. To gain admission for a stay in any of them it would be unwise even to list your religion as Jewish on visa applications and other official documents.

A sunlit fringe reef bursting with healthy stony coral.

Local Dive Etiquette and Customs

Eilat's tiny stretch of coastline has been intensively dived for longer than almost any other part of the Red Sea, and the wear and tear of decades of sustained diving activity has placed a great strain on the area's reefs. Active steps are underway to preserve Eilat's underwater ecosystem, and the cooperation of visiting divers is a crucial part of this strategy. It is vital that you avoid all contact with the reef, maintain good neutral buoyancy, and keep well clear of the reef at all times. Pay careful attention to your finstrokes, and never sit or stand on coral.

1 DOLPHIN REEF

Location: South of the port on the Eilat–Taba road.
Access: Shore entry from Dolphin Reef Dive Centre.
Conditions: Very protected, easy access.
Average depth: 9m (30ft)
Maximum depth: 15m (50ft)
Average visibility: 12m (40ft)

Dolphin Reef, a 10,000-sq m (107,000-sq ft) area of sea, averaging 12m (40ft) deep and fully enclosed by buoyed nets, is home to a school of Bottlenose Dolphins (*Tursiops truncatus*) that have been rescued from Russia and Japan. The school lives happily together and has even bred its own young. The dolphins can jump the net to freedom if they so wish, and often do so only to return later with fresh propeller scars on their backs.

The enclosure also contains a wreck and reef fish, including some interesting species rescued from fishermen, such as Cobia and large habituated stingrays. Sea lions from a smaller enclosure beside the dolphin enclosure regularly jump the net to join in the fun.

A member of staff must accompany all participants; snorkellers enter the enclosure over the net, but divers enter through a sliding curtain facing the shore at the bottom. The dolphins are sensitive to the noise of the curtain being opened and immediately appear, energetically passing by at high speed with lots of clicking and shrieking. Do not expect them to pose; once they have had a quick inspection of the newcomers and searched the accompanying staff for titbits, they go back to their boisterous play, occasionally preying on reef fish hiding in the sand.

Over the course of a day, the dolphins see hundreds of divers and snorkellers and soon become bored with them. Therefore, it is best to book the first dive of the day – before the sand gets stirred up and when the dolphins have not had human contact overnight – when they are likely to be more curious.

Opposite: *Porcupine Pufferfish (*Diodon hystrix*) among Dendronephthya Soft Tree Corals.*

Dolphin Reef

Eilat's Dolphin Reef is an unusual site by any standards. It is a commercially operated scuba and snorkelling centre where the main attraction is a pod of semi-wild dolphins. The philosophy behind the centre is equally unusual: despite the huge commercial potential of such a site, the management policy is to make this a place where the dolphins' needs come first.

Uniquely, the bottlenose dolphins here are not captive; they are free to leave at any time, by jumping over the nets. The dolphins receive an incentive to hang around – in the form of regular feedings of fresh fish – but the surprising thing is how willing they are to interact with humans. For example, the dolphins perform a variety of tricks at four daily training sessions, yet they are not rewarded for this behaviour with gifts of food. It is precisely this type of behaviour that makes Dolphin Reef a mecca for dolphin study. A team of research students, funded by a German university, operates a comprehensive year-round research programme at the centre's fully equipped behavioural lab.

This is a superb chance for divers to learn more about one of the most fascinating creatures in the sea.

2 SUFA MISSILE BOAT

★★★

  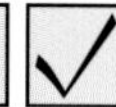

Location: About 2km (1¼ miles) south of Dolphin Reef (Site 1), north of the Village Pub.
Access: Motor transport from Eilat dive centres, then shore entry.
Conditions: Rocky bottom offers loose footing on entry/exit.
Average depth: 25m (80ft)
Maximum depth: 30m (100ft)
Average visibility: 12m (40ft)

This is a wreck site, on a navy missile boat which was purpose-sunk here in 1994. About 50m (165ft) offshore, the boat is 46m (150ft) long and it sits in an upright position on the seabed. Its stern lies in 30m (100ft) of water. The boat's highest point is the mast top in just 15m (50ft) of water.

Coral growth has already begun on the hull and superstructure; obviously the faster-growing soft corals

predominate, but you can also make out the first polyps of stony coral colonies. The ubiquitous sea urchin is also present in large numbers, so watch where you put your hands. Fish life is fairly good, although the wreck has not yet really become a settled habitat.

The wreck has been prepared for divers: access to hazardous areas has been closed off, and attempts made to keep the wreck as safe as possible for underwater visitors. Consequently, if there's an entrance, it's safe to go in. This is a nice site for novice wreck divers to hone their skills, with its relatively shallow profile and user-friendly layout.

3 YATUSH – GUNBOAT WRECK

★★★

Location: About 400m (1310ft) south of the Sufa wreck site (Site 2).
Access: Motor transport from Eilat dive centres, then shore entry.
Conditions: Some current possible.
Average depth: 28m (90ft)
Maximum depth: 33m (110ft)
Average visibility: 12m (40ft)

This wreck, a small naval gunboat, lies at an angle at the bottom of an offshore drop-off. It is situated just in front of the Aquasport Diving Centre — the reef here is a

SUFA MISSILE BOAT

The missile boat wreck is an enjoyable dive, and many divers are happy to leave it at that, without wondering about what the boat is and how it got there. However, a little research turns up a fascinating piece of local history.

The wreck is one of five Sufa missile boats bought by the Israeli government from France in the mid-1960s. Delivery of the boats was indefinitely postponed due to a French arms embargo in force at the time, but in the wake of the Six Day War the Israeli navy was desparate to take delivery. When the Israelis realized that they were not going to get their boats through diplomatic channels, they hatched a daring plan: to take the boats (which, after all, were bought and paid for) in a military mission.

And so, in late 1967, that was exactly what they did. A small Israeli military force went to Cherbourg and took possession of the boats, breaking them out of the harbour and sailing them back to Israel.

It is particularly apt to note that the commander of the mission was a man who would later be a driving force behind the growth of sport diving in Israel, Gadi Ben Zeev, the man in charge of Red Sea Sports Club, Eilat's largest dive centre.

A minor footnote: the wreck was also the site of the 1995 Guinness record for most divers on a wreck at one time – 155 divers managed to cram themselves on board.

*Twobar Anemonefish (*Amphiprion bicinctus*) cluster around the host anemone.*

shallow slope from shore to 5m (15ft), after which it drops steeply to 30m (100ft); the boat lies at the foot of this drop. The boat's stern is at about 33m (110ft), with its shallowest point at the bows in 25m (80ft) of water. The wreck is around 15m (50ft) long; built of aluminium, intact and in good condition, having been purposely sunk for divers.

The wreck houses a good collection of reef fish, including lionfish, scorpionfish and stonefish, wrasse, triggers, butterflyfish and damselfish. There are some nice morays, and the area below the boat is home to a resident potato grouper at least 1m (3ft) in length. Shovelface lobster can sometimes be seen here, and jacks, tuna and barracuda occasionally cruise by in search of a meal.

Being made of aluminium, the wreck itself boasts no coral. There are, however, a number of mixed, mostly stony coral heads scattered on the sandy bottom, with attendant clouds of small reef fishes.

4 CORAL BEACH

★★★☆☆☆

Location: About 200m (655ft) south of the Yatush wreck (Site 3).
Access: Motor transport or walk from Eilat dive centres, then shore entry.
Conditions: Some mild currents possible.
Average depth: 20m (65ft)
Maximum depth: 40m (130ft)
Average visibility: 12m (40ft)

This is a wide sloping reef, gently dropping from the inshore shallows to 10m (35ft) over the space of about 150m (490ft). Beyond this point, the reef drops steeply to a maximum at around 40m (130ft).

The reef composition throughout the site is mixed coral patches over sand; the deeper sections offer better coral cover, and the lip of the offshore drop-off boasts three large pinnacles.

Coral growth tends toward the stony species, although there is some soft growth.

Entry to the site is at the north edge of the nature reserve fence, and the dive is entirely within the reserve's boundaries.

A shallow inshore reef runs the length of the shoreline, offering excellent snorkelling in depths of 3m (10ft) and less. The site's southern boundary is a footbridge crossing this reef, allowing access from shore without treading on delicate coral.

Fish population at the site is good and varied. Along with the usual reef species, careful attention will turn up some rarities and oddities, including frogfish, ghost pipefish and occasional seahorses.

Scorpionfish, lionfish and stonefish are common, including the Filament-finned Stinger.

5 NATURE RESERVE/MOSES ROCK

★★★☆☆☆☆☆☆

Location: Just south of the Coral Beach site (Site 4).
Access: Motor transport or walk from Eilat dive centres, then shore entry through a nature reserve, for which an entrance fee is payable.
Conditions: Some mild currents possible.
Average depth: 20m (65ft)
Maximum depth: 40m (130ft)
Average visibility: 12m (40ft)

This, one of the finest sites in Eilat, has really benefited from its protected status as part of the nature reserve. Coral and fish life here outshine most local sites, even those lying just a few hundred metres away.

The site's profile and layout are almost identical to the Coral Beach site to the north. A shallow inshore reef provides good snorkelling, while the reef slopes gently outward to an offshore drop-off. The slope is dotted with coral heads, and there is a large pinnacle in 8–9m (25–30ft) of water near the drop-off. This is Moses Rock, for which the site is named.

The entire site boasts a wealth of coral species. Of particular interest are the *Acropora* tables on the drop-off section from 15–30m (50–100ft). There are also numerous sponges and anemones.

Fish life keeps up the pace with big scorpionfish (*Inimicus filimentosus*), stonefish and lionfish, frogfish, trumpetfish, pipefish, puffers, moray eels, yellowtail barracuda, jacks, fusiliers, needlefish, and a hundred and one smaller reef species. There is also an assortment of rays, which can include eagle rays, Bluespotted Ribbontail Rays and even electric rays.

6 JAPANESE GARDENS

★★★★☆☆☆☆☆

Location: Between Moses Rock (Site 5) and the underwater observatory.
Access: Motor transport from Eilat dive centres. An entry fee is charged.
Conditions: Some currents; take care near observatory's automatic doors.
Average depth: 20m (65ft)
Maximum depth: 45m (150ft)
Average visibility: 12m (40ft)

Japanese Gardens is a continuation of the coastal reef that stretches south from Coral Beach (Site 4). Like the sites to the north, it begins with a shallow reef which slopes to 10–15m (35–50ft) over the space of about 100m (330ft). The pattern of a sharp drop-off from 10m (35ft) is continued here, and the drop-off section is so steep as to resemble a wall. This wall area is densely packed with corals, as is the shallow inshore reef. The coral cover is good.

The southern section of the site lies among the buildings of the underwater observatory. Special care should be taken here to avoid injury, particularly in the area of the observatory's submerged automatic doors. You should not come within 5m (15ft) of these doors.

The corals here are exceptional and fish life is as good as you will find in the Eilat area, with a wide range of species and good distribution and population density. Along with the plethora of Red Sea reef species you find rarities such as the frogfish, fascinatingly ugly stonefish, and steamroller-flat crocodilefish. Jacks, schooling barracuda and other open water hunters often cruise by, and even Whitetip Reef Sharks have been spotted here, a real rarity in shark-poor Eilat.

If you had only one dive to do in Eilat, this would be the one to go for.

7 THE CAVES/THE LIGHTHOUSE

★★★★

Location: About 1km (½ mile) south of Japanese Gardens (Site 6), just north of the Princess Hotel.
Access: Motor transport from Eilat dive centres, then shore entry.
Conditions: Some mild currents.
Average depth: 4m (15ft)
Maximum depth: 6m (20ft)
Average visibility: 12m (40ft)

This very shallow site, lying to the south of Coral Beach (Site 4) on the way to the Egyptian border, is based on a large pinnacle, the largest of many in the area, lying in just 4m (15ft) of water. Reaching almost to the surface, it is pierced by two cracks or caves – hence the name. Only one of these is suitable for entry; the second is rather too small.

The cave pinnacle sits on a very shallow sloping reef; the site is dotted with various coral formations, from soft coral patches to fire corals, with quite a good range of stony corals. Fish life on the site is very similar to the range of species at the Coral Beach sites, with the usual small reef fishes and some added variety in the form of frogfish, scorpions and small colourful nudibranchs. The caves are home to large schools of sweepers.

This site's very limited profile may disappoint some divers, but it is a very nice venue for night dives, when depth is not really a factor.

8 TABLE CORAL

★★★★★★

Location: About 50m (165ft) north of the Egyptian border checkpoint, offshore from the large concrete blocks.
Access: Motor transport from Eilat dive centres, then shore entry.
Conditions: Some slight currents.
Average depth: 18m (60ft)
Maximum depth: 30m (100ft)
Average visibility: 12m (40ft)

This site boasts a decent range of corals and some very particular attractions among its fishy residents. It is a sloping reef in a two-tiered profile, with a shallow inshore reef slope giving way to a steeper drop-off some distance offshore. The inshore reef here is quite well covered, with a good range of corals and reef fishes for snorkellers to explore. Out past the drop-off, there are pinnacles, coral spurs interspersed with sandy gullies, and the *Acropora* tables for which the site is named — three or four of them quite large, 2–3m (5–10ft) wide, lying at depths between 14–20m (45–65ft).

For fish watchers, this site has some surprises to offer. A good local guide will be able to point out unusual species, such as frogfish, stonefish, shovelhead lobster, octopus, squid, and several different types of cowries and other molluscs.

*A rare photograph of two fighting giant moray eels (*Gymnothorax javanicus*).*

Israel

How to Get There

By air: Although there is a small airport in the middle of Eilat, most tourists use the military airport at Ovda, 40 minutes north of Eilat. Ovda is served by a wide range of charter flights at some of the cheapest prices in the region. It is possible to fly to Tel Aviv and travel on by road.
By boat: Car/passenger ferry from Cyprus/Greece/Italy.
By road: You can also enter Israel overland from both Jordan and Egypt, but do not use the same passport for travel to other Arab countries. Through-bus or shared taxi services are available from both countries, and their border crossings are very close to Eilat.

Transport in Eilat is simple; most of the central part of town is compact enough to walk, while buses and taxis, both inexpensive, are available for longer trips. The dive centres arrange shuttle transport from hotels, so you can avoid paying for transport to your chosen dive base.

Where to Stay

Accommodation is plentiful, but it can be shockingly expensive when compared with that of other Middle Eastern countries. The cheapest option is **camping** – you can set up a tent in designated areas along the coast road, or there are basic chalet-style campgrounds – one of these is just south of the Red Sea Sports Club. There is a collection of private hostels and cheap guest houses near the bus station which are cheap, but some are pretty grotty.

Eilat's mid-range accommodation, which would be luxury-price in any other country in the region, includes places like the **Red Sea Sports Hotel** complex, the **Aqua Sport Dive Centre**'s accommodation, or the **Etzion Hotel** in the town centre. Top-range places charging several hundred dollars a night include the **King Solomon's Palace Hotel** and the **Royal Beach Hotel**.

The Ambassador Hotel PO Box 390, Coral Beach, Eilat; tel 972 8 6382222/fax 972 8 6374083; email info@ambassador.co.il/info@redseasports.co.uk; www.ambassador.co.il/www.redseasports.co.uk/www.redseasports.co.il.

Aqua Sport Divers' Lodge Aqua Sport International, PO Box 300, Eilat 88102; tel 972 8 6334404/fax 972 8 6333771; email info@aqua-sport.com; www.aqua-sport.com.

King Solomon's Palace Hotel Eilat North Beach, Eilat 88000; tel 972 8 6363444/fax 972 8 6334189.

Royal Beach Hotel PO Box 765, North Beach, Eilat; tel 972 7 636 8888/fax 972 7 636 8811; email royal-beach@isrotel.co.il; www.isrotel.co.il.

Where to Eat

Eilat has some fine restaurants, as well as a full range of budget eats. By the seafront in the main hotel area you will find a range of fast food joints; there are also plenty of Israeli-style snack places. Up by the Shalom centre on Hatzmarim Street, there are a scattering of sidewalk cafés, or for something more adventurous there's the moderately priced Yemeni **Nargile Restaurant**, at the top of Hatzmarim next to the bus station. For one of the finest steaks in the Middle East, look no farther than **Pedro's** on Ye'elim Boulevard (tel 972 7 6379504). There are also some high-quality restaurants in the more expensive hotels, including Thai, Chinese and other international cuisines. Most dive centres have snack bars on or near the premises.

Dive Facilities

Eilat has gained a reputation as the diving classroom of the world, with several busy centres of varying size and standards of service. The excellent **Red Sea Sports Club** is the largest, with an enthusiastic, international staff, tuition in a variety of languages, technically exceptional facilities and equipment, a hotel on the premises, and a solid reputation. If you're thinking of learning to dive, or of extending your qualifications, this is a good place to do it. **Dolphin Reef** is not just an environment for dolphins, it is also a fully fledged dive centre and school. **Aqua Sport International** is also well regarded and is conveniently located near to the dive sites.

Aqua Sport International PO Box 300, Eilat 88102; tel 972 8 6334404/fax 972 8 6333771; email info@aqua-sport.com; www.aqua-sport.com. Certifications: PADI, BS-AC and CMAS.

Dolphin Reef Eilat PO Box 104, Southern Beach, Eilat; tel 972 8 6371846/fax 972 8 6375921; email: info@dolphinreef.co.il; www.dolphinreef.co.il. Certifications: PADI, CMAS, and ANDI Nitrox and Tri-Mix.

Marina Divers PO Box 599, Coral Beach, South Marina, Eilat 88000; tel 972 7 6376787/fax 972 7 6373130; email marinad@netvision.co.il. Certification: PADI.

Red Sea Sports Club PO Box 390, Coral Beach, Eilat 88102; tel 972 7 6379685/fax 972 7 6373702; email info@redseasports.co.uk; www.redseasports.co.il/www.redseasports.co.uk. A PADI 5-star IDC Center; certifications: PADI, BS-AC and CMAS.

Hospitals

Israel's medical system is the most advanced in the Middle East. The **Yoseftal Hospital** (tel 972 8 6358011/fax 972 8 6370149) is very high-tech, but correspondingly expensive – make sure you have insurance.

Diving Emergencies

There is a fully equipped **recompression chamber** at the hospital; no dive site in Eilat is more than 12 minutes from the chamber. You can contact the chamber through the hospital switchboard, and ambulances and emergency services can be reached by phoning 101. The direct line for the chamber is 972 8 6358067.

The Israelis were the pioneers of hyperbaric medicine in the region, and much of the training for recompression facility staff in places as far away as Eritrea was done by Israeli experts.

Local Highlights

Eilat is a tourist town without many tourist attractions aside from the sun and sand.

If the diving begins to wear thin, you may need to head out of town to find much of interest. There are, however, a couple of places you may want to visit in the area.

Coral World is a great place to experience the underwater world while taking a break from diving or snorkelling. There are large tanks with sharks, rays, turtles and many other colourful sea creatures.

Even better, you can see what goes on in the **Coral Beach Nature Reserve** from the underwater observatories situated some 90m (300ft) offshore, accessed by the pier. You can snorkel or dive here but, if you prefer not to get wet, you can experience the wonders of the deep on a high-tech submarine which departs from the North Beach marina. (The submarine is rather expensive so, instead, you could try the glass-bottom boats which cost substantially less and are equally thrilling.)

If you fancy something different you could visit the **Aerodium**, behind the Sport Hotel on North Beach. A powerful jet of air keeps you suspended in a simulated sky-diving state, 3–4m (10–12ft) above ground. Included in the price of your visit is one hour of instruction. You must be reasonably fit to try this unusual, exhilarating activity.

JORDAN

Some of the finest diving in the northern Red Sea is packed into Jordan's one small stretch of coastline and, as a result of Jordan's pivotal role in the Middle East peace process, the underwater bounty of this tiny region is attracting the attention of divers from all over the world.

Jordan's coastline consists of only 27km (15 miles) of beaches and commercial ports at the northern end of the gulf of Aqaba, opposite Eilat in Israel. Until recently, divers on either side of the border could look but not touch, although you can clearly see Eilat's high-rise hotels from the beach in Aqaba. It was only with the signing of the peace treaty between the two countries that it became possible to cross the few kilometres that separate the two towns.

The People and the Culture

The Jordanian people are charming, hospitable and friendly, wonderful ambassadors for Arab culture and gracious hosts to the growing stream of foreign visitors to their homeland. English speakers will find no problem with communication in Jordan, although even a few words of Arabic will open doors for you.

Climate

The climate of Jordan's Red Sea coast is very similar to that of the Israeli Red Sea coast. Summer highs can reach 40°C (104°F), while the winter temperature hovers around a relatively pleasant 20–25°C (68–77°F), even when temperatures just inland drop to freezing or below. Throughout the year, humidity is very low. The air on the Red Sea coast is dry enough for dive gear to dry out between dives, even in winter.

Marine Life

Coral is really what diving in Jordan is about. You will find a better density of fish life, and clearer visibility, elsewhere in the northern Gulf of Aqaba, but the condition and quality of

Opposite: *A group of divers pile into a Zodiac to travel to a dive site.*

Above: *Anemonefish are called clownfish because of their gaudy colours and clownish antics.*

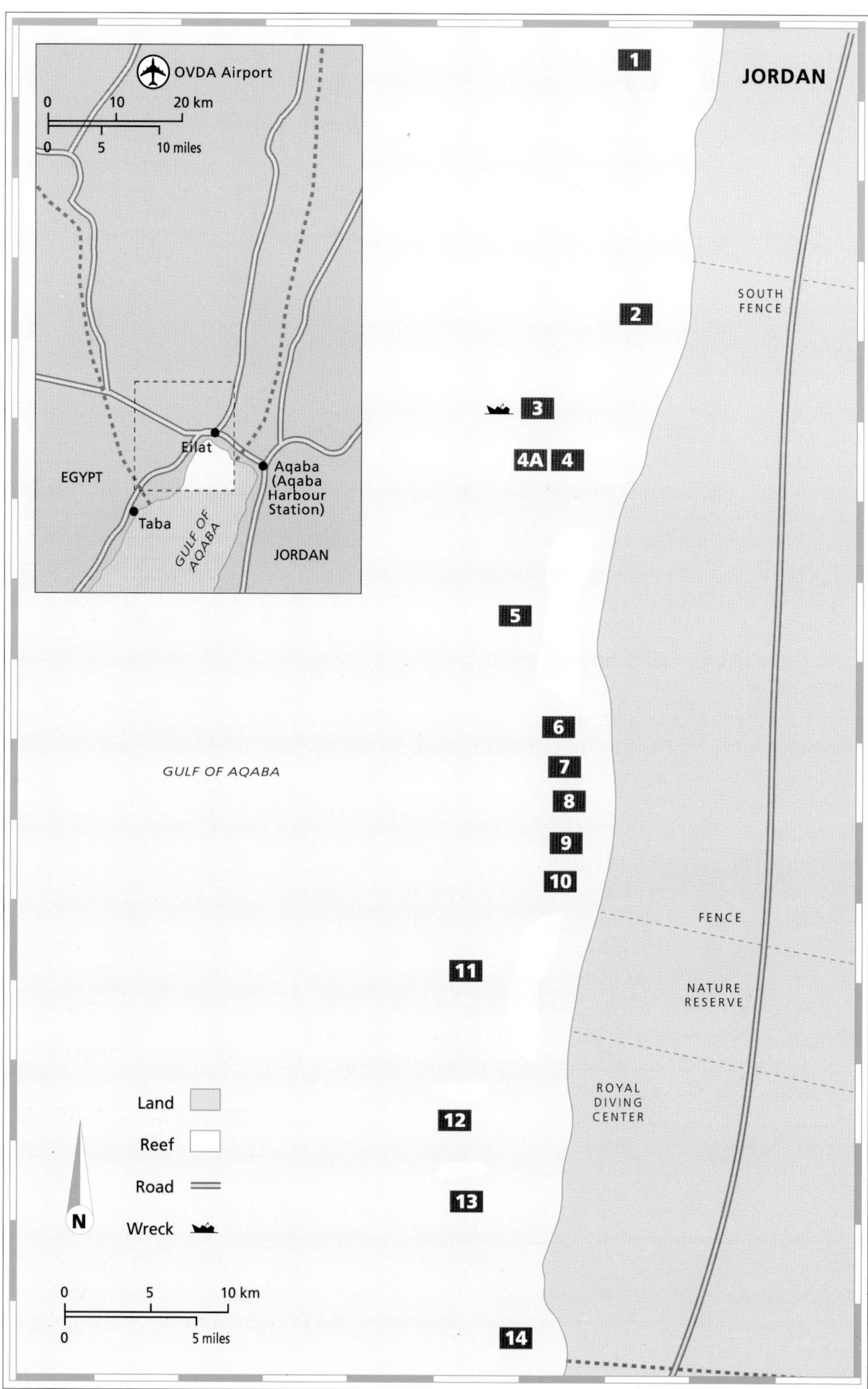
OVDA Airport
0 10 20 km
0 5 10 miles
Eilat
EGYPT
Aqaba (Aqaba Harbour Station)
Taba
GULF OF AQABA
JORDAN
1
2
3
4A 4
5
6
7
8
9
10
11
12
13
14
SOUTH FENCE
FENCE
NATURE RESERVE
ROYAL DIVING CENTER
GULF OF AQABA
Land
Reef
Road
Wreck
N
0 5 10 km
0 5 miles

coral growth in Jordan are really second to none, with stunning coral vistas in a near-perfect state of preservation. This is especially encouraging given the concentrated nature of diving activities here. Aqaba has avoided the severe deterioration of the reef that plagues Eilat or Sharm el Sheikh, and is taking active steps to preserve its unique marine resources for future generations.

Aqaba's reefs achieve a near perfect balance between soft and stony corals, represented by an exuberantly diverse range of species. All of the area's corals can be found in concentrations unusual elsewhere in the northern Red Sea, with extensive fields of soft corals, huge bommies or pinnacles of exquisitely preserved massive corals like *Porites* or *Favites*, and cabbage coral formations the size of a small house. *Acropora* and other branching corals are abundant, and waving heads of colourful *Dendronephthya* compete with expanses of gently pulsing *Xeniid* soft corals in carpets that cover wide swathes of the reef face. Delicate branching tables and antler forms are also common, with sponges and anemones adding colour and interest.

The fish life is diverse and Jordan's reefs are scintillating examples of the sheer range and vibrancy tropical reef fishes can achieve. Common species include angel and butterflyfish, venomous lion and scorpionfish, parrotfish, and a range of groupers that includes abundant Lyretail Groupers. Schooling species such as jacks, snapper and fusiliers are all present, as are moray eels.

CONDITIONS

Diving in the Aqaba area has little in the way of adverse conditions, aside from the occasional strong wind at the surface. Currents tend to be slight, and visibility is generally good, averaging around 20m (65ft) and frequently much better. Temperatures range between summer highs of 26°C (80°F) or more, to a decidedly chilly winter low of 20°C (68°F). While this may sound warm to northern divers, a couple of dives a day in winter-time Aqaba will have you craving a decent wet suit.

JORDANIAN FOOD

Like most countries in the northern Red Sea, Jordan shares a culinary heritage with the rest of the Arab world, and many dishes found in the country are identical to those found in Cairo or Khartoum. Some dishes, though, are uniquely Jordanian, and a few of these are listed below.

- **Mansaf** is a dish of lamb stewed in a yoghurt-based sauce, flavoured with turmeric, cardamom and other spices. Its long preparation time makes the lamb succulent and tender. It is served in large chunks and the meat comes away from the bone easily, making a knife and fork unnecessary.
- **Maklouba** is an elaborate dish of rice, meat and vegetables, slow-cooked together in a large pot, then turned out onto a serving tray. Preparation can take several hours. Diners then dig into the steaming mountain of rice, discovering the delicacies layered throughout the dish.
- **Bukhari rice** is a tasty yellow rice preparation, not dissimilar to Indian biryani or pullao. Turmeric or saffron-coloured rice is slow-cooked with chickpeas and onions; the rice can be served with meat, or as an accompaniment to other dishes.
- **Kofta** is a ground meat dish, but unlike the standard Arab equivalent, Jordanian Kofta is baked in a casserole, often with potato and tomato.
- **Kebab halabi** is the Jordanian name for what other Arabs call Kofta – ground spiced meat grilled on skewers.

ACCESS

Jordan is easily accessible to Western visitors with international airports in Amman and in Aqaba itself both served by direct flights from Europe and elsewhere. The land border with Israel is now fully open, and border formalities are quite streamlined. Many visitors take advantage of lower charter airfares by flying into Eilat, then crossing the border to Aqaba for their holiday. In addition, ferry services link Aqaba with Nuweiba in Egyptian Sinai, making connections from Aqaba to any of the northern Red Sea resorts quick and simple.

Dive Operators and Facilities

Aqaba offers a selection of accredited dive centres, providing organized dives and dive tuition. All offer a high level of service, with well-maintained equipment, experienced guides and transport to the local sites. Most are based in Aqaba tourist hotels or shopping centres, which makes them easy to find; however, the down side of their central location is the long commute from the centres to the dive sites. There is one exception, the Royal Diving Club, which has a prime location on the southern coastline, with walk-in access to some excellent dive sites and very short commuting times to the others. This is an obvious advantage, but it does mean spending the whole day at the centre; the town is too far away to pop back for lunch between dives.

Local Dive Etiquette and Customs

Most diving in the Aqaba region is done from the shore, with minibuses taking you from the centres to the dive sites. With only 27km (17 miles) of coastline to choose from, commute times are less rigorous than in many Red Sea diving areas, but two dives a day won't leave you much time for a leisurely lunch between dives.

You should be aware that Jordanian regulations prohibit diving in these waters without supervision by a local dive guide. This is provided by the Aqaba centres as part of their dive packages, but independent divers should not expect to get their tanks filled and then head off on their own.

1 PRINCE ABDALLAH REEF

★★★★★★★

Location: Directly offshore at the government campsite, Aqaba south coast.
Access: By minibus from Aqaba dive centres, then shore entry; also possible by boat from some centres.
Conditions: Some wind and waves; also, watch out for sea urchins.
Average depth: 15m (50ft)
Maximum depth: 30m+ (100ft+)
Average visibility: 20m (65ft)

The campsite management controls access to the entry point, so many clubs tend to ignore this site. This is a pity, since the reef here extends several hundred metres out from shore, with excellent if patchy coral cover over a sandy bottom. The reef shows some slight damage, possibly from the 1995 earthquake (see page 50), but boasts a very wide range of species.

After a shallow shore entry, the reef is marked by a series of small, shallow ravines at about 2–3m (7–10ft), through which divers can swim to reach the deeper reef. This area is also a good spot for snorkelling. Beyond the ravines, the reef slopes off very gradually to maximum depths beyond 30m (100ft), offering a very broad scope for exploration.

Dozens of morays can be seen on the reef, as can triggers, goatfish, groupers and angelfish, scorpionfish, lionfish, and a large number of wrasse species including birdnose, checkerboard and clown coris. Butterflyfish, damsels, clownfish and a host of anthias and basslets make up the small end of the spectrum, and the odd Bluespotted Ribbontail Ray can often be seen on the sand.

2 BLACK ROCK

★★★★★★★

Location: At the southern edge of the government campsite, Aqaba coast.
Access: By minibus from Aqaba dive centres, then shore entry; also possible by boat from some centres.
Conditions: Be aware that the shoreline is within the campsite boundaries and you may have a long swim to the exit point.
Average depth: 18m (60ft)
Maximum depth: 30m (100ft)
Average visibility: 20m (65ft)

A sand and rubble slope at the entry point leads to a marker buoy tethered just opposite the boundary fence; from here, a right turn takes you onto the reef. As you swim north, you will encounter large pinnacles and tower formations in the shallows – the reef is generally very contoured, and boasts a steeper slope than most sites in the area.

The reef composition is particularly varied, with many different corals, both stony and soft. Some damage is evident, possibly from the 1995 earthquake, and there is also a moderate amount of debris in the inshore sections, originating from the campsite onshore. However, the reef is healthy and attractive, with lots of cabbage coral, massive forms, plenty of *Dendronephthya, xeniid*, elephant ear and other soft and semi-soft corals, sponges, anemones, and some very nice branching stony corals.

One big attraction is the likelihood of spotting a turtle or two. There are lots of emperors and snapper, lyretail and other grouper, small triggerfish, wrasse and parrotfish, lions and scorpionfish; boxfish are prevalent, along with puffers of several types, and Sailfin Surgeonfish and butterflyfish are common.

3 CEDAR PRIDE

★★★★

Location: 4km (2½ miles) north of Royal Diving Club, Aqaba coast.
Access: By minibus from Aqaba dive centres, then shore entry; also possible by boat from some centres.
Conditions: Some wind and waves possible; watch out for sea urchins on entry.
Average depth: 20m (65ft)
Maximum depth: 30m (100ft)
Average visibility: 20m (65ft)

Built in Spain as the *Mona Dos* in 1964, this 74-m (245-ft) freighter went through various owners and names before *Cedar Pride*. After a mysterious fire at the port of Aqaba in 1982, the vessel remained as a floating hulk. With royal patronage she was finally cleaned up and purposely sunk for divers in November 1985. She now lies on her port side across two raised sections of the seabed; there is thus a swim-through under the wreck.

JORDAN'S MARINE PEACE PARK

As a result of a 1994 peace agreement and special arrangements for Aqaba and Israel in 1996, the RSMPP (Red Sea Marine Peace Park) was set up as a joint undertaking by the governments of Israel, Jordan and the USA. Israel and Jordan share 41km (25 miles) of shoreline around the northern Gulf of Aqaba. Jordan has established a marine park off the shores of Aqaba and has designated a protected coral reef strip stretching 7km (4½ miles) from south of the port to just north of the Saudi Arabian border on the eastern side of the Gulf of Aqaba. Israel has set aside the southern part of the Eilat coast for nature conservation.

A 4-km (2½-mile) 'marine protected belt' lies in the sea, approximately parallel to two on-shore nature reserves that stretch from the southern end of the city of Eilat to the border crossing with Egypt at Taba.

*Two Coral Groupers (*Cephalopholis miniata*) square up for a confrontation.*

The wreck is marked by a surface marker buoy, and lies about 50m (165ft) offshore at the foot of a sand and sea grass slope. On the seaward side, the deck, superstructure and cargo areas offer the most interesting diving; the large tank areas can be swum inside, and much of the superstructure can be penetrated. The view from the north is particularly impressive, with the ship's stern rising dramatically from the bottom, complete with propeller. At the bow end, the remains of what appears to be the ship's lifeboat lie on the bottom. On the wreck there is good soft coral growth.

The site boasts a good range of reef fish. Jacks and barracuda are regular visitors from deeper waters, and the smaller reef species such as damsels and basslets are well represented.

4 HUSSEIN REEF

★★★★★★★

Location: 3.8km (2½ miles) north of Royal Diving Club.
Access: By minibus from Aqaba dive centres, then shore entry; also possible by boat from some centres.
Conditions: Some wind and waves may complicate entry.
Average depth: 18m (60ft)
Maximum depth: 20m (65ft)
Average visibility: 20m (65ft)

Located just to the south of Cedar Pride (Site 3), a very colourful reef with a gently sloping profile. Generally well contoured, with some steeper sections, particularly around 20–25m (65–80ft). The reef's gentle undulations are broken by some large bommies, outcrops and large coral heads. Inshore, the shallow sections of the reef offer good snorkelling possibilities.

Throughout, the site boasts some excellent coral. Fish life is equally exciting, with large numbers of lionfish, morays, angelfish, groupers, boxfish, pufferfish, trumpetfish, scorpions, pipefish and lizardfish. Clown and other anemonefish defend their patches, while jacks dart in silvery flashes along the reef.

4A BARGE CRANE C 4368 TAIYONG

★★★

Location: Just offshore of the Hussein Reef area, known as the Japanese Gardens by some operators.
Access: By boat.
Conditions: Choppy with moderate to strong currents.
Average depth: 50m (165ft)
Maximum depth: 57m+ (187ft+)
Average visibility: 20m (65ft)

Located some distance from the shore, the Barge Crane C 4368 *Taiyong* was a container barge owned and operated by the Arab Shipping Co. Her owner died and in 1997 the authorities decided to scuttle her. Now located between 35–57m (115–187ft) beneath sea level, she is lying on her starboard side with the bow towards shore. The port side is between 35–40m (115–130ft) and the top of the derrick is at 57m (187ft). Only accessible by boat, access is restricted to technical divers using more than one scuba cylinder and with Enriched Air Nitrox for staged decompression procedures.

5 GORGONIAN I

★★★★★★★★★

Location: 3.2km (2 miles) north of Royal Diving Club.
Access: By minibus from Aqaba dive centres, then shore entry; also possible by boat from some centres.
Conditions: Some strong wind and waves possible at the surface.
Average depth: 20m (65ft)
Maximum depth: 30m+ (100ft+)
Average visibility: 20m (65ft)

This is another gently sloping reef, extending offshore for a considerable distance as it angles slowly down to depths of 30m (100ft) or more.

Coral growth here is exquisite. Everything imaginable grows in profusion and dense concentration. This is easily one of the finest coral sites in the Gulf of Aqaba. The fish life is stunning too, with lionfish, scorpions, angelfish, grouper, parrots and butterflyfish providing plenty of colour, and sea turtles, mostly hawksbill, frequently visiting the reef.

Gorgonian I really is unmissable for novices and experienced divers alike.

6 GORGONIAN II

★★★★★★★

Location: 3km (2 miles) north of Royal Diving Club.
Access: By minibus from Aqaba dive centres, then shore entry; also possible by boat from some centres.
Conditions: Possibility of wind and waves at surface.
Average depth: 18m (60ft)
Maximum depth: 40m+ (130ft+)
Average visibility: 20m (65ft)

Just south of Gorgonian I (Site 5), this site is in many ways similar. It is another gentle slope reef with a wide range of corals and a good, varied population of reef fishes.

The gorgonian for which the site is named lies in the deeper water of the reef's northern section. Other coral attractions include some big bommie formations, and mixed pinnacles formed of a variety of stony corals. *Acropora*, *Favites*, *Porites*, plate and cabbage

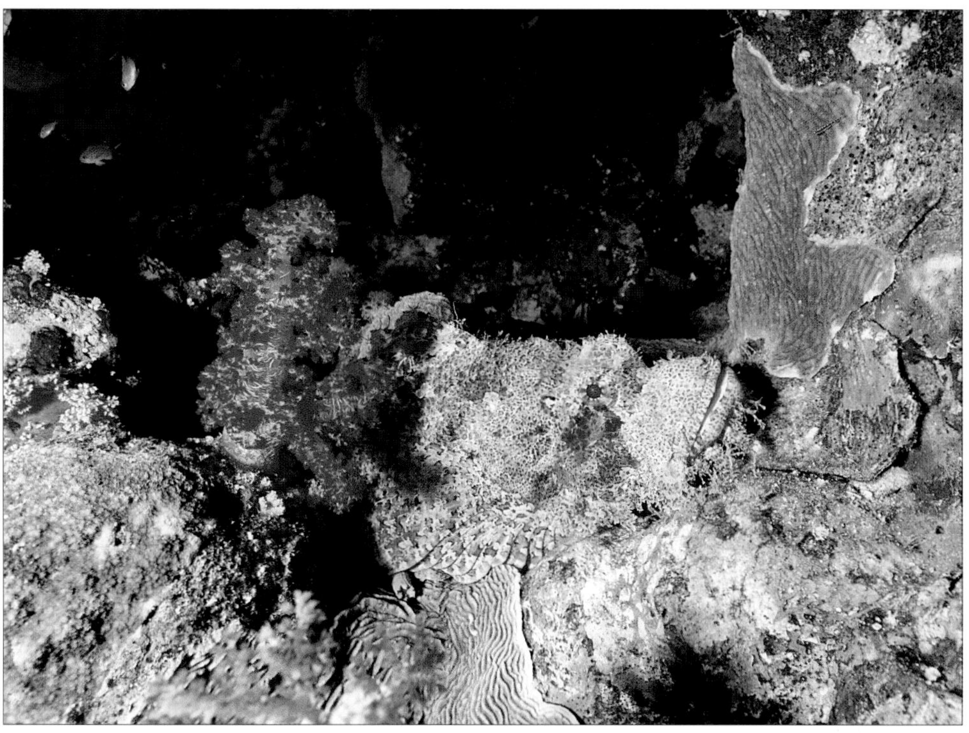

Above: *The bearded scorpionfish is virtually undetectable when nestling among rocks and coral.*
Below: *Anthias swarming around coral.*

corals are all present, along with a few good soft coral sections.

Fish life is quite dense, and the site offers some surprises, including at least one large Yellowmouth Moray, several other morays, interesting small pipefish, scorpions of several types, trumpetfish, wrasse, angelfish and Lyretail Groupers. There are a great many damsels and other small reef species, including some spectacular concentrations of colourful anthias and basslets.

7 NEW CANYON (OLIVER'S CANYON)

★★★☆☆☆

    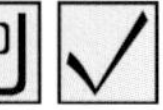

Location: 2.7km (1¾ miles) north of Royal Diving Club.
Access: By minibus from Aqaba dive centres, then shore entry; also possible by boat from some centres.
Conditions: Wind and waves at the surface can complicate access.
Average depth: 18m (60ft)
Maximum depth: 40m+ (130ft+)
Average visibility: 20m (65ft)

This site, at the southern edge of Gorgonian II (Site 6), is on a very flat sloping reef, with a profile almost horizontal in places. The reef touches depths of 30m (100ft) or more several hundred metres offshore, but reaching these depths on the reef face will require a long swim. The canyon for which the site is named is a wide, steep-walled valley whose sandy bottom drops steeply to depths well over 40m (130ft). At 6m (20ft) there is the shell of an Anti-Aircraft Tracked Vehicle – 'the tank' – sunk in 1999 by King Abdullah.

Due to its relatively undived state, the reef boasts better coral quality than many sites in the area. There are lots of bommies (large, spherical coral heads), and heads of massive corals, including *Favites* and *Goniopora*; plate, mushroom and cabbage corals are also widespread, and there are extensive areas of dense, soft coral growth. Fish life can be sparse, but there are some attractions: dozens of big scorpionfish, large lionfish and many lizardfish make their homes here.

8 CANYON (EEL CANYON)

★★★☆☆☆

Location: 2.4km (1½ miles) north of Royal Diving Club.
Access: By minibus from Aqaba dive centres, then shore entry; also possible by boat from some centres.
Conditions: Some wind and waves possible.
Average depth: 25m (80ft)
Maximum depth: 40m+ (130ft+)
Average visibility: 20m (65ft)

This site begins on a reef slope which angles gently out to a drop-off about 60m (195ft) offshore. Beyond the drop-off, a reef wall descends to a flat plateau at 40m (130ft). The entire reef is split by the canyon for which the site is named: a large, steep-sided valley running perpendicular to shore from the reef shallows to the open water beyond the drop-off.

The usual reef species are to be found on the reef face and wall, while the proximity of open water brings in jacks and schooling surgeonfish. The site is well covered with corals, tending more to the stony species.

9 BLUE CORAL

★★★☆☆

Location: 1.6km (1 mile) north of Royal Diving Club.
Access: By minibus from Aqaba dive centres, then shore entry; also possible by boat from some centres.
Conditions: Some wind and waves.
Average depth: 20m (65ft)
Maximum depth: 40m+ (130ft+)
Average visibility: 20m (65ft)

This site, named for a type of blue-tinged lacy coral, lies to the south of the Canyon site (Site 8) in the middle of the bay. It is a sloping reef about 30m (100ft) wide, bounded to either side by deeper sand patches. The reef runs down to a maximum depth of 40m+ (130ft+), but plenty of interest can be found in the shallower sections from 15–25m (50–80ft).

Coral cover is the usual excellent selection of stony and soft species, with a fair number of branching types, cabbage and plate coral, and some soft formations.

Fish life is quite good, with parrots, grouper, angelfish, butterflyfish, wrasse and many other reef species. Small basslets and anthias abound, and you can often see Bluespotted Ribbontail Rays.

10 MOON VALLEY

★★★☆☆

Location: About 700m (½ mile) north of Royal Diving Club.
Access: By minibus from Aqaba dive centres, then shore entry; also possible by boat from some centres.
Conditions: Some wind and waves can complicate entry.
Average depth: 20m (65ft)
Maximum depth: 30m+ (100ft+)
Average visibility: 20m (65ft)

This site, just off the shore to the north of the nature reserve fence, is a gentle, undulating slope reef, with slight rolling ridges running perpendicular to the shoreline. The reef is interspersed with sand valleys, which give the site its name.

The site boasts a good range of corals, with respectable if slightly patchy cover. Both stony and soft corals are well represented.

Growth in the shallower areas is marred by some damage and litter, but the deeper sections of the reef are in good condition.

There are plenty of fish here. Some notable residents include schooling jacks, fusiliers and snappers, groupers and coral trout, angelfish, trumpetfish, lots of moray eels, box, puffer and porcupinefish, many types of wrasse, basslets and dottybacks, and dozens of lionfish.

11 LONG SWIM

Location: From the Moon Valley site to the Royal Diving Club 700m (½ mile) south.
Access: By minibus from Aqaba dive centres, then shore entry; also possibly by boat from some centres.
Conditions: Good air consumption and careful depth monitoring are essential.
Average depth: 12m (40ft)
Maximum depth: 30m+ (100ft+)
Average visibility: 20m (65ft)

This site is on the shallow part of the reef stretching between Moon Valley (Site 10) and the jetty at the Royal Diving Club.

It covers a distance of 700m (2295ft) or more, so is suitable only for divers with very good air consumption, or for snorkellers comfortable with long swims. The site extends along the coast of a fenced nature reserve, so exit/entry is possible only at Moon Valley to the north or the jetty to the south.

The northern reef is rather patchy, similar in some ways to the Moon Valley site; to the south, coral growth becomes denser, with some very profuse growth.

There are several sandy areas, including a couple of wide, barren valleys, along the reef's length. The reef does slope down to depths of 30m (100ft) or more, but given the constraints of air supply and distance, you would be ill advised to drop this deep – most divers set a maximum depth of 12m (40ft) or less.

A sea grass field marks the end of the dive; here you find the mooring of a surface marker buoy, which is the locator point for the jetty.

All the coral on this site is in excellent shape, perhaps due to the protection of the nature reserve. Even the patchy areas to the north display very clean, healthy growth, and the denser southern section is spectacular.

Fish life at this site is also good, with a fine assortment of reef species such as parrotfish, puffers, boxfish, lionfish, lots of morays, sand gobies and pipefish, groupers, angelfish, butterflyfish and schools of fusiliers and snappers. Nudibranchs can be spotted all over the site.

12 AQUARIUM

★★★★★★★

Location: The northern house reef at Royal Diving Club.
Access: Shore entry from Royal Diving Club jetty.
Conditions: Take care when entering from the jetty; the bottom can be too shallow if you are overweighted or negatively buoyant.
Average depth: 20m (65ft)
Maximum depth: 37m (120ft)
Average visibility: 20m (65ft)

This is an exceptionally good site for a house reef, with good coral growth, prolific fish population, and a range of depths to suit everyone from novice snorkeller to experienced diver. The reef is gently sloping to around 30–37m (100–120ft).

Coral is the usual first-class variety of species, with some big patches of very nice *Dendronephthya* soft coral, cabbage coral, *Acropora* branching coral, lots of anemones and sponges, and some black coral at depth.

There are plenty of fish to see: pufferfish, groupers, lionfish, scorpions, nice angelfish, snappers and lots of emperors, sweetlips, trumpetfish, pipefish, damsels and brilliantly coloured anthias, dottybacks and basslets. On the sand it is possible to find stingrays, and even flounder-like flatfish.

13 THE GARDENS

★★★★★★★

Location: Just south of the jetty at Royal Diving Club.
Access: Shore entry from the jetty.
Conditions: Some mild currents; wind and waves can be strong.
Average depth: 18m (60ft)
Maximum depth: 25m (80ft)
Average visibility: 20m (65ft)

This site, the southern section of the house reef at the Royal Diving Club (see Site 12), is a gently sloping flat reef made up of distinct heads and coral formations on a sandy bottom. The variety of corals here is less wide-ranging than at some sites. There is some evidence of damage from the earthquake in 1995, but most coral heads are in good shape. Soft corals, such as *Dendronephthya* and *Xeniids,* are much in evidence, and the stony corals are also very well represented.

Fish life is up to the usual standard for this stretch of coast, with the usual reef fish complemented by some smaller attractions, like several types of pipefish, seahorses and interesting sand gobies.

Easy shore access makes this a prime, and therefore popular, site for snorkellers.

14 SAUDI BORDER

★★★★★★★★★

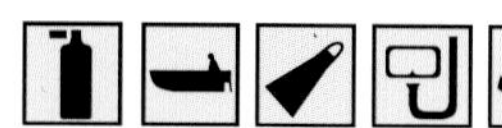

Location: About 300m (985ft) north of the Jordan/Saudi Arabia border.
Access: By minibus from Aqaba dive centres, then shore entry; also possible by boat from some centres.
Conditions: Some mild currents possible.
Average depth: 20m (65ft)
Maximum depth: 50m+ (165ft+)
Average visibility: 20m (65ft)

This site has a moderate to steep sloping profile, running from the reef shallows inshore to a sand bottom beyond 60m (195ft). The inshore section offers good, if patchy, coral growth down to about 7m (25ft). Beyond this point the reef slope steepens and coral growth becomes dense.

Coral cover is excellent, in an exquisite state of preservation, with an almost perfect balance between stony and soft species. The best of the coral lies beyond the drop-off at 7m (25ft) or more, beyond comfortable snorkelling range for most.

Fish life is good, if not as spectacular as the coral. Damsels and clownfish are everywhere and there are thousands of tiny basslets and anthias, small wrasse, butterflyfish, boxfish, porcupines and large pufferfish. Regal and other angelfish are present, and large Napoleon Wrasse are a common sight.

This is one of the best coral sites in Jordan and is definitely not to be missed.

GULF OF AQABA QUAKE

In late 1995, a severe earthquake rocked the northern Red Sea. Richter scale estimates vary wildly, but the quake, whose epicentre was in the central Gulf of Aqaba offshore from Nuweiba, was certainly powerful enough to damage buildings and roads all over the northern Gulf. Shock waves were felt as far away as Cairo and hotels in Eilat were split down the middle. Aqaba and Nuweiba saw serious structural damage and injuries occurred as far south as Sharm el Sheikh.

A less obvious victim of this destruction was the reef ecosystem. Coral damage was seen throughout the region, with particular upheavals along the Aqaba shore. Fortunately, there was no tsunami or tidal wave associated with the quake, or the damage could have been irreparable.

The stony corals were the worst hit and several sites lost prized formations. But overall the immediate damage was less extensive than some had feared, with reef damage mostly localized and generally light. The long-term effects are harder to predict; some die-off will be inevitable, but given the Red Sea's perfect conditions for coral growth, there is every chance for a rapid regrowth. Time will tell.

*A female Bicolor Parrotfish (*Cetoscarus bicolor*) tucks up in a hole for the night.*

How to Get There

By air: Jordan's only port, Aqaba, has an international airport just north of the city for charter flights from Europe, North America and the Far East. However, most divers fly to the capital's Queen Alia International Airport at Amman and then connect for Aqaba. In general, this route is more expensive than using the low-cost flights to Eilat and the cost of crossing the border, but the security hassles that Eilat's Ovda Airport imposes on tourists make it preferable to fly directly to Jordan if you can afford it.
By ferry: Aqaba also has a passenger and vehicular ferry service to Nuweiba in Egypt; this was until recently the only link between the Arab states east of the River Jordan and the north African Arab states. This will change with the opening of the Jordan/Israel border, but currently the ferry still carries most of the cross-Red Sea trade, and is packed with freight trucks on every crossing.
By road: With the peace agreement between Israel and Jordan now firmly in place, the land border between Eilat and Aqaba is fully open to foreign tourists and their vehicles. Future plans call for the establishment of an international free zone linking Aqaba, Eilat and Taba in Egypt, with minimal border formalities between the three; how this works out, only time will tell.

Where to Stay

Aqaba has a number of luxury tourist hotels, as well as a range of less expensive options. The overall standard of accommodation is high; even in mid-range rooms you will generally find colour TV, air-conditioning and even a refrigerator. Top-end possibilities include the **Aquamarina I Beach Hotel Club**, **Aquamarina II City Hotel**, **Aqaba Gulf**, **Nairoukh II** and **Alcazar Hotel**.

In the mid-range, plenty of smaller hotels are scattered around the town centre; one of the nicest of these is the **Red Sea Hotel**, tucked away behind the Ali Baba restaurant and the Ata Ali patisserie. Most rooms here have en suite bathrooms and balconies. Also in this range is **Nairoukh I**. Real budget-priced options also exist; several can be found in the same street as the Sitt el Sham restaurant in the town centre.

Alcazar Hotel PO Box 392, Aqaba 77110; tel 962 3 2014131/fax 962 3 2014133; email alcsea@alcazar.com.jo; www.alcazarhotel.com.
Al Amira Hotel PO Box 383, Aqaba; tel/fax 962 3 2012559; email amira@hotmail.com.
Aqaba Gulf Hotel PO Box 1312, Aqaba 77110; tel 962 3 2016636/fax 962 3 2018246; email aqgulfhtl@index.com.jo; www.aqabagulf.com.
Aquamarina I Beach Hotel Club PO Box 96, King Hussein Blvd, Aqaba; tel 962 3 2016250/fax 962 3 2032630; email aquama@go.com.jo.
Aquamarina II City Hotel PO Box 96, Al Nhada St, Aqaba; tel 962 3 3155165/fax 962 3 2032633; email aquama@go.com.jo.
Aquamarina III Royal Hotel Manara St, Aqaba; tel 962 3 2032634/fax 962 3 2032639; email aquama@go.com.jo.
Nairoukh Hotel I PO Box 1138, Aqaba; tel 962 3 2019284/fax 962 3 2019285.
Nairoukh Hotel II PO Box 1138, Aqaba; tel 962 3 2012980/fax 962 3 2012891.
Red Sea Hotel PO Box 65, Aqaba; tel 962 3 2012156/fax 962 3 2015789; email redseahotel@firstnet.com.jo.
A 54-room hotel is being constructed at the Royal Diving Club.

Where to Eat

Probably the nicest restaurant in Aqaba is the **China Restaurant**, upstairs just next to Grindlays/ANZ Bank. Good places for lunch or dinner are the **Tikka Chicken** and the **Mankal Chicken Tikka**, just up the road. Also good in this area is the **Chili House**, an American-style burger place.

The square behind the Red Sea Hotel, near the post office, has a couple of good Jordanian cafeterias; **Sitt el Sham** is the best, with daily special meals of home-style Jordanian cooking. Just downhill from here, the boulevard above the mosque has a range of eateries; among these are the **Syrian Restaurant** and **Ali Baba's**, where you can sip a beer or glass of wine with your meal. Next door to Ali Baba's, the **Ata Ali** patisserie does a range of delicious pastries; you can sit on the terrace with a cup of tea or Turkish coffee and watch the world go by.

Dive Facilities

The excellent **Royal Diving Club**, 15km (9 miles) south of town, is the only operator situated near the dive sites; its spacious grounds contain a fully equipped dive centre, classrooms, swimming pool, snack bar and one of the few beaches in the Aqaba region where women can sunbathe freely. Staffed by a mixed English and Jordanian crew, the centre is friendly and professional.

Two centres are based in hotels: the **Aquamarina**, in the Aquamarina I hotel, and **Seastar Watersports** in the Alcazar Hotel.

Aquamarina Diving Center 110 PO Box 96, Aqaba; tel 962 3 2016250/fax 962 3 2032630; email Aquama@go.com.jo; www.aquamarina-group.com/Diving.html. PADI 5-star facility.
Dive Aquaba PO Box 1061, Aqaba 77110; tel/fax 962 3 2034849; email diveaqaba@diveaqaba.com.
Royal Diving Club Southern Coastal Road, Aqaba; tel 962 3 2032709/fax 962 3 2017097; email info@jptd.com.jo. PADI 5-star IDC Center.
Seastar Watersports/Alcazar Hotel, PO Box 392, Aqaba 77110; tel 962 3 2014131/fax 962 3 2014133; email alcsea@alcazar.com.jo; www.seastar-watersports.com. PADI 5-star IDC Center; BS-AC.

Hospitals

The **Princess Haya Hospital**, on the hill in the centre of town, is among the best in the country. It also houses the recompression and diving emergency centre.

Diving Emergencies

Aqaba boasts one of the best recompression centres in the Middle East. A six-bed Dräger **recompression chamber** is run by a professionally trained medical team at the hospital; a single-patient portable chamber with docking facilities can be used to transport patients to the main chamber. Contact the hospital on tel 962 3 2014111.

Local Highlights

There is not a great deal to do in Aqaba itself beyond simply relaxing and enjoying the local atmosphere. One possibility is the tiny **local museum**, on the seafront just south of the town centre. Next door is an impressive, partially restored **14th-century fort**, its gateway boasting massive, iron-studded doors and the Hashemite coat of arms carved in the stone above. The town also boasts an **archaeological site** with ruins dating back to AD 650 and earlier.

There are **beaches** at some of the larger hotels where women can sunbathe reasonably freely. The beach at the **Royal Diving Club**, south of town, is far better: its remote location and a strict entry control policy make it a completely hassle-free zone.

Further afield, there are two major attractions within easy reach of a day trip from Aqaba. The first is **Petra**, the spectacular ghost town carved from solid stone by the Nabateans more than 2000 years ago. A vast complex of temples, façades and other edifices carved directly into the solid valley walls, this site is rightly considered one of the wonders of the world. Jordan's other, natural, wonder is the supreme desert canyon of **Wadi Rum** – an amazingly rich spread of superb desert, with some almost unbelievable views.

SAUDI ARABIA

Saudi Arabia is really one of diving's last frontiers. Very few Westerners have ever managed to dive here, despite the best efforts of many. The appeal of diving almost untouched, barely explored reefs, far from the hustle and bustle of the western Red Sea's tourist resorts, is undeniable. Unfortunately, there are barriers that prevent you from doing so (see Visas overleaf).

With by far the longest coastline on the Red Sea – over 79 per cent of the eastern shoreline – Saudi Arabia holds a wealth of diving possibilities. From the Jordanian border on the northern Gulf of Aqaba to the Yemeni border in the far south, there are probably as many reefs concentrated in Saudi waters as in the rest of the Red Sea. Most organized diving is done in the area around Jeddah, which has a large expatriate community, but there are immense stretches of coastal reef along the entire coast to be explored. There are also innumerable offshore patch reefs and islands. Reef quality is reported to be excellent offshore, with little damage from industry or construction and none whatsoever from over-diving.

Water quality varies somewhat, given the extensive length of the coastline. In general, the northern reefs offer similar visibility to that found on the opposite coast, while the southern reefs become progressively less clear. Inshore reefs throughout much of the region tend to be turbid and heavily sedimented. The best diving is on seaward reefs and offshore patch and fringe reefs, where the muddy inshore conditions are absent.

Very little commercial fishing has been done by the Saudis since the petrodollars started rolling in. There is a fair amount of small-scale local fishing with hand lines or small nets, but almost no large-scale exploitation of fish stocks. This leaves large stocks of reef and pelagic fishes undisturbed for divers to enjoy. However, with the downward trend in oil prices the Saudi government has begun exploring its coastal resources, and intensive fishing may once again become common here. Another worrying trend is the reported introduction of blast fishing, supposedly carried out by foreign workers from Southeast Asia, where the technique is widely used. Spear fishing by Southeast Asian guest workers is common on the fringing reefs.

Opposite: *Stony and soft corals compete for light and space.*

Above: *Yellowsaddle goatfish (*Parupeneus cyclostomus*) forage in small groups or large schools.*

MARINE LIFE

Fish distribution is similar to that of the western Red Sea coast, with all the familiar Red Sea reef fishes represented, including groupers, wrasse, parrotfish, surgeons, triggerfish, angel, and butterflyfish. There are also considerable numbers of pelagic fish: jacks, tuna, Spanish mackerel and barracuda are all reported, and many of these species have substantial breeding grounds in Saudi waters. The area also supports several shark species, both reef and open-water; the southern shark population, however, has come under some pressure from Yemeni shark fishermen, who also fish Eritrea's Dahlak Islands.

The Saudi coast supports the same range of coral species as on the west coast; particularly well-represented species include *Acropora* in several growth forms, *Porites*, *Stylophora* and *Pocillopora*, and a range of soft corals including *Dendronephthya* and the *Xeniid* family. Growth is reportedly most dense in the northern half of the country, with reef quality decreasing toward the more heavily sedimented south.

The more remote regions, in particular, are very seldom dived, since most dive operations are based around Jeddah and cater for expatriate weekend divers. Some important Saudi reefs are the Jezirat Ruweijil fringe reef off Al Humaideh in the Gulf of Aqaba; the islands of Sanafir and Barqan in the Straits of Tiran; the Wejh Bank, on the north coast between Wejh and Qalib; and the Jeddah reefs, such as Shi'b al Kebir, Abu Faramish, Mismari Reef and Abu Madafi. There are very many other reefs in Saudi waters that await exploration by recreational divers, and a big part of the pleasure of diving here is the possibility of discovering virgin sites.

CONDITIONS

Sea temperatures range from lows of 20°C (68°F) or less in the Gulf of Aqaba in winter to over 35°C (95°F) off the south coast in summer. This is mirrored by surface air temperatures, which can range from 10°C (50°F) or less on the coast in winter to a blistering 50°C (122°F) in summer.

VISAS

Until recently, the Saudi Arabian government discouraged foreign tourism – the traditionalist regime did not want relaxed Western morals to pollute the country's strict Islamic purity. Only Muslims on a pilgrimage, guest workers with a work permit sponsored by a Saudi Arabian employer, or those on a short transit visa were allowed in. Visitors have been known to manage to dive while passing through on a transit dive, but only on fringing reefs. Single women are not allowed to enter the country on a transit visa – all women on a transit visa must be accompanied by their husbands. Overland groups buy Muslim marriage licences in Amman (Jordan) as a way around this problem.

However, as the oil revenues have dropped, a tiny amount of tourism has been allowed and the main people to benefit from this change have been cruise ship passengers and divers. So far, tourist diving only occurs at sites covered by Saudi Arabian dive operators and they must act as your sponsor in obtaining a visa. Do not try to enter Saudi Arabia without a visa or rely on the promise of anything other than a transit visa, as nothing less works.

THE PEOPLE AND THE CULTURE

Saudi Arabia is a strictly traditional country. The Wahhabi branch of Islam practised here is acknowledged even by hard-line Muslims to be the strictest on Earth, and the country recognizes no other faith. Non-Muslims may not hold Saudi citizenship and are barred from many parts of the country, including all mosques and from the entire region surrounding the holy cities of Mecca and Medina.

Regulations Concerning Women

Contact between men and women, and the public activities of women, are regulated by strictly enforced guidelines, and the country's laws ensure that there are no transgressions. Foreigners get no special concessions. Westerners, both male or female, are required to adhere to Saudi standards of legal morality in dress, demeanour and behaviour.

Couples walking together in public may be asked for proof of marriage. Men and women are also strictly prohibited from swimming together, and this restriction most definitely also applies to diving.

A special religious police force, the Matawwa, exists to enforce Islamic morality. They are the public arbiters of what is decent and proper. Standards of modest dress are often violently enforced to the extent that foreign women with exposed arms or legs have received beatings or have had their offending flesh spray-painted.

For women who are still determined to dive (and there are women who dive regularly), great care must be taken to avoid legal problems. The Matawwa is known to pay special attention to dive parties.

Dive Operators and Facilities

Jeddah has a number of diving centres and educational facilities. There are several PADI instructors working in the area and courses are regularly arranged for locals and expatriates. The dive centres organize fairly regular dive trips on Jeddah's local reefs and occasional trips further afield.

*Surgeonfish (*Acanthurus sohal*) are plentiful along the shallows of the fringing reef.*

SHORE DIVES IN JEDDAH (Sites 1-3)

In recent years there has been so much building development in the Jeddah area that sites for shore dives are limited. Instead, most people now dive from private beaches, where an entrance fee is paid for the day to use the facilities. Regrettably there has also been considerable development north of Jeddah, including a large amount of dredging, which has had an adverse effect on visibility. However, this situation has improved recently.

The places described on the following pages have been selected as extremely good dive sites. Divers must have permits issued by the Saudi government's Ministry of Agriculture and Fisheries (see page 59) and must obey all local laws and be sensitive to local customs. It is important to be aware that diving groups attract attention at the Corniche dive sites (Sites 1 and 2) as they are public places and favourite picnic areas for locals at weekends.

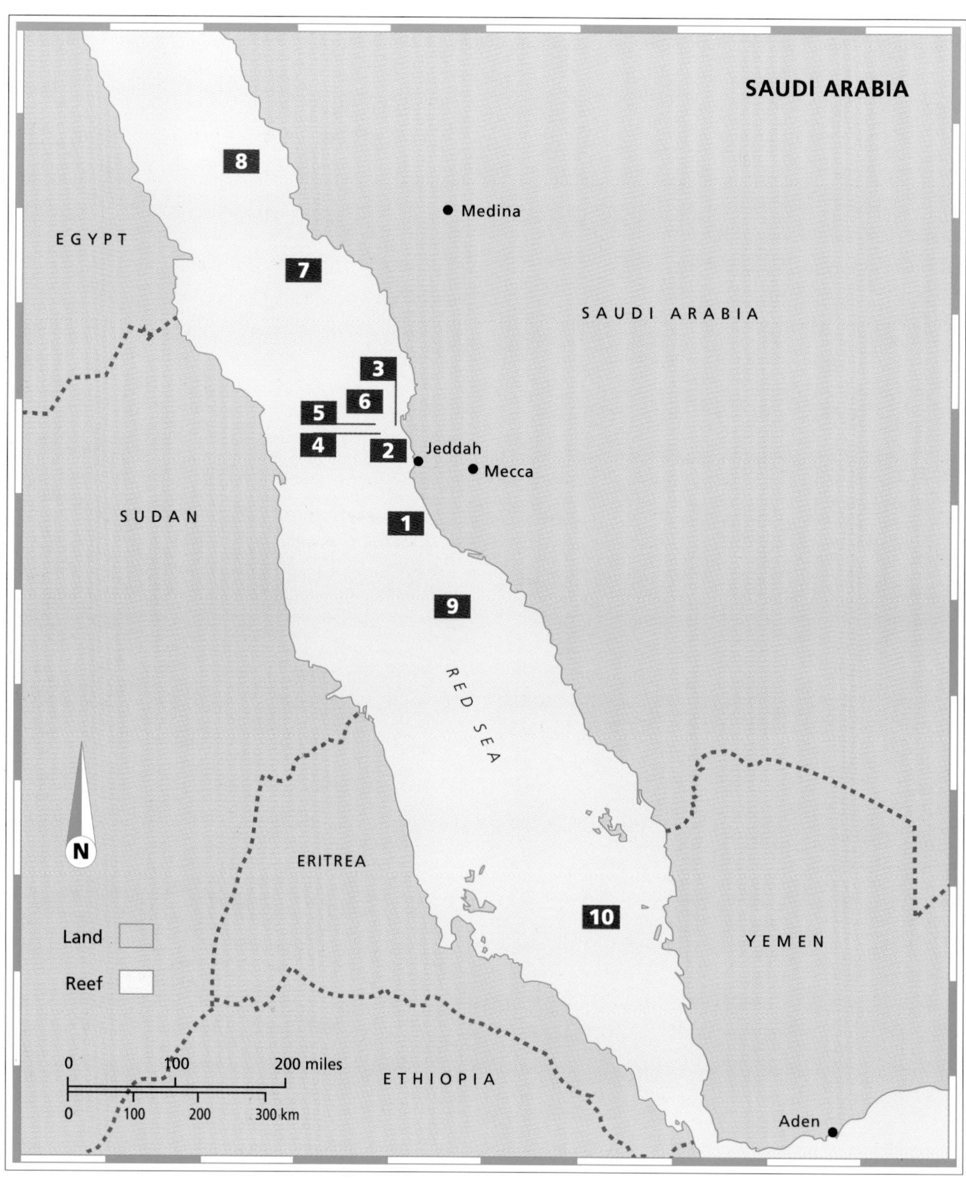

1 JEDDAH, SCHWAIBA (SCHU'AIBA)

★★★★

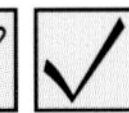

Location: Drive toward Makkah and turn right toward Taif on the Christian bypass. Turn right again after 500m (530yd) toward Jizan. About 40km (25 miles) along this road is a police checkpoint. After the checkpoint turn right along a road that follows a line of big pylons serving the plant. Stay on this road until you reach the de-salination plant, then drive south across the desert to the beach, which stretches a few kilometres south to a coastguard station.
Access: By car, a four-wheel drive is required.
Conditions: Best in the early morning, before the on-shore wind picks up, causing swell and surf.
Maximum depth: 45m (150ft) after the second drop-off.
Average depth: First plateau 15–25m (50–80ft). Sandy bottom with occasional coral heads and pinnacles.
Average visibility: 15–20m (50–65ft)
Schwaiba is a nice place to camp and night diving is excellent. Always notify the Coastguard before diving, and show them your papers. If they are in order you will receive the cooperation of the Coastguard and enjoy a very pleasant, trouble-free time.

2 JEDDAH, WHEAT-SHEAVES MONUMENT, AL-CORNICHE ROAD

★★★

Location: On the Corniche Road, 2km (3 miles) north of the Sheraton and Al-Bilad Hotels.
Access: By car. Parking is readily available.
Conditions: As with all shore dives in Jeddah, conditions are best in the early morning before the onshore winds pick up. The wind causes swells, surf, poor visibility, and longshore currents of various strengths. (These are rarely too strong to swim against and are not hazardous.)
Maximum depth: 45m (150ft)
Average depth: 15–20m (50–65ft) on the first plateau.
Average visibility: 20m (60 ft)
Since the Corniche Road was built there has been very little commercial development in this area that affects the aquatic habitats, and the environment has made a good recovery. However, divers should be careful of people fishing. It is best to notify the Coastguard before making your dive to prevent problems arising at a later stage.

This site has some interesting caves to explore. The constant current provides the abundant coral life and filter feeders with nutrients.

3 JEDDAH, THE AL-NAKHEEL BEACH

★★

Location: On the coastline north of Obhor Creek, 200m (220yd) past the petrol station. It is marked by a signboard in the central reservation of the road.
Access: By car. There is ample parking inside the beach complex.
Conditions: It is always best to dive in the early morning along the shoreline in Jeddah. In the afternoon, the swell and surf start to build, making exit over the reef more hazardous. This beach can become quite crowded in the afternoon, so the earlier you arrive the better.
Maximum depth: 45m (150ft)
Average depth: 15–25m (50–80ft) on the first plateau.
Average visibility: 20m+ (65ft+)
There are many private beach complexes along this stretch of coast. Al-Nakheel remains one of the most reasonably priced and offers a good range of facilities, including a dive shop with rental and air fills, a retail outlet, a restaurant, a swimming pool, sunbeds, changing rooms, and a jetty that takes you to within 30m (100ft) of the reef. It has a pleasant beach. There is an admission fee, which is higher on the Islamic weekend of Thursday and Friday. This site is a favourite night-diving spot and the facilities stay open until late.

BOAT DIVES IN JEDDAH (Sites 4-6)

Most of the best dive sites in Jeddah are off the coast and accessible only by boat. There are sites suitable for everyone, from the novice to the experienced diver, and there are many fascinating wrecks to explore.

These offshore sites are mostly unspoilt and are all well known to the captains of the various dive boats, most of which operate out of Andalus Playa Marina. Dive boats can be booked through the listed dive shops or directly through the marina, and can be organised for groups of any size. Individual divers can also be accommodated on trips.

Trip prices include lunch and refreshments, and overnight cruises are possible.

4 JEDDAH, TOWER REEF SOUTH TIP

★★★★

  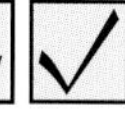

Location: 33km (18 nautical miles) west from the mouth of Obhur Creek, Jeddah.
Access: This site is only accessible by dive boat.
Conditions: The weather is usually fairly calm in the morning, with increasing wind in the afternoon.
Maximum depth: The second drop-off goes down to 50m (165ft). Beyond, there is a secondary coral garden rich in marine life, with black coral on the wall.
Average depth: 12–15m (40–50ft), a large plateau right on the south tip of the reef.
Average visibility: 20m (65ft)

This is one of the classic dive sites outside Jeddah. The currents from the north embrace the reef. A rich marine life includes large coral formations and many fish, ranging from anthias to large predators, which come from the south and hunt where currents meet at the tip.

5 JEDDAH, TOWER REEF NORTH TIP

★★★★

Location: 33km (18 nautical miles) west of the mouth of Obhur Creek, Jeddah. The compass heading from the mouth of the creek is a straight 270°.
Access: This site is only accessible by dive boat.
Conditions: The prevailing wind is northwest, building up in the afternoon. It is only possible to anchor on the east side of the reef (inside). Dive through the passage between a smaller northern coral formation and the main reef to the outside of the reef. Watch out for the current in the afternoon and during bad weather.
Maximum depth: 35–40m (115–130ft)
Average depth: 18–25m (60–80ft)
Average visibility: 20m (65ft)

This dive site has a lot to offer: a wealth of marine life, great photographic opportunities, a wreck and a chance to see sharks. A large column in the middle of the canal is completely covered with gorgonians and large red soft corals, surrounded by multitudes of small coral reef fish. As you come out on the reef's west side, head north and there is a three-hatch Greek cargo ship, the *Stephanos.*

6 JEDDAH, ABU FARAMISH

★★★★★

Location: These two reefs are 53km (29 nautical miles) northwest of Obhur Creek in Jeddah. You have to leave early in the morning in order to get there in decent time before the wind starts to build up. You can go 270° to Tower Reef and then head 290° to find the two reefs.
Access: This site is only accessible by dive boat.
Conditions: Most of the time the water is fairly calm.
Maximum depth: 25m (80ft)
Average depth: 15–20m (50–65ft)
Average visibility: 20m (65ft)

This is one of the 'far horizons' dive sites for divers from Jeddah. It is best known for rich coral reefs and friendly sharks. Visibility is usually good and on favourable days the water is extremely clear. You can find anything, from garden eels to black corals and even the odd shipwreck.

7 YANBU, BARRACUDA BEACH, NORTH OF THE CREEK

★★★

Location: At N24° 08.80′ and E037° 31.45′. Drive north from Yanbu, pass the airport, and at the next petrol station turn off the tarmac road to the left. Follow a worn dirt track about 2km (3 miles), pass a shallow mangrove swamp, continue until you see two small concrete blocks 500 m (530yd) apart, go through the gap, and you come to an old asphalt road system. Barracida Beach is at the end of the third east–west tarmac road.
Access: A 30-minute trip by four-wheel drive vehicle.
Conditions: Mainly morning dive sites are the best, since the sea will build up in the afternoon.
Maximum depth: 42m (140ft)
Average depth: The first plateau is at 18m (60ft)
Average visibility: 20m (65ft)

With easy access from the beach, this is one of the favourite dive sites in the Yanbou region. Large congregations of barracuda, jacks, large tuna and sailfish frequent this reef. If you swim over the edge of the first drop-off and explore the outer wall, there are large red soft corals, fan corals and garden eels.

8 SOUTH TIP OF WEDJ (WEJH) BANK, MASHABI ISLAND

★★★★★

Location: South of Mashbi (Masahib) Island.
Access: Only by a well-equipped, live-aboard offshore dive boat and after permission from the Saudi authorities to travel along the shoreline.
Conditions: Exposed to west winds and sea. This site is best visited in good weather conditions.
Maximum depth: 25m (80ft)
Average depth: 10–12m (35–40ft)

The richness of the colours in the water and on the reef, plus the assortment of fish and large predators, make the Bank's southern tip one of the top dive sites in the Red Sea.

9 SHI'B 'AMMAR, NORTHERN PART OF THE FARASAN BANKS

★★★★★

Location: South-southwest from the small village of Al-Lith, at the northern tip of the Farasan Bank, approximately 77km (42 nautical miles) from the shore.
Access: Only by an offshore dive boat, and after permission from the Saudi Arabian authorities.
Conditions: There is safe anchorage and diving within the lagoon, regardless of weather conditions.
Maximum depth: 27m (90ft)
Average depth: 14–17m (45–55ft)
Average visibility: 15m (50ft)
A top dive site because of its varied fish and marine life and because it can be visited and dived in all weathers. The south tip of the lagoon entrance is the best area to dive. Night dives in the lagoon are exhilarating.

10 JABAL AT TAIR, OFF THE YEMENI COAST

★★★★★

Location: South-southwest from Jizan, at N15°30' and E41°45'.
Access: Only by a well-equipped live-aboard, offshore dive boat.
Conditions: Generally calm weather. There are no strong currents.
Maximum depth: 32m (105ft)
Average depth: 14–18m (45–60ft)
Average visibility: 15m (50ft)
A virgin reef. Few divers have been in the water, so the fish are curious and approachable. We saw mantas, stingrays, sharks, barracuda and garden eels. The water has exceptional clarity and the coral is spectacular.

Saudi Arabia

HOW TO GET THERE

By air: Jeddah airport has excellent connections with Europe and most of the Middle East, but as it is purely a business destination, except for Muslims on pilgrimage, there are no cheap flights.
By ferry: There are ferries that mainly carry pilgrims and guest workers between Jeddah and Jordan, Egypt and Sudan.
By road: Saudi Arabia's road borders are open with Jordan, Yemen and the United Arab Emirates. For Yemen, if you are not Yemeni or Saudi Arabian nationals, you may only use the border along the coast road. There are many restrictions and, unless you have a work permit, you will be limited to a short transit visa.

GOVERNMENT PERMIT FOR DIVING IN SAUDI ARABIA

Dive permits for Saudi Arabia are issued by the Ministry of Agriculture and Fisheries, but first you must get an application from the Coastguard Headquarters at the Hovercraft Station, located on the Corniche road, south of the Sari Street junction.

Having obtained this form, it has to be completed and stamped by your company (tourists from overseas will have this permit arranged for them by their Saudi Arabian dive operator) before being returned to the Coastguard to be stamped. The Coastguard will ask you to sign a declaration that you will not in any way damage or remove anything from the underwater environment, and that you will notify the Coastguard before diving.

The stamped application form is then to be taken to the Ministry of Agriculture and Fisheries (located at Kilo 7, Makkah Road) along with: four passport-size photographs; a photocopy of Iqama (Government ID card for foreigners); copy and original of dive licence (PADI, BS-AC etc.); copy and original of diving wall licence (PADI, BS-AC etc.); a letter from your company giving permission for you to dive (must be stamped by the Chamber of Commerce). These documents should be taken to the Ministry in a standard green legal-size hanging file and the licence will normally be ready for collection next day.

WHERE TO STAY

Most of the large international hotel chains have a presence in Jeddah, but if you have a work permit you will already have accommodation, and if you are a tourist, your visa sponsor will arrange your accommodation.

WHERE TO EAT

There are many restaurants in Jeddah, but as there is effectively no public nightlife, most tourists eat at their accommodation.

DIVE FACILITIES

Two companies in Jeddah specialize in organizing tourist diving visas as well as diving packages, daily dive trips and diving permits. **Desert Sea Divers** Saudi Underwater Services, PO Box 50817, Jeddah, KSA 21533; tel 966 2 6561807/fax 966 2 6561288; email info@desertseadivers.com; www.desertseadivers.. **Saudi Divers** Sameria Commercial Centre, PO Box 7101, Jeddah 21462; tel 966 2 6646301/fax 966 2 6677153; email alireza@naseej.com.sa or saudidivers@yahoo.com. PADI 5-star Center. Also: **Sea Squirt Divers** 7 Birch, Al Hada Compound, Al Khobar; tel/fax 966 59 2704695; email enquiries@seasquirtdivers.com; www.seasquirtdivers.com.

For those divers who are already in the country, the dive shops in Jeddah and Yanbu offer training, rental and retail equipment. **Arab Circumnavigator** PO Box 4582, Jeddah 21412; tel/fax 966 2 6608224. **New Red Sea Divers** PO Box 8787, Jeddah 21492; tel 966 2 6606368/fax 966 2 6602064. **Red Sea Coral Diver** PO Box 8711, Jeddah 21492; tel 966 2 6612140/fax 966 2 6837946. **Yanbu Divers** PO Box 1083, Radwa Holiday Inn, Yanbu; tel 966 4 3224246/fax 966 4 3227281.

HOSPITALS & DIVE EMERGENCIES

The only recompression (hyperbaric) chamber available to foreigners is at **GNP Hospital** PO Box 4553, Prince Sultan Street, Jeddah 21412; tel 966 2 6823200/fax 966 2 6830289. There is a mono-chamber that can only accept emergencies at King Faisal Specialist Hospital and Research Centre, PO Box 3354, Riyadh 11211; tel 966 1 4647272.

LOCAL HIGHLIGHTS

There are several interesting old buildings in Jeddah itself.

EGYPT

Egypt boasts some of the finest diving in the whole of the Red Sea, from the coral playgrounds of southern Sinai to the offshore splendour of the deep south. Well-known diving areas like the Râs Muhammad National Park have received the lion's share of international attention, but even in the most intensely dived resort areas, there are still little-dived reefs. And with over 1500km (930 miles) of coastline covering most of the northwestern Red Sea, there is certainly no shortage of pristine dive sites further afield.

Marine Life

Think of any coral species and you will almost certainly find a living example in the Egyptian Red Sea. Even if you concentrated on the species to be found on a single site, the list would be unending. The fish are as unbelievable as the coral, and every dive is like a visit to the world's best aquarium.

The People

The Egyptians are a blend of peoples as disparate as Bedouin Arabs and Nilotic Africans, with a mix of cultures that combines Islam, Coptic Christianity and the rich traditions of a dozen ancient Mediterranean empires. Rooted in the rich soil of religious faith and cultural tradition, Egyptian society is nonetheless adapting to meet the needs of a modern world. And what all Egyptians seem to share is an open, friendly outlook which is as warm as the Egyptian sun.

Climate

Egypt's climate is one long summer, with an average rainfall of less than 2in (5cm) a year. Blue skies and baking sun are the norm the year round. Temperatures may fluctuate from below freezing in the desert in winter to 50°C (122°F) or more in the southern Egyptian summer, but clouds are a rare occurrence in any season.

Opposite: *Late evening sun illuminates the almost lunar landscape of the Sinai desert.*
Above: *The beautiful emperor Angelfish (*Pomacanthus imperator*).*

CONDITIONS

Below the surface, the endless summer continues. Water temperatures rarely fall as low as 20°C (68°F) in the depths of winter, and summer highs can be well over 30°C (86°F). Visibility is generally a superb 20m (65ft) average for most of the country, with highs of 30m (100ft) or more. Current movement is generally moderate throughout but individual sites may experience strong localized currents. Surface conditions are also generally benign, but the autumn wind change – from late September on – can bring big waves and swells that make access to isolated offshore sites difficult.

NORTH SINAI

North Sinai, as the term is used in this book, means the north Egyptian coast of the Gulf of Aqaba. There is a big chunk of Sinai that lies further to the north, traditionally referred to as North Sinai, but it does not reach the Red Sea. The Egyptian coast of the Gulf of Aqaba stretches from Taba, the Israeli border post, to the northern section of Râs Muhammad National Park at Nabeq; it encompasses the towns of Dahab and Nuweiba, and includes some of the Gulf of Aqaba's finest dive sites. Like the rest of the Sinai, the coast is populated by Bedouin tribes whose ancestors migrated here from the Arabian peninsula centuries ago.

THE PEOPLE AND THE CULTURE

The Bedouin speak a colloquial form of Arabic and follow a semi-nomadic lifestyle; they are adopting an increasingly settled way of life, and Sinai has a number of permanent

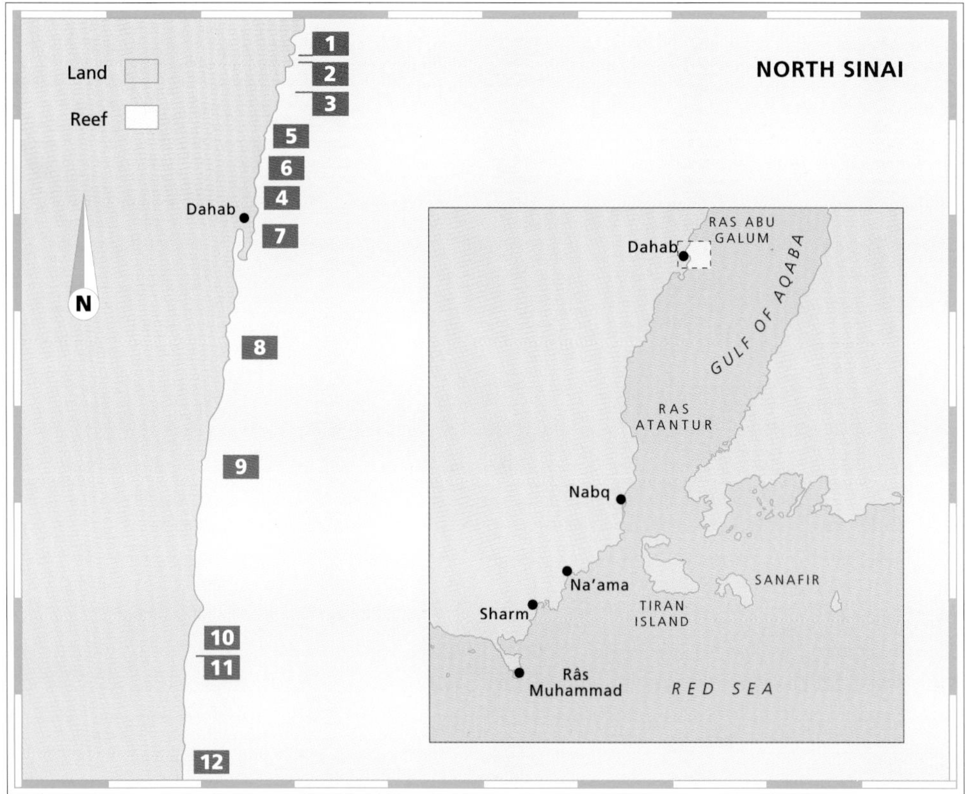

Bedouin settlements such as those at Dahab and the coast near Nabeq. The arrival of the tourist industry, however low-key, has brought with it an influx of Egyptian newcomers, who have invested heavily in the new resort areas, and who tend to hold the lion's share of tourist-industry jobs.

CLIMATE

The Sinai is an arid, mountainous desert. The coast follows the same weather patterns as the rest of the peninsula, receiving little precipitation and experiencing extremely hot, dry summers and winters marked by warm days and cooler evenings, with temperatures often falling sharply toward freezing during the night.

DIVE HIGHLIGHTS

Here you will find some of the least spoiled reefs on the Egyptian coastline, with none of the hustle and bustle of the more developed diving areas to the south. Luxuriant coral gardens and sheer offshore canyons attract a dense population of reef fauna, and the clear waters bring crystal visibility to add to your diving pleasure.

MARINE LIFE

The area's reefs are home to a dazzling array of Red Sea reef species, from huge Napoleon Wrasse to tiny, glittering anthias. The range of pelagic species is also more than respectable. In addition, sea turtles and dolphins frequent North Sinai reefs, lending every dive the excitement of a possible encounter.

The reefs are shining examples of tropical coral at its best, with a vast, lush range of stony and soft corals including exquisite table *Acropora*, *Stylophora*, massive *Porites* and *Goniopora*, fire coral, low-lying cabbage coral, graceful gorgonians and pulsing *Xeniid* soft corals.

Swimming with dolphins is one of the highlights of Red Sea diving.

CONDITIONS

A steady north wind blows on to the Sinai coast for much of the year, raising waves which can at times make access to the best sites difficult. As autumn moves toward winter, these onshore winds can be especially troublesome, but even during the worst weather there are plenty of sheltered sites to enjoy.

ACCESS

Access to the Egyptian dive sites in the Gulf of Aqaba is almost exclusively from shore. This is partly a result of the prevailing winds which, combined with the area's sheer coastline, make it impossible for boats to anchor. However, since the best sites lie within a few metres of the coastline this is not a problem.

DIVE OPERATORS AND FACILITIES

There are a number of professional dive operations. The bulk of these are clustered in Dahab, the area's main resort town, but others can be found in Nuweiba and even Taba. Most are of a high technical standard, offering tuition through a number of certification agencies and employing multi-lingual Western and Egyptian dive staff. Jeeps or pickup trucks ferry divers to the dive sites, and a full range of rental equipment is available.

LOCAL DIVE ETIQUETTE

Because shore entries are the norm here, it is especially important to take care when entering the water. Caution is needed, not just to prevent injury to yourself, but also to safeguard the fragile reef. Try to do as little damage as you can to the delicate reef table as you make your way to and from your dives.

EGYPTIAN FOOD

Many people are familiar with Middle Eastern food, which has become widely available in Western countries in recent years. While Egyptian food bears many similarities to the other cuisines of the region, it has unique characteristics. The following should give you an idea of what is on offer in the average Egyptian eating place.

- **Aish** is bread (it also means 'life'). It resembles pita bread and is also called khubz. It is eaten in huge quantities at all meals.
- **Fool** (or Foul, or Ful) is the Egyptian staple – boiled fava beans served in any number of different ways. At its most basic, it is a bowl of boiled beans with a little oil and lemon; at its most refined, it is a delicately spiced purée accompanied by onions, tomatoes and sometimes meat. It is used as a filling in pockets of aish for quick snacks, or served on its own or as part of a more substantial meal.
- **Ta'amiya** is better known in the west as felafel, crunchy balls of puréed chickpea, deep fried and often served in **aish** pockets.
- **Tahina** is sesame seed paste mixed with lemon and spices. It is used as a dip or as a dressing in sandwiches.
- **Hummus** means chickpea. It can be served whole or mashed into a paste with tahina and spices.
- **Shawarma** is the Egyptian equivalent of gyros or doner kebab: grilled meat stacked on a rotisserie spike, then sliced thin and served in aish pockets.
- **Kofta** is ground meat, grilled on skewers or made into meatballs.
- **Kushari** is a mix of rice, macaroni, lentils and tomato sauce topped with fried onion.
- **Shorba** is soup; shorbat 'addis, or lentil soup, is the classic Egyptian soup.
- **Coffee** is qahwa or gahwa, served Turkish style in tiny glasses. *Masbout* means medium sweet. *Bidoon sukr* means without sugar.

1 THE BELLS

★★★★★★★

Location: Several km/miles north of Dahab village, just north of the Blue Hole (Site 2).
Access: By car to the Blue Hole, then a short walk to the entry point on the shore.
Conditions: Waves can complicate access despite protected entry.
Average depth: 20m (65ft)
Maximum depth: 50m+ (165ft+)
Average visibility: 20m (65ft)

A true vertical wall, full of overhangs and fissures, with lots of swim-throughs and cavelets. Toward the Blue Hole in the south the reef profile softens to a steep slope.

The dive begins in a small slot in the reef table, about 100m (330ft) north of the Blue Hole lagoon. After reaching your maximum depth on the sheer wall section just south of the entry, ascend slowly and then follow the reef south to the lip of the Blue Hole lagoon, in about 6m (20ft) at the top of the reef. This will be your exit point.

Coral cover on the wall section is not abundant, but there is quite good growth of plate and cabbage coral, black coral bushes and white soft corals.

Although the fish life here is reasonable, there are many sites with greater diversity and larger populations.

Like all wall sites, this one should be treated with caution. It is easy to be seduced by the sheer profile and far exceed your planned maximum depth. You should also remember that the exit point is only a few hundred metres/feet from the entry and is easily missed.

STONEFISH

The well-camouflaged Stonefish features high on the list of divers' worst nightmares, but the fact that they are very common and that very few divers have trouble with them should ease the minds of many.

Thought to be the world's most venemous fish, the Stonefish's spines contain a toxic venom that can kill a child or a highly allergic adult. Stonefish are found on the top of reefs or on the sand, so the people most at risk are local fishermen who tread on them while walking over the reef collecting shellfish.

True Stonefish remain still in a horizontal position for long periods of time, such that, depending on the habitat, they either allow algae to grow on their body or sand to cover it for further camouflage. They are usually only visible if they move.

CROCODILEFISH

The crocodilefish is one of the real oddities of the tropical reef. Lurking on the sandy bottom between coral patches, its subtle camouflage and flattened, low-lying body make it almost impossible to spot. It is often only the twinkle of the fish's eyes that gives it away.

There are several species of crocodilefish in the Indo-Pacific region. In the Red Sea, the predominant species is *Papilloculiceps longiceps*, the Indian Ocean crocodilefish. It is a large fish, growing to 70cm (28in). Like all crocodilefish, it has a laterally flattened body, two dorsal fins, and is covered with brownish, mottled markings on a lighter background. Its head features upturned eyes and bony ridges; fringe-like *papillae* lie above the eyes, and a spine lies below it. The fish's broad, horseshoe-shaped mouth is clearly visible from above. It feeds on crustaceans and small fishes which it captures with lightning-quick lunges from its concealment on the seabed.

2 BLUE HOLE

★★★★★★★

Location: A few km/miles north of Dahab village.
Access: By car from Dahab, then shore entry.
Conditions: Generally an easy and relaxed dive, but attempts to dive deep into the hole are extremely dangerous.
Average depth: 20m (65ft)
Maximum depth: 50m+ (165ft+)
Average visibility: 20m (65ft)

A pleasant but not outstanding site, with the greatest attraction lying not in the Blue Hole – the lagoon – but on the rich, sloping reef outside.

Entry to the site is through a large lagoon in the reeftop, about 50m (165ft) across. This lagoon is the 'blue hole' that gives the site its name. It is, in fact, the top of a vertical shaft which is reported to descend over 300m (985ft) straight down. A shallow lip at about 6m (20ft) leads from the lagoon to the outer reef. Deep within the hole, an arched passage also links the reef face with the hole.

The reef slope is fairly rich in stony corals – particularly the reef section to the south of the lagoon, which has *acropora* and brain corals – and, to a lesser degree, in soft corals.

Triggerfish, jacks, unicornfish, parrotfish, angelfish, groupers and surgeonfish are all part of the variety of fish life on the outer reef. Within the lagoon, with its sparse coral growth, there is little marine life of any kind.

For safety reasons divers are discouraged in the strongest possible terms from exceeding maximum depth limits in the Blue Hole.

3 THE CANYON

★★★★★★★

Location: Several km/miles north of Dahab, about halfway to the Blue Hole (Site 2), and just in front of the

Canyon dive centre.
Access: By car from Dahab, then shore entry.
Conditions: Entry can be complicated by wind and waves. Divers entering the canyon should take standard cave diving precautions.
Average depth: 20m (65ft)
Maximum depth: 50m+ (165ft+)
Average visibility: 20m (65ft)
This site takes its name from a long, narrow and very beautiful canyon that runs north to south from the shallow reef just offshore to depths of around 50m (165ft) on the reef slope further out. Access to the site is through a shallow (3-m (10-ft) lagoon lying a few steps from the shoreline. Note the prominent treetrunk-like pinnacle just outside the lagoon entrance – a good landmark for locating the exit point.

The entrance to the canyon is marked by a large coral mound lying some 10m (35ft) out from the reef face, in around 12m (40ft) of water. A man-sized opening in this coral hummock gives on to the top chamber of the canyon, a fishbowl-like enclosure filled with sweepers.

From here the canyon drops through various twists and turns to a depth of 50m (165ft). Open water is visible along most of its length through the narrow opening in the roof, but there is no opening large enough to exit through until 30m (100ft) depth.

Outside the canyon the reef has good coral cover but inside the canyon there is little, if any, coral growth to see.

Among the large range of reef fish here, some notable residents include pufferfish, unicornfish, snappers, groupers, basslets and rabbitfish. Jacks can often be seen along the reef, and beautiful, jewel-like schools of sweepers inhabit the canyon.

Note that only divers with considerable deep diving experience should consider swimming through the canyon to exit at depth. There is plenty for less experienced divers to see without risking a long, hazardous penetration. Even very experienced divers are strongly discouraged from proceeding beyond the 30m (100ft) exit. This deeper section is another of Dahab's diving fatality blackspots.

4 LIGHTHOUSE

★★★★★

Location: In front of the lighthouse, Dahab bay.
Access: By car from Dahab dive centres, then shore entry.
Conditions: Easy sheltered entry, but some surge likely even at moderate depth.
Average depth: 18m (60ft)
Maximum depth: 30m+ (100ft+)
Average visibility: 20m (65ft)
This is a fine dive, with a good range of features and depths to suit all levels of diver. Located just offshore at the lighthouse in Dahab bay, it features a sloping reef extending north around an out-thrust point of land. This section, while excellent in profile and layout, is looking a bit tired and worn. Large pinnacles extend out from the point, reaching depths of more than 25m (80ft) before tailing off to a series of smaller coral heads reaching into the depths. The reef then gives way to a wide, featureless sand slope before reaching a second sloping coral wall to the north.

This second reef slope is very interesting, with a flat reef top at around 4m (15ft) and a lower limit of around 20m (65ft), beyond which there is bare sand with a few coral patches. A shallow lagoon cuts the reef top at this reef's southern edge, hosting a varied fish life; the reef here is healthier overall than the southern section.

Both sections of the reef show a lot of secondary growth, with live coral patches over a visible base of skeletal corals. Both stony and soft species are well represented, particularly in the richer northern section. Fish life is diverse, if somewhat sparse, with big trumpetfish, wrasse, groupers, surgeonfish and unicornfish, lionfish and parrots all prevalent. Turtles and rays are frequently spotted here.

Divers and snorkellers please take note: because of the site's popularity as a windsurfing venue, do take extra care when surfacing and while at the water surface.

5 ABU HILAL/SMALL CANYON

★★★★★★★

Location: Between Dahab village and The Canyon dive site (Site 3).
Access: By car from Dahab, then shore entry.
Conditions: Wind and waves can make entry tricky.
Average depth: 20m (65ft)
Maximum depth: 50m+ (165ft+)
Average visibility: 20m (65ft)
This extensive site features an inshore reef top dropping steeply to 10-12m (35-40ft). The entry point, just south of an out-jutting spit of reef which acts as a breakwater for northerly wind-driven waves, leads onto a sheltered sandy lagoon with a bottom of 12m (40ft). Swimming straight out from here, divers will cross a shallow coral bar or threshold at around 4m (15ft), descend to their maximum depth along the rolling slope, then turn north and slowly ascend.

The canyon for which the site is named begins at a depth of more than 30m (100ft). It is extremely narrow and twisting, with severely limited exit points; beginning as it does at considerable depth, and reaching much

Opposite: *Longnose hawkfish (*Oxycirrhites typus*) find ideal refuge on a gorgonian coral.*

greater depths before an exit is possible, it lies beyond the scope of sport diving, and penetration should not be considered.

Beyond the canyon, a large uprising leads the way back to shore. A second large sandy area lies between the site's northern edge and the reef spit sheltering the entry point; swim either around the base or over the top, and you will arrive back at the entry lagoon.

Coral throughout the site is excellent, both in density and variety, and in excellent condition.

Fish life is equally diverse: among the hundreds of reef species; notable residents are unicornfish, wrasse, big groupers, triggerfish, lionfish and big starry puffers. Sea turtles are also a common sight.

6 EEL GARDEN

★★★★★★

Location: Offshore at the north end of Dahab's Bedouin village.

Access: By car from Dahab, then shore entry.

Conditions: Some surf may complicate entry; stonefish are common on the reeftop.

Average depth: 18m (60ft)

Maximum depth: 30m+ (100ft+)

Average visibility: 20m (65ft)

Entry to this site is through a small lagoon, which descends from the reeftop to an exit point on the reef at about 7m (25ft). Little more than 1.5m (5ft) wide at some points, this entry lagoon can act as a funnel for wave surge or runout from falling tides, so divers should be prepared for a strenuous swim.

Once outside the lagoon, a wide sandy slope leads off to the left (north), covered with literally thousands of the garden eels that give the site its name. Across the sand lies a sloping reef wall with scattered coral heads on the sand at its 18–20m (60–65ft) base; south of the sand, the reef continues, with lots of fine coral growth but no exit point until the lighthouse.

There is an excellent selection of coral growth along both reef sections, with stony and soft species including *Acropora*, plate, cabbage coral, *Dendronephthya* and *Xeniids*. Anemones are pretty common here.

As well as the eponymous garden eels, the site boasts large numbers of lionfish, Bluespine Unicornfish, damsels and basslets, parrots, groupers and plenty of sand gobies.

7 THE ISLANDS

★★★★★★★★★

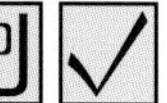

Location: On the Dahab coast, next to the Lagona Hotel.

Access: By car from Dahab, then shore entry.

Conditions: Entry can involve a long walk on the reef top at low tide.

Average depth: 12m (40ft)

Maximum depth: 16m (50ft)

Average visibility: 20m (65ft)

The Islands is a dense concentration of coral pinnacles and patch reefs in a sheltered location along the Dahab shore, a labyrinthine range of peaks, valleys, corridors, sand patches, bowls, amphitheatres, deep wells and coral peaks.

This intricate seascape is densely covered with absolutely pristine coral; the reef practically glows with a jewel-like quality. The range, condition and density are awesome – this is probably the most diverse and well-preserved selection of corals in the Sinai area. Every conceivable stony coral is present, with a diversity of soft corals to match.

Stunning as the coral is, it is rivalled by the fish life. Huge schools of barracuda, snappers, surgeonfish and unicornfish vie with scintillatingly coloured reef species. Sea bream, emperors, big triggerfish, rabbitfish, Birdnose Wrasse and a hundred and one other species round out the picture, with the occasional turtle thrown in for good measure. One particular highlight is a large, sand-bottomed amphitheatre halfway along the reef, where giant schools of immature barracuda congregate, circling like a flashing silver tornado.

8 THE CAVES

★★★★★★★

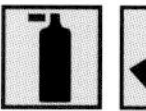

Location: On the Red Sea coast, 5km (3 miles) south of Dahab southern military checkpoint.

Access: By car from Dahab, then shore entry.

Conditions: Entry and exit can be tricky, especially in strong surf.

Average depth: 20m (65ft)

Maximum depth: 50m+ (165ft+)

Average visibility: 20m (65ft)

This site centres on a large, open-fronted chamber, or cavern, deeply undercutting the reef table close to shore. A small, semicircular shelter or windbreak by the track marks the entry point.

Entry to the site is effected by basically throwing yourself off the reef edge into deep water at the top of the cavern. Frequent strong waves at the surface may make it advisable to don your fins in the water, rather than risk losing your balance in the surf. On exit, you will need to judge wave patterns and allow yourself to be carried onto the reef top by the swell.

Once in the water, the cavern is directly below you. The undercut sections can be entered on either side of the sandhill; on the right, or south, side, a very contoured shallow reef section, with many inlets and surf tubes, leads onto the sloping body of the main reef; while to the north, a deeply undercut extension of the cavern leads down the side of the sandhill to the northern continuation of the reef slope.

The reef sections are as interesting as the cave, with good cover of stony and soft corals, and a lively population of reef and schooling fishes. Divers should make a personal judgement as to whether the entry/exit is within their scope.

*A bigeye (*Priacanthus hamrur*) hovers near to the reef at night.*

9 GABR EL BINT

★★★★★★

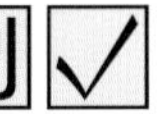

Location: On the coast south of Dahab, several km/miles beyond The Caves (Site 8).

Access: A ten-minute car ride, then one hour by camel from Dahab.

Conditions: The site's position is sheltered by the bay arm from the north swell.

Average depth: 20m (65ft)

Maximum depth: 50m+ (165ft+)

Average visibility: 20m (65ft)

Part of the attraction of this site is the novelty of the

commute – by camel along the inaccessible coastline between Dahab and Nabeq to the north of Sharm el Sheikh. The sight of a train of camels, driven by Bedouin in full regalia and loaded down with high-tech dive gear, is an unforgettable one.

The site is a sheer wall running around the north point of a curving bay. Following the coastline, the wall drops to depths well past 50m (165ft). Within the bay, the wall begins at depths from 8–20m (25–65ft), above which a gently sloping reef flat leads to shore, dotted with sand flats and *acropora*. North around the point, the upper reef slope widens, encompassing a veritable forest of soft corals which blanket the reef completely in places, as well as numerous huge gorgonians in the 2–3m (5–10ft) range. Inshore, a large sandy lagoon dotted with coral heads lies just past the point, an excellent place to spot rays and numerous large crocodilefish.

There are abundant soft and stony coral formations. Most species of fish are sparsely represented.

This is one of the most unusual sites along the Sinai coast, and well worth the effort. Trips are regularly arranged by Nesima Diving Center (see page 71).

10 END OF THE ROAD REEF

★★★★★☆☆☆☆☆

Location: At the extreme end of the Nabeq coastal road north of Sharm el Sheikh.
Access: By jeep from Sharm el Sheikh.
Conditions: Reef top entry may be hazardous, especially in windy and wavy conditions.
Average depth: 20m (65ft)
Maximum depth: 60m+ (200ft+)
Average visibility: 30m (100ft)

Onshore winds make entry very difficult, and even highly experienced divers are often injured during entry and exit. Also bear in mind that a serious injury this far from civilization could be life threatening.

The dive is on a submerged island about 10–15m (35–50ft) offshore, with its top in about 3m (10ft); a deep canyon extends down the southern side of the island to depths beyond 65m (215ft), while a narrow sandy channel with a bottom at 10m (35ft) separates the reef from shore. This channel broadens into a sandy plateau north of the reef, while the east side of the reef is a steep sloping wall to 50m (165ft) and beyond.

Coral cover is excellent throughout, with an amazing variety of species. All the corals are dense and profuse, and in an excellent state of preservation – this is one of the healthiest reefs in the region. Fish life is of the same order of excellence, with all the usual reef fish in abundance. The site also boasts one of the widest ranges of wrasse species in the Sinai area.

Note: when driving north of Sharm el Sheikh, there is a very real danger from minefields – do not stray off marked roads for any reason whatsoever.

11 OVER THE HILL (RÂS ATANTUR BAY)

★★★★★☆☆☆

Location: 23km (14½ miles) north of the Bedouin village, on the Nabeq coastal road. About 1.6km (1 mile) south of End of the Road (Site 10).
Access: By jeep from Sharm el Sheikh, then shore entry from reeftop.
Conditions: Access is difficult, as at site 10.
Average depth: 20m (65ft)
Maximum depth: 60m+ (195ft+)
Average visibility: 30m+ (100ft+)

A rich and well-preserved site, with a phenomenal density and diversity of fish and coral life. In the centre of a small bay, just beyond the bluff of Râs Atantur, the dive is on a small reef promontory extending into the bay. This reef has a steeply angled profile and is surrounded by steep sand slopes.

These slopes are dotted with coral heads while the reef has every conceivable type of coral, in staggeringly dense formations. This is probably the best site for stony corals in the entire region.

Note: when driving in this area, you must not leave marked roads, due to danger from mines.

12 NABEQ

★★★★☆☆☆

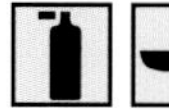  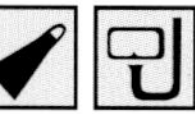 

Location: About 20km (12 miles) north of Sharm el Sheikh.
Access: By car from Sharm el Sheikh, then shore entry.
Conditions: Easy and sheltered, but involves a long walk through shallow water to entry point.
Average depth: 10m (35ft)
Maximum depth: 18m (60ft)
Average visibility: 15m (50ft)

This site is a large group of coral heads and pinnacles in shallow water off the coast at Nabeq. The site is intricate and labyrinthine, with plenty of scope for exploration among the scattered coral blocks.

On a flat, sandy bottom covered with eelgrass, the blocks, heads and pinnacles range from 1-m (3-ft) babies to monsters that nearly reach the surface.

These blocks, composed of a wide range of stony and soft corals, host an equally wide range of reef fishes. Jacks, groupers, triggers, rabbitfish and many others are all present, and the isolated nature of the individual heads seems to concentrate the fish in a way that would be impossible on a more open reef. Turtles are also regular visitors to the reef.

Note: do not stray from marked roads.

How to Get There

By air: Getting to North Sinai is straightforward. With international airports at Râs Nusrâni (for Sharm el Sheikh), Râs el Naqb and another just across the Israeli border north of Eilat, there is a huge number of flights to choose from. A taxi ride from either airport to Dahab takes about 1 1/2 hours; border formalities between Israel and Egypt, though very streamlined, will add around 45min to the trip. From within Egypt, there are luxury buses available from Cairo and other western cities.
Getting around: Within Dahab there is little need for transport, as it is easy to get around on foot and local dive centres arrange transport to the dive sites. Taxis will take you to other parts of the Sinai coast.

Where to Stay

Originally a Bedouin village with a few huts catering to backpackers, Dahab is now a full-scale resort with luxury facilities. The town still retains its original, alternative flavour, and much of the accommodation in the area is still pitched towards a younger, budget market. The town is full of 'camps' with basic bungalows of a relatively homogenous standard. A few names to look for include **Crazy Camel**, **Dolphin** and **Lighthouse** camps.

The **Nesima Hotel**, an addition to the dive centre and restaurant of the same name, is possibly the nicest place to stay in Dahab, with lovely stone architecture and a high standard of accommodation. Other top-range options include the **Hilton** and the **Novotel**, which are both a little way out of town.

Hilton Dahab South Sinai, Dahab; tel 20 69 3640 310/fax 20 69 3640 424; email dahab@hilton.com; www.hilton.com.
Nesima Hotel Dahab, South Sinai; tel 20 69 3640 320/fax 20 69 3640 321; email nesima@menanet.net; www.nesima-resort.com.
Novotel Coralia Dahab PO Box 23, South Sinai; tel 20 69 3640 301/fax 20 69 3640 465; email h1718@accor-hotels.com.

Where to Eat

Dahab's culinary range is not the widest you will find in Egypt. Like the accommodation, the restaurants provide a very similar selection of dishes at budget prices. Dozens of places are ranged along the beach in town, offering seafood, kebabs and some rather fanciful interpretations of Western cuisine. One shining exception to this homogenous diet is provided by the restaurant of the **Nesima Diving Center** where you will find an extensive, imaginative menu.

Dive Facilities

Dahab has various dive centres, ranging from basic filling stations to purpose-built dive resorts. One place that stands out from the crowd is **Nesima Diving Center**, a friendly and professional operation which employs an international staff and has a full range of facilities, including a good restaurant and a bar for after diving hours.

Club Red PO Box 12, Dahab, South Sinai; tel/fax 20 69 3640 380; email club-red@club-red.com; www.club-red.com. PADI 5-star IDC Center.
Fantasea Divers PO Box 9, Dahab, South Sinai; tel 20 69 3640 483/ tel/fax 20 69 3640 043; email fdc@link.net; www.fantaseadiving.net. PADI 5-star IDC Center.
INMO Divers Home PO Box 15, Dahab, South Sinai; tel 20 69 3640 455/fax 20 69 3640 372; email inmo@inmodivers.de; www.inmodivers.de. Certification: PADI.
Nesima Diving Center Mashraba, Dahab, South Sinai; tel 20 69 3640 320/fax 20 69 3640 321; email nesima@menanet.net; www.nesima-resort.com. PADI 5-star facility.
Reef 2000 Bedouin Moon Hotel, PO Box 60, Dahab, South Sinai; tel/fax 20 69 3640 087; email info@reef2000.com; www.reef2000.com. Certification: PADI.

Hospitals

There are excellent facilities across the border at Eilat and at Sharm el Sheikh, which are preferable for serious non-diving emergencies.

There is now a good, nine-person recompression chamber at Dahab next to the Dahabeya Hotel. Emergency number (9.30–6pm), 069 3640536; 24-hour emergency number 010 143 3325.

Diving Emergencies

Again, the closest facilities are in Sharm el Sheikh (tel 20 69 3660 922/3/fax 20 69 3661 011) or Eilat (tel 972 8 6358023). Bear in mind that the road to Sharm el Sheikh crosses a very high pass, and therefore poses a threat when transporting suspected DCS victims.

Local Highlights

While many visitors to Dahab seem content to spend their time having a smoke on the beach, there are plenty of other options. **Horse stables** cater for aspiring cowboys and girls, while the local Bedouin arrange **camel treks** of all descriptions, from a half-hour jog round the village to trips of several days to **Râs Abu Gulûm** or the **wadis** inland. Jeep safaris follow similar routes, taking in attractions such as the coloured canyon near **Nuweiba** or the **Ain Khudra Oasis**.

St Catherine's Monastery

The monastery is situated at 1,570m (5150ft) at the head of the valley in the shadow of Mount Sinai (where Moses is believed to have received the Ten Commandments from God). The Greek Orthodox monastery was founded in AD527 by the Emperor Justinian, who in AD552 also built the Church of St Catherine. The church was built near the place where Moses is believed to have confronted the Burning Bush; and there is a rather stark chapel commemorating the event. The interior of St Catherine's Church is richly decorated with paintings, marble and carved wood – the decorations are nearly all 18th-century. The impressive marble tomb of St Catherine, which contains her skull, stands in the church sanctuary.

Today, the monastery is run by 15 monks and, as it is still a working establishment, it is not possible for tourists to roam at will over the entire site. However, if you write ahead and ask permission, it may be possible to get special authorization to see the treasures of the library and museum. Outside, the gardens are stocked with olive, cherry, apricot and plum trees and are definitely worth a look.

Nearby attractions along the coast include the ancient **Crusader castle** on Pharaoun Island. Captured from its Christian builders in the 12th century, it was expanded and fortified by the Arab hero, Saladin, as a deterrent against Christian expansion from the Holy Land into the Red Sea region.

Other possibilities include a trip to **St Catherine's monastery** (see box above).

Dahab is internationally renowned as a **windsurfing** venue, and for those wanting to give the sport a try, numerous watersports centres rent equipment and give tuition.

SOUTH SINAI

Home to the fabled Râs Muhammad National Park, the southern tip of the Sinai peninsula has fascinated the world's diving population for decades. With dozens of world-class dive sites, dedicated aficionados return year after year. Despite the huge volume of diving traffic, the area still hides some virtually undiscovered diving gems.

'South Sinai' here refers to the southernmost tip of the peninsula, from Sharm el Sheikh to the western edge of Râs Muhammad National Park. As well as the huge number of shore or coastal diving sites, the area also includes the Strait of Tiran, with its spectacular string of offshore reefs. Away from the coast, the South Sinai region contains some of the world's most stunning desert scenery, with rugged mountains forming a hauntingly beautiful backdrop to the beaches and cliffs of the Sinai coast. The resort town of Sharm el Sheikh forms the hub of tourism in the region, and acts as the base for most visitors to Sinai.

THE PEOPLE AND THE CULTURE

The Sinai was until recently the domain of the Bedouin, a nomadic people whose origins lie in the Arabian peninsula, and whose distinctive lifestyle and appearance have remained unchanged for millennia. Recent developments, particularly the massive growth of tourism in the region, have sparked an influx of new arrivals, mostly Egyptians from Cairo and other Nile Valley cities. These newcomers have built up much of the tourist industry in South Sinai, and in the process have become targets for a certain amount of resentment. Many Bedouin feel they have been sidelined in their own homeland and consider it unjust that the new wealth arriving in the area should go largely into the pockets of these new arrivals.

CLIMATE

Sinai weather is characterized by hot, dry summers and cool, dry winters. Summer highs reach 40°C (104°F) or more, while winter lows in December and January can fall close to freezing in the desert, though the coastline tends toward more moderate daytime temperatures of 20°C (68°F) or more. Rainfall is minimal, and sunny skies are the norm in summer or winter.

MARINE LIFE

From the tiny, glittering jewels of basslets to the stately grandeur of a 2-m (6½ ft) Humphead wrasse, these reefs encompass the full range of northern Red Sea coral reef fishes. Sharks abound in some seasons, with Grey Reefs, Hammerheads, Blacktip and Whitetip Reef Sharks cruising along the coastal reefs, while other marine species such as hawksbill turtles and even dolphins are frequently sighted. Invertebrates such as octopus, cuttlefish and squid are also common.

Best known for its pristine walls of exquisite stony corals, South Sinai offers an equal wealth of soft corals

SLEEPING IN THE DESERT

The Sinai coast is full of accommodation possibilities, from basic huts to the most luxurious of tourist-class hotels. Given all this choice, it might seem odd to choose instead to spend the night breathing camp fire smoke in a sand-blown patch of desert, far from the amenities of the tourist centres. Yet for many locals and visitors one of the biggest of the region's attractions is the chance to do just that.

Camping in the desert does not necessarily mean roughing it. There is any number of options, from hiking up a wadi with your sleeping bag to embarking on a five-star, air-conditioned desert tour, complete with five-course meals and cultural entertainment shows. Local travel agents can arrange trips. Even better, local residents may invite you to join them for an evening out.

Whichever way you choose to go, the experience of a night beneath the vast, star-filled desert sky, surrounded by absolute peace and quiet, is an opportunity you shouldn't pass up. If you get the chance, try to fit in a night in what locals appropriately call the 'million-star hotel'.

among its hugely varied repertoire of reefs. With reef profiles ranging from sheer, undercut cliffs to gently undulating coral fields, the area is a living encyclopedia of tropical corals.

CONDITIONS

The great depth and sheer walls of the southern Gulf of Aqaba give the Sinai coast admirably clear waters for most of the year. Visibility is in the 20 to 30m (65–100ft) range, with occasional seasonal reductions due to algal or planktonic blooms. Sea temperatures fall between a summer high of 28°C to 29°C (82–84°F) and winter lows in the low 20s°C (70s°F). Wet suits may be optional in summer – although repetitive dives make the warmest water feel cold – but in winter a 5–7mm (⅕–¼in) suit with hood would be reasonable. Some divers use dry suits.

ACCESS

With few exceptions, organized diving in South Sinai is done from dive boats and access is usually a simple matter of jumping overboard. Trips are generally done on a two-dive per day basis, with a hot meal cooked on board between dives. Many of the sites can also be accessed from shore, and for the fully equipped, experienced diver with access to a vehicle, this can be an excellent way of avoiding the crowds.

DIVE OPERATORS AND FACILITIES

Sharm el Sheikh boasts a large and growing number of dive centres of international quality. Equipment, facilities and level of training are all generally superb, and, with so much competition around, there is enough pressure to keep standards high and prices reasonable.

LOCAL DIVE ETIQUETTE AND CUSTOMS

As a new arrival, you may be asked to go on a checkout dive before moving on to the prime dive sites; this precaution is for your safety and in the interest of preserving the delicate ecology of local reefs. As a responsible diver you should graciously accept it as a small price to pay for visiting these natural marvels. You should also note that it is standard practice for local centres to ban any diver who is seen destroying coral on a dive.

To ease both the diving pressure on the reefs and the ship traffic in the busy shipping lane, some of the reefs in the Strait of Tiran are limited to diving from local day boats only. Night diving is forbidden in the Râs Muhammad National Park.

1 JACKSON REEF

Location: The northernmost of four reefs extending down the centre of the Strait of Tiran.
Access: By local boat from Sharm el Sheikh or other ports.
Conditions: As with all Tiran sites, strong currents are a very real possibility.
Average depth: 20m (65ft)
Maximum depth: 40m+ (130ft+)
Average visibility: 20m (65ft)

On the northern edge of the reef, the wreck of a grounded freighter, the *Lara*, stands as a warning to shipping in the busy strait. Most of its hull has been salvaged for scrap, leaving only a skeletal hulk. A fixed mooring exists at the southern end of the reef; dives begin from this point and proceed generally northward along the east side of the reef.

Current tends to run from the north, and generally picks up strength as you approach the point on the east side. Most divers will want to make this the northern limit of their dive, and turn back to the south here. Strong swimmers with good air consumption and experience in currents can round the point, after which the current slackens, and continue their dive along the reef's north edge. This should only be done by prior arrangement with your dive guide, and great care should be taken, since divers have been swept off the reef here.

The steep-sided walls of Jackson Reef are among the finest in the Sinai region; the current-swept reef is densely grown with a real profusion of stony and soft corals, with special accents provided by luxuriant gorgonian fans, sea whips and black corals, and vivid growths of soft coral.

Fish life, not surprisingly, is excellent. The strong current brings plenty of nutrients for reef and schooling fish; current and profile combine to tempt pelagic fish in from the open water, and large schools of barracuda and jacks are common here, as are larger predators including several species of shark. The smaller reef species on which these pelagic visitors feed are profuse.

SHARK BEHAVIOUR

If you spend much time diving in the Red Sea, as sure as the sun shines, you will see sharks. While this will thrill many divers, for some the idea of being in the same water as a shark is fraught with horror.

Sharks are not sea-devils, as they are often portrayed. They are simply large fish, and their behaviour is no more dangerous than that of any other large predatory species, once you understand it.

On the whole, sharks are rather less dangerous than dogs on land, and their behaviour is as easy to understand. With very few exceptions, sharks attack for only two reasons – self defence or feeding. Humans, particularly divers, do not resemble sharks' natural prey, so unless you trigger a shark's defences, you are safe in their presence.

When sharks feel threatened or territorial, they exhibit clear signalling behaviour. This takes the form of exaggerated swimming movements, with extreme side-to-side twisting and tail-thrashing. If you see a shark exhibiting this behaviour, stay calm, remain on the reef face or the bottom; make yourself look as large as possible, close up to the other divers to appear larger, and slowly move up the reef out of the shark's terrirtory.

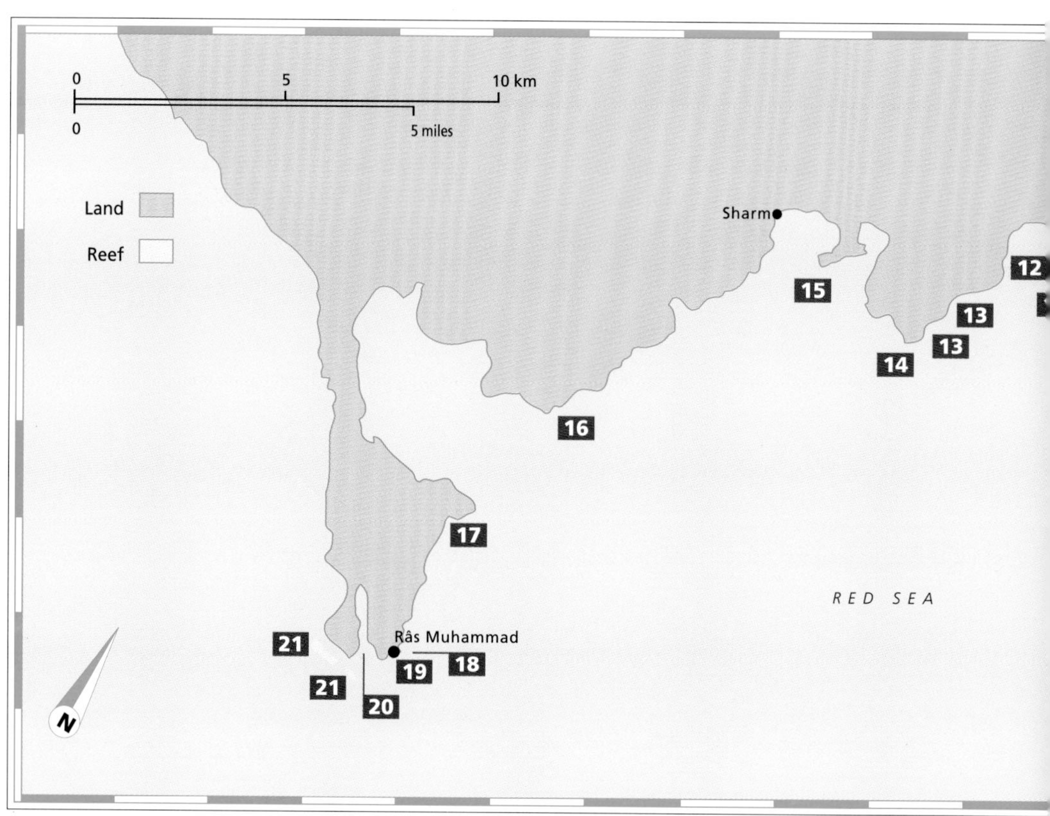

2 WOODHOUSE REEF

★★★★★★

Location: Second from the north in the Strait of Tiran reef chain.
Access: Local boat from Sharm el Sheikh, Na'ama Bay or other ports.
Conditions: Strong current possible.
Average depth: 15m (50ft)
Maximum depth: 40m+ (130ft+)
Average visibility: 20m (65ft)

Lying between Jackson and Gordon Reefs, Woodhouse is a long, narrow reef running at an angle from northeast to southwest. From its shallow reef top, the reef drops at a sharp angle on all sides; although it is less than vertical throughout the reef's length, the angle steepens still further beyond 25m (80ft).

Woodhouse is generally dived as a drift along the reef's eastern side. The current is usually moderate, but can pick up speed at certain phases of the Moon, particularly toward the northern channel between Woodhouse and Jackson. Care should be taken not to get pulled around the point here, as you could be swept off the reef into the main shipping lane.

Coral cover is excellent throughout the reef, with dense growth all over; there are a few sandy patches at depths of around 20m (65ft). Many species are present but because of the sheltered position of the reef, away from the main current, a certain amount of sedimentation has affected the corals here.

Pelagic fish include big tuna and schools of trevally or jacks. Fusiliers, snappers, surgeons and unicorns also school here, along with thousands of other reef fish.

3 THOMAS REEF

★★★★★★

Location: Second from the south in the Strait of Tiran reef chain.
Access: By local boat from Sharm el Sheikh, Na'ama Bay or other ports.
Conditions: Current can be strong.
Average depth: 20m (65ft)
Maximum depth: 50m (165ft)
Average visibility: 20m (65ft)

This site is on a generally steep sloping reef, which includes some plateau sections and a very deep canyon running along the reef's southern section. It is the smallest of the four Tiran reefs, and its position in the chain leaves it exposed to some fairly vigorous currents.

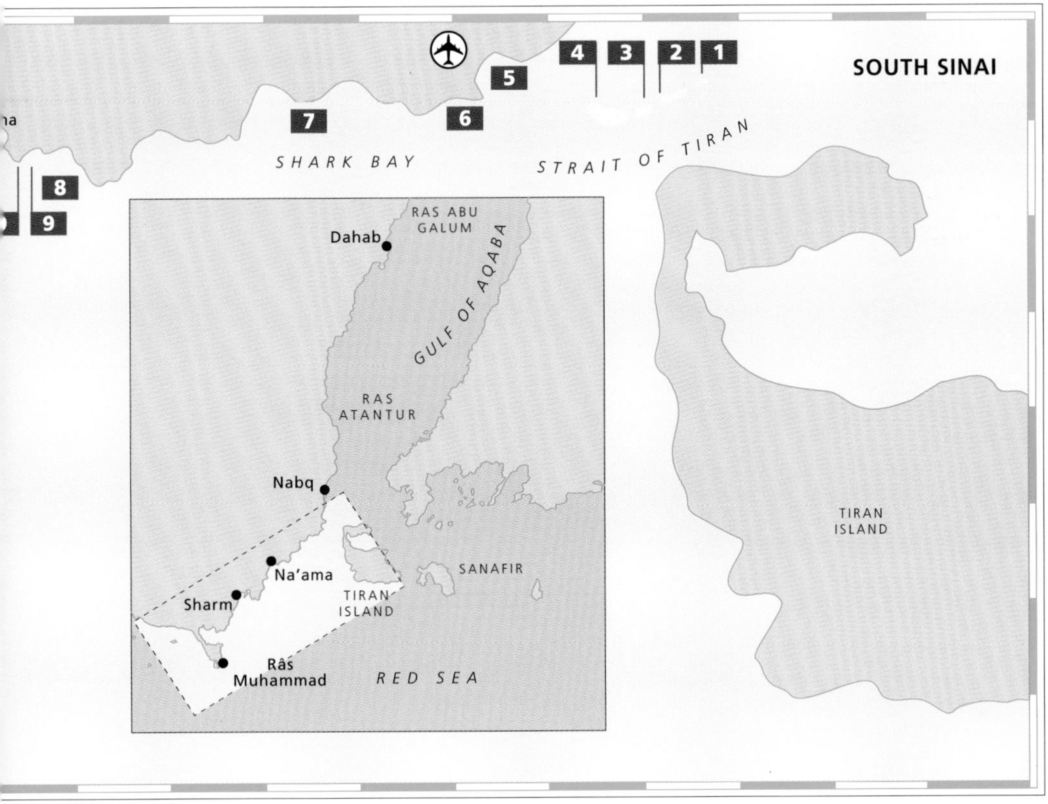

SOUTH SINAI

4 3 2 1 5 6 7 8 9

SHARK BAY

STRAIT OF TIRAN

TIRAN ISLAND

RAS ABU GALUM

Dahab

GULF OF AQABA

RAS ATANTUR

Nabq

Na'ama

Sharm

TIRAN ISLAND

SANAFIR

Râs Muhammad

RED SEA

The reef's upper section is a riot of colour, encompassing some of the finest soft coral growth in the Sinai region. Huge, densely packed fields of *Dendronephthya* of every imaginable hue are spread across the reef, along with fine *Stylophora*, some *Acropora* and many other stony coral forms.

Fish life is also rich, with the greatest concentration in the shallows. Lyretail and other groupers grow to great size, and many varieties of rabbitfish and wrasse congregate along the reef face, accompanied by box and pufferfish.

The only reason to go much deeper than 20m (65ft) at Thomas Reef is to explore the canyon, but this is an option only for very experienced deep divers. You should not even consider this hazardous feat without consulting your dive guide.

YELLOWBAR ANGELFISH

One of the quintessential reef fish of the Red Sea is the Yellowbar Angelfish; its brilliant blue body is marked by a vertical yellow band.

Its Latin name is *Pomacanthus maculosus*, and it closely resembles the Arabian Angelfish, *Pomacanthus asfur*. It grows to a reported maximum length of 50cm (20in), and like all Pomacanthus angelfish it subsists on a diet of sponges supplemented by small invertebrates and algae.

This fascinating fish inhabits coastal reefs and bays, and tends to favour silty conditions - the sediment-rich waters of Eritrea's Dahlak archipelago boast one of the densest populations in the Red Sea.

Juveniles of the species are marked by an almost psychedelic arrangement of blue and white bars, which gradually fade to uniform blue; the characteristic yellow bar does not appear until the fish reaches about 6cm (2¼in).

4 GORDON REEF

★★★★★★★

Location: Southernmost of the Strait of Tiran reefs.
Access: By local or live-aboard boat from Sharm el Sheikh, Na'ama Bay or other ports.
Conditions: As with all Strait reefs, can be swept by current.
Average depth: 15m (50ft)
Maximum depth: 35m+ (115ft+)
Average visibility: 20m (65ft)

Like Jackson to the north, this reef is marked by the wreck of a large commercial freighter, the *Loullia*. At the southern end of the reef there is also a light beacon to keep other ships off the reef. A permanent mooring point lies just offshore, near the light.

The dive site encompasses a wide, oval, sloping patchy reef which extends to the south and east of the shallow circular reef top, rather like the sloping brim of a baseball cap. The reef composition is quite varied, with patchy sections, sand beds and fully fledged coral gardens. In the centre of the reef slope, a 'shark amphitheatre' or bowl dips to 24m (80ft). A variety of shark species can be seen sleeping on the sandy bottom.

The site boasts a very good range of corals, with lots of branching varieties. All of the corals are well preserved, in densely growing patches that often show a remarkable mix of different species.

Fish life is not the most profuse in the Strait of Tiran, but there are some notable surprises, including a huge moray eel. Triggerfish abound, while surgeonfish and jacks swim in moderately large schools, and angelfish, parrotfish and small wrasse are all present in good numbers. Large Napoleon Wrasse can often be seen.

The reef slope is suitable for relatively inexperienced divers, and more experienced divers can make the most of the incredible experience to be enjoyed down in the shark amphitheatre.

5 RÂS NUSRÂNI

★★★★★★★

Location: Western mainland point at the southern end of the Strait of Tiran.
Access: By shore, or by local boat from Sharm el Sheikh, Na'ama Bay or other ports.
Conditions: Current can be fierce – novices beware.
Average depth: 20m (65ft)
Maximum depth: 40m+ (130ft+)
Average visibility: 20m (65ft)

This site is a sloping wall at the point of Râs Nusrâni (Arabic for Christian Headland). In profile, it varies between very steep to moderately sloping, depending on location: the steepest wall section lies south of the point, while the reef to the north flattens somewhat. Inshore, a shallow mini-wall follows the edge of the reef top.

The reef is well covered in dense stony and soft corals, with lots of massive coral heads, some good branching forms, and a nice selection of colourful soft corals. Fish life is spectacular, with a huge range of reef and pelagic species. Morays hide in reef crevices, fusiliers, jacks, surgeonfish and barracuda school off the reef, and needlefish shimmer near the surface. Large turtles are also a common sight, paddling lazily along the reef slope.

Opposite: *A diver plunges into the surreal depths at Paradise Reef, South Sinai (Site 13).*

6 WHITE KNIGHTS

★★★★★★★★

Location: Just south of Râs Nusrâni (Site 5).
Access: By local boat from Sharm el Sheikh, Na'ama Bay or other ports.
Conditions: Some deeper sections require caution.
Average depth: 15m (50ft)
Maximum depth: 35m+ (115ft+)
Average visibility: 20m (65ft)

This site, lying inside the bay formed by Râs Nusrâni to the north, has numerous points of interest. Just inshore from the boat mooring, a deep canyon extends down from the shallows, while to the north of this, mixed sand and coral patches lead to a wide sand slope colonized by garden eels. To the south, a wooden wreck adds even more interest.

Most dives begin at the entrance to the canyon, a narrow opening leading down from an inshore sand patch. The narrow, sand-bottomed canyon descends steeply, passing through a series of overhangs and two covered swimthroughs, one at around 15m (50ft) and a second, for advanced divers only, leading out to the reef face at 35m (115ft).

After leaving the canyon, there are two options. Turning right takes you south along the reef to the

NAPOLEON WRASSE

One of the largest and most impressive fishes you are likely to meet in the Red Sea is the Napoleon Wrasse, *Cheilinus undulatus*. Also known as the Humphead Wrasse, a quick look at a fully-grown example will explain the names – as the male matures, it develops a pronounced hump or protuberance on its forehead, looking remarkably like the outline shape of Napoleon's hat.

Unlike the Bumphead Parrotfish, which uses its head to break off chunks of the coral it feeds on, no explanation has been found for the Napoleon's hump. Like all *Cheilinus* wrasse, the Napoleon feeds primarily on molluscs and small invertebrates, which it sucks up through protruberant, fleshy lips. Along with its usual diet, it has been known to eat boxfish and even the toxic Crown-of-Thorns Starfish.

Fully grown Napoleon Wrasse can reach recorded lengths of 2.29m (7½ft), and can weigh as much as 190kg (419lb). Their stubby, deep-bodied shape makes them appear even more massive; certainly, a close approach from a mature Napoleon is something few divers will soon forget. While naturally wary, these fishes are also naturally curious, and in areas where fish-feeding has been practised, Napoleons in search of handouts will often make unnervingly close approaches to divers.

*Sweetlips (*Plectorhinchus gaterinus*) are mostly reef dwellers that shelter in caves or wrecks.*

wreck, while a left turn takes you across the reef slope to the eel garden and a series of beautiful, shallow reef patches.

Swimming south and gradually ascending, you will see a dense assortment of species, including cabbage corals, staghorn and table *Acropora*, and several varieties of soft coral. At about 14m (45ft), ten minutes' swim south from the canyon, you will encounter the upturned bulk of a wood-hulled wreck, the *Noos 1*, a local dive boat that sank in 1994 after an electrical fire in the engine room.

7 SHARK BAY

★★★☆☆☆

Location: On the coast at Shark Bay, south of Râs Nusrâni (Site 5).
Access: By shore, or by local boat from Sharm el Sheikh, Na'ama Bay or other ports.
Conditions: Easy shore entry, but watch out for boat traffic.
Average depth: 20m (65ft)
Maximum depth: 60m+ (195ft+)
Average visibility: 20m (65ft)

This site, lying just in front of the Shark's Bay Diving Club, is a sloping reef broken by a large sandy area that houses the dive centre's jetty and boat area. To the south, the reef has a moderate slope and is well covered in coral; north of the jetty is a shallow area good for relaxed snorkelling.

Directly in front of the sandy shore entry point, a deep canyon drops through the reef; its mouth lies at the foot of the reef wall, forming the sand slope's southern edge. The canyon's steep and sandy floor descends rapidly to depths of 60m (195ft) and more – take care not to be drawn too deep.

Exiting the canyon, you can explore the moderately sloping reef to the south, gradually ascending before turning back to the north. This section shows dense growth of both stony and soft corals, although less pristine than at some places along this coast. Fish life is diverse and interesting, with angelfish, parrotfish, groupers, wrasse and morays on the reef, and rays and flatfish lying on the sandy entry slope.

8 FAR GARDEN

★★★☆☆☆

Location: On the coast between Shark Bay and Na'ama Bay.
Access: By local boat from Sharm el Sheikh, Na'ama Bay or other ports.
Conditions: Generally calm.
Average depth: 18m (60ft)
Maximum depth: 30m+ (100ft+)
Average visibility: 20m (65ft)

This site is a garden-like reef of colourful corals running northwest to southeast. The northwest portion of the reef is steeply sloping with a sharp drop-off towards the point, while the southwestern section has a more gradual slope. Pinnacles and outcrops dot the reef, and the tops of these, together with the shallow inshore reef top, make for excellent snorkelling.

Coral growth throughout the site is concentrated in small patches, with strong growth of dozens of species, from relatively hardy staghorn coral to the delicate *Dendronephthya*.

Fish life is good in this site, with lots of wrasse – Napoleons in particular – and big parrotfish and groupers. Hawkfish, scorpionfish, fairy basslets, damselfish, and many types of triggerfish share the reef, while goatfish, lizardfish and crocodilefish can be found on the many sandy areas.

9 NEAR GARDEN

★★★☆☆

Location: Just south of Far Garden (Site 8), to the north of Na'ama Bay.
Access: By local boat from Sharm el Sheikh, Na'ama Bay or other ports.
Conditions: Like Far Garden, no adverse conditions are likely.
Average depth: 15m (50ft)
Maximum depth: 30m+ (100ft+)
Average visibility: 20m (65ft)

This site begins on an inshore mini-wall that drops from the surface reef table to about 15m (50ft). From here, the reef slopes gently outward, maintaining an even profile to 25m (80ft), where the slope steepens considerably. A huge number of pinnacles, heads and coral clumps dot the reef as it descends, hosting populations of colourful small reef fish. The larger reef fish are also present, and Bluespotted Ribbontail Rays rest half hidden on the sandy bottom.

The undemanding profile of this reef and its ample sandy areas make it an excellent venue for novice divers, and the shallow reeftop and upper reef mini-wall are perfect for snorkellers. Advanced divers will find plenty of scope for exploration on the deeper reef slope.

10 TOWER

★★★☆☆☆

   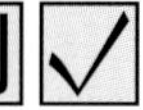

Location: Just south of Na'ama Bay on the Sinai coast.
Access: By shore entry or local boat from Sharm el

Sheikh, Na'ama Bay or other ports.
Conditions: Shore entry can be tricky at low tide.
Average depth: 20m (65ft)
Maximum depth: 40m+ (130ft+)
Average visibility: 20m (65ft)
This site, named for a tower-like rock formation on shore, lies just below the Tower resort complex.

For shore entries and exits, especially at low tide, it is worth knowing about a short cut. Halfway across the reef top, directly out from the steps, is a small submerged cave mouth. This opens out into a passage leading through to the open water, cutting out half of the awkward clamber across the reef top.

The reef is most interesting in its upper reaches, with the exception of the canyon which drops to depths of 40m (130ft). Coral in the top 20–25m (65–80ft) is excellent, with a very wide variety of species. Quality is good, particularly in terms of the luxuriant soft coral growth, which is in fine condition. The reef shallows host almost every fish you can imagine and reef sharks have been known to visit the reef's deeper sections.

This is a particularly nice site to dive in the morning, when the sun's rays reach down into the canyon and the deeper reef slopes.

11 PINKY'S WALL

★★★★★★★★

Location: On the Sinai coast, between Tower and Turtle Bay sites (Sites 10, 12).
Access: By shore, or by local boat from Sharm el Sheikh, Na'ama Bay or other ports.
Conditions: Shore access is physically demanding.
Average depth: 20m (65ft)
Maximum depth: 60m+ (195ft+)
Average visibility: 20m (65ft)
Access from shore requires a four-wheel-drive vehicle to get to the cliff top, then a rather strenuous scramble down a narrow wadi. You will then need to make a surf entry across the jagged reef top. This shore entry should only be attempted by fit divers experienced in rough shore entries.

Once in the water, conditions are near perfect; generally clear visibility reveals a beautiful sheer wall dropping to great depths, with excellent coral growth, particularly the pink soft corals for which the site is named.

Coral growth, especially soft corals like *Dendronephthya*, is what this site is all about. Stony coral growth is not as dense as at many sites near here, but the profusion of soft species more than compensates. Sweepers hide in shimmering schools in the recesses and overhangs, while schooling fish hang off the reef face. There are also good numbers of parrotfish, rabbitfish, groupers and wrasse.

TRIGGERFISH ATTACK

Most of the potential hazards of tropical diving have been well publicized and most divers are equipped to avoid common dangers such as scorpionfish and fire coral. But one common Red Sea troublemaker may be relatively unknown to most divers: the common, seemingly innocuous, triggerfish.

Normally shy and retiring, these colourful reef fish undergo a complete personality change during their mating and nesting cycle. Instead of hiding in a crevice or swimming off into the deep, a nesting triggerfish can and will aggressively attack a diver many times its size. Such behaviour might seem comical, but the sharp teeth and strong jaws of the triggerfish make an attack anything but funny.

Titan triggers and blue triggers are all likely to display aggression, so if you see one of these fish patrolling a depression in the sand or coral rubble, you would be best advised to swim slowly away, giving it a wide berth. If you are attacked, try to turn your fins to face the fish. The triggerfish will very likely direct its aggression at your moving fins, rather than to your more vulnerable flesh.

This site is exceptional for several reasons: as a wall site in a region of generally sloping reefs, as one of the limited numbers of sites with shore access, and as one of the most concentrated growths of soft coral on this stretch of coast.

12 TURTLE BAY

★★★★★★

Location: Sinai coast, between Pinky's Wall and Paradise sites (Sites 11 & 13).
Access: By shore, or by local boat from Sharm el Sheikh, Na'ama Bay or other ports.
Conditions: Generally easy, although shore access can be tricky at low tide.
Average depth: 30m (100ft)
Maximum depth: 35m+ (115ft+)
Average visibility: 20m (65ft)
This is a medium sloping reef, bounded inshore by a mini-wall to around 10m (35ft), and a shallow reef top 30–40m (100–130ft) wide in places. The reef face is well covered with outcrops and pinnacles and boasts an excellent variety of coral species.

Fish life is equally diverse, including many sedentary reef fish – scorpions, stonefish, lizardfish, hawkfish and others – and the usual vast array of free-swimming reef species.

When accessing the site from shore, particularly at low tide, the long walk across the reef table can be exasperating. In all but the lowest tides you can in fact swim across the reef top with your fully inflated BCD and scuba gear extended in front of you.

Like many sites along this stretch of coast, the route

to the shore access point is via a constantly shifting network of jeep tracks. Check with local dive centres for up-to-date route information.

13 PARADISE/FIASCO

★★★☆☆☆

Location: On the Sinai coast, between Turtle Bay and Râs Umm Sid sites (Sites 12 & 14).
Access: By shore, or by local or live-aboard boat from Sharm el Sheikh, Na'ama Bay or other ports.
Conditions: Some strong currents – drift diving is a good possibility.
Average depth: 20m (65ft)
Maximum depth: 35m+ (115ft+)
Average visibility: 20m (65ft)

This is really a combination of two dive sites. The southernmost, Fiasco, lies just north of the point at Râs Umm Sid, while Paradise is the northern extension of the same reef.

The Paradise section has some amazing outcrops – like a garden of abstract sculptures. To the south, the pinnacles continue, interspersed with some very nice *acropora* tables. A very good density of soft corals is complemented by a wide range of stony species. The quality of coral at this site, particularly inshore, is among the finest on the coast.

Big jacks and barracuda of more than 1m (3ft) can be seen here when the current is running, as can schooling and solitary reef fish. Sandy sections host interesting bottom-dwellers, such as crocodilefish and Bluespotted Ribbontail Rays.

Unless a decent current is flowing, the site can be somewhat dull, as water movement brings out the full variety of fish life. With a strong current it is possible to drift from the north end of Paradise almost to the point of Râs Umm Sid on one tank.

14 RAS UMM SID

★★★☆☆☆

   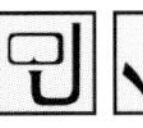 

Location: Râs Umm Sid point, southeast of Sharm el Moiya/Sharm el Sheikh town.
Access: By shore, or by local or live-aboard boat from Sharm el Sheikh, Na'ama Bay or other ports.
Conditions: Strong currents possible; shore entry difficult due to wide reef flat.
Average depth: 20m (65ft)
Maximum depth: 35m+ (115ft+)
Average visibility: 20m (65ft)

This is a steep sloping wall, extending from the point at Râs Umm Sid inward toward the bay to the west. The reef follows the shoreline and is marked by intermittent sand patches, coral heads and pinnacles.

Coral attractions include gorgonians, *acropora*, fire corals, dense soft coral patches and some substantial coral formations. Fish life is more than acceptable, with lots of big and small jacks/trevally, emperor and regal angelfish, various parrotfish, picasso and other triggerfish, surgeons, Napoleon wrasse, moray eels and lionfish on the reef, and crocodilefish and stingrays on the sand.

Black Corals

The so-called black corals, which are widely used for jewellery, are of the family *Ceriantipatharia*, and can be distinguished by their very fine, branching structure, resembling small branching shrubs or bare twigs. Contrary to the expectations of some divers, living black corals do not appear black; it is the inner horny skeleton of the coral which is black, and the harvested corals must be ground and polished to reveal this colouration.

15 TEMPLE

★★★☆☆☆

Location: West of Râs Umm Sid, at the entrance to Sharm el Moiya.
Access: By shore, or by local or live-aboard boat from Sharm el Sheikh, Na'ama Bay or other ports.
Conditions: Gentle and sheltered, with easy profile.
Average depth: 15m (50ft)
Maximum depth: 35m+ (115ft+)
Average visibility: 20m (65ft)

This is a flat, sloping reef with two major, and a few minor, pinnacles adding contour to the reef face. The largest of the pinnacles is The Tower. Its bulk is split by two major fissures, one of which can be swum through. The second should not be entered, to avoid damaging the delicate gorgonians growing along its sides. All the pinnacles hide a surprisingly rich variety of reef animals.

Coral growth throughout the site is good, with a density and mix of species difficult to match in the immediate area. The fish are as pleasant a surprise as the coral, with a truly amazing range of species colonizing the reef.

The surprising richness and diversity of this site make it one of the region's most underrated sites.

16 RAS GHOZLANI

★★★★★☆☆☆☆☆

Location: At the north edge of the mouth of Mersa Bareika, Râs Muhammad.

Access: By local or live-aboard boat from Sharm el Sheikh, Na'ama Bay or other ports.
Conditions: Generally easy; some currents are possible.
Average depth: 18m (60ft)
Maximum depth: 30m+ (100ft+)
Average visibility: 20m (65ft)
This site lies at the mouth of Mersa Bareika, the large shallow bay that nearly separates Râs Muhammad from the Sinai mainland. The reef follows the shoreline at the bay's northern point. A sheer but shallow inshore wall gives way to a sloping, patchy reef face below about 15m (50ft).

It is hardly worth listing the vast array of coral at this site. If it exists in the Red Sea, you will find it here. Fish life is abundant all across the reef in a riot of scintillating colour. This is possibly the nicest spot on the southern coast for small reef species.

Unlike the popular but overcrowded sites, such as Shark Reef (Site 21), this superb site is not visited by hordes of divers each day, so its delicate beauty has been preserved.

17 RAS ZA'TIR (RAS ZA'ATAR)

★★★★☆☆☆☆

    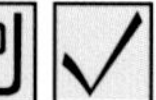

Location: Râs Muhammad, across the mouth of Mersa Bareika from Râs Ghozlani (Site 16).
Access: By local or live-aboard boat from Sharm el Sheikh, Na'ama Bay or other ports.
Conditions: Generally easy, but visibility can be poor due to sediment.
Average depth: 20m (65ft)
Maximum depth: 30m+ (100ft+)
Average visibility: 20m (65ft)
The reef at this site is similar but more contoured than Râs Ghozlani, with many cracks and fissures, some forming small caves which can be entered.

There is a reasonable range of coral species, both stony and soft, and a large-scale growth of *xeniid* soft corals. Coral quality is generally good, but suffers from silting and sandfall, particularly to the north. Fish life is excellent. The dense and diverse fish population of this site outshines Râs Ghozlani.

The rich selection of Red Sea fishes makes the site a real attraction and more than compensates for the somewhat lacklustre condition of the coral.

18 JACKFISH ALLEY

★★★★☆☆

  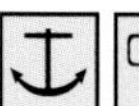  

Location: Râs Muhammad, just south of Râs Za'atir (Site 17).
Access: By local or live-aboard boat from Sharm el Sheikh, Na'ama Bay or other ports.
Conditions: Wind, waves and currents can all be strong making access tricky.
Average depth: 20m (65ft)
Maximum depth: 40m+ (130ft+)
Average visibility: 20m (65ft)
This site, also called Fisherman's Bank or Stingray Alley, begins on a sheer wall. The early section of the wall is very porous, with lots of small holes and crevices, and boasts a couple of penetrable caves, each featuring separate exit and entrance holes.

Proceeding southward, the wall gives way to a sandy plateau at around 20m (65ft), well covered with coral heads and outcrops. After widening out considerably, this plateau narrows at its southern end to form a small channel or alley. Further out from the wall, a second, deeper plateau can be found.

Coral growth is good overall and the fish population is excellent, with plenty of the jacks and stingrays that give the site at least two of its names and all the usual reef fish.

19 SHARK OBSERVATORY

★★★★☆☆☆☆

     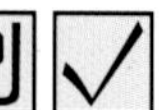

Location: Râs Muhammad, just south of Jackfish Alley (Site 18).
Access: By shore, or local or live-aboard boat from Sharm el Sheikh, Na'ama Bay or other ports
Conditions: Strong currents can cause problems, especially for shore access.
Average depth: 20m (65ft)
Maximum depth: 40m+ (130ft+)
Average visibility: 20m (65ft)
The site stretches from the foot of the observatory cliff in the north, across the mouth of a shallow box-shaped inlet, to the beginning of the Anemone City (Site 20) to the south. There are two possible shore entry points, one inside the inlet and a second in the small cove at the foot of the cliff. Both can be reached by road.

In the past it was possible to see sharks here just by looking down from the cliff top, but with the advent of dive tourism and its attendant boat traffic, the sharks have mostly moved on.

The site is a vertical wall, sloping outward at its foot. The rugged profile is most dramatic in the northern section where the reef face is especially contoured, with fissures, inlets and crevices to explore. Coral growth is good with lots of variety among both soft and stony species.

The steep profile does not encourage dense populations of smaller reef species, so quality and quantity of fish are somewhat dependent on currents and the pelagic life they encourage. Jacks, barracuda and the occasional Grey or Blacktip Reef Sharks liven things up when the current is running; snappers, surgeonfish and unicorns are present in schools of varying size, and larger reef fish such as big groupers and Napoleons are usually to be seen.

Divers should be careful of the strong currents which are common in this area, and those who enter from shore should be doubly cautious. Once beyond the point to the north, there is no shore exit point – do not round the point if current could prevent you from returning to the exit point.

20 ANEMONE CITY

★★★★★☆☆☆☆

    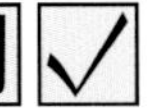

Location: Râs Muhammad, just inshore from Shark Reef (Site 21).
Access: By shore, or by local or live-aboard boat from Sharm el Sheikh, Na'ama Bay or other ports.
Conditions: Some strong currents and mild downdrifts; shore entry can involve a long wade.
Average depth: 18m (60ft)
Maximum depth: 40m+ (130ft+)
Average visibility: 20m (65ft)

Anemone City is one of the nicest sites in the Râs Muhammad area. The reef is steeply sloping, cut by deep bays and inlets. The sharply angled profile is broken by a number of plateaux or large shelves, on which densely grown pinnacles and coral heads stand. Coral growth is very rich, particularly on the portion of the reef stretching to the right from the shore entry point, in the direction of Shark Reef.

There are of course huge numbers of anemones, with attendant anemonefish. The site also boasts some prolific fish life, particularly in the mornings when the site is bustling with activity. Near the surface, barracuda and silvery needlefish hang patiently in the water.

Shore access, from a parking area at the edge of the shallow inshore bay, can be rather tiring at low tide as it involves crossing the shallows in the bay. The easiest route is along the left edge of the bay as you face the sea.

21 SHARK REEF/JOLANDA REEF

★★★★★☆☆

Location: The southern tip of the Sinai Peninsula, at the south end of Râs Muhammad National Park.
Access: By shore, or by local or live-aboard boat from Sharm el Sheikh, Na'ama Bay or other ports.
Conditions: Very strong currents are common.
Average depth: 20m (65ft)
Maximum depth: 50m+ (165ft+)
Average visibility: 20m (65ft)

When divers think of Sinai, they think of Shark Reef and Jolanda. The two reefs are, in fact, the twin peaks of a single coral seamount rising just off the Râs Muhammad coast and separated from the mainland by a shallow channel.

Shark Reef, the easternmost of the two, boasts a sheer wall dropping to well past 50m (165ft) along its northeast and eastern sides, giving way to a steep reef slope as the reef proceeds southwest toward Jolanda. A shallow saddle lies between the two reefs at 18–20m (60–65ft); a second shallow patch lies south of Jolanda. This second flat patch is the site of what remains of the Jolanda, a wrecked freighter; the ship slipped into the deep in 1986 after a severe storm, but a little of its cargo remains incongruously strewn across the reef.

Coral is excellent, with good if sparse growth on the wall sections and dense coral gardens on the shallower flat areas. Big pelagics and schooling fish swarm these reefs in their thousands. The most impressive concentration is on the wall at Shark Reef. Big sharks of many species – hammerheads, grey and blacktip reefs among them – can be seen in the blue, particularly off the northeast corner of Shark Reef. On the reef, hundreds of different reef fishes can be spotted as can moray eels of a metre (3ft) and bluespotted and blackspotted stingrays.

As a boat dive, the two reefs are normally done as a drift, with the boat collecting you from the shallows beyond Jolanda; this alleviates many of the current-related problems common here. You can also dive the site from shore, entering at Anemone City (Site 20) and swimming across the channel to Shark Reef; this should only be attempted if current is manageable, and extreme care should be taken to conserve enough air for the return trip. Shore entry option is inadvisable if you are not a strong swimmer.

Red Sea bannerfish tend to swim in pairs.

South Sinai

How to Get There

By air: The southern Sinai's international airport is at Râs Nusrâni for Sharm el Sheikh, the region's undisputed capital of tourism, and receives a huge number of scheduled and charter flights. Charter fares from Europe are generally very competitive and often cheaper than comparable flights to Cairo or other Middle Eastern cities.
By road: Luxury bus lines link Sharm el Sheikh to Cairo and the rest of mainland Egypt, with through connections to Israel, Jordan and many other long-haul destinations. Taxis in the South Sinai region are among the most expensive in Egypt, as much as ten times higher than in non-tourist areas.
By ferry: A direct ferry service runs from Sharm el Sheikh to Hurghada on the mainland Egyptian Red Sea coast, and the Nuweiba to Aqaba (Jordan) ferries are only 1$^1/_2$ hours from Sharm by car.

Where to Stay

Sharm el Sheikh and its upmarket satellite resort, Na'ama Bay, have experienced an orgy of building, with luxury tourist accommodation appearing everywhere. Budget possibilities are more limited (see box on page 73), though some mid- to low-range places can be found.

At the top end of the scale, multinational chains such as **Hilton**, **Marriott**, **Intercontinental** and **Mövenpick** dominate.

In the mid- to low-range, the pick of the lot is definitely the **Sanafir Hotel** – one of the first, and still one of the best in the range. **The Pigeon House** is another in this range with a good reputation, and it is popular with divers.

Camel Hotel PO Box 10, Na'ama Bay, Sharm el Sheikh; tel 20 69 3600 700/fax 20 69 3600 601; email info@cameldive.com; www.cameldive.com/camel-hotel.htm.
Gafy Land (Days Inn) PO Box 76, Na'ama Bay, Sharm el Sheikh; tel 20 69 3600 210/ fax 20 69 3600 216; email gafyland@sinainet.com.eg.
Hilton Fayrouz Resort Na'ama Bay, Sharm el Sheikh; tel 20 69 3600 140/fax 20 69 3601 040; email fayrouz@sinainet.com.eg; www.hilton.com.
InterContinental Garden Reef Resort El Pasha Bay, PO Box 186, Sharm-El-Sheikh; tel 20 69 3600 006/fax 20 69 3600 009; email garden_reef@intersharm.com.
Kanabesh Hotel Na'ama Bay, Sharm el Sheikh; tel 20 69 3600 186/fax 20 69 3600 185.
Marriott Hotel Sharm el Sheikh; tel 20 69 3600 190/fax 20 69 3600 188.
Mövenpick Hotel Jolie Ville Na'ama Bay, Sharm el Sheikh; tel 20 69 3600 100/fax 20 69 3600 111; email resort.sharm-el-sheikh@moevenpick.com; www.moevenpick-hotels.com.
Novotel Aquamarine Na'ama Bay, Sharm el Sheikh; tel 20 69 3600 173/fax 20 69 3600 177.
Pigeon House Na'ama Bay, Sharm el Sheikh; tel 20 69 3600 996/fax 20 69 3600 995.
Sanafir Hotel Na'ama Bay, Sharm el Sheikh; tel 20 69 3600 197/fax 20 69 3600 196; email sanafir@sinainet.com.eg; www.sanafir.com.

Where to Eat

The concentration of restaurants in Sharm el Sheikh/Na'ama Bay is the best you will find anywhere in Sinai.

Na'ama Bay
Na'ama Bay has most of the upmarket restaurants, including the excellent **La Fleur** à la carte restaurant at the Mövenpick hotel, a great place for a splurge or celebration. In the Mall in Na'ama, the **Chinese/Korean** does good Korean barbecues; opposite, the Sanafir Hotel houses a branch of the quality **Peking Chinese** restaurants. The **Tam Tam** restaurant is a wonderful place to eat real Egyptian food, and is also one of the only places in Na'ama that has not inflated its prices to cash in on the tourist boom.

Sharm el Sheikh
One to try is the excellent but underrated **Flampe** restaurant, which does tasty grilled meats and seafood, soups and other delicacies at half the price and with twice the service of similar establishments in Na'ama. Also in Sharm town, the **Sinai Star** is a big barn-like place that specializes in fresh seafood; **Suleiman's**, just down the road, is a bit more refined and offers a similar menu of fresh fish, squid, prawns and lobster, grilled or fried, with a full accompaniment of Egyptian salads for surprisingly low prices. Many of the big hotels have set-price buffets; for a bit of a morning treat, the breakfast buffets at the **Mövenpick** are excellent.

Evening entertainment can be found at the **Pirates Bar** in the Fayrouz Hilton, a mock-nautical theme pub with imported draft beer which acts as the watering hole for local dive guides and instructors. For something more active, the **Bus Stop** disco in the Sanafir gets going later in the evening; quieter options include the sidewalk cafés and beach bars found along the promenade.

Dive Facilities

A complete listing of the many operations offering organized diving in South Sinai would fill a book on its own. This list is only a pick of some of the best around, and is by no means comprehensive. One of the oldest and friendliest centres is the **Camel Dive Club** – with a warm, hospitable and knowledgeable management, an international staff of highly trained, multilingual dive guides and instructors, and a superb blend of casual atmosphere and professional organization, Camel comes highly recommended. **Emperor Divers** are regularly voted top (or near top) Red Sea Dive Centre by readers of *English Diver* magazine. **Sinai Divers** is another old-timer, very professional and operates several Red Sea live-aboards.

Anemone Dive Center Pigeon House Hotel, Na'ama Bay, Sharm el Sheikh; tel 20 69 3600 999/fax 20 69 3600 725; email anemone@sinainet.com.eg. Certifications: PADI and SSI.
Camel Dive Club Na'ama Bay, Sharm el Sheikh; tel 20 69 3600 700/fax 20 69 3600 601, email info@cameldive.com; www.cameldive.com. Certifications: PADI and SSI.
Colona Divers PO Box 49, Sharm el Sheikh (club at Amar Sina Hotel, Râs Umm Sid); tel 20 69 3600 670/fax 20 69 3600 546; email sharm@colona.com; www.colona.com. Certification: PADI.
Divers International tel 20 69 3600 865/fax 20 69 3600 176; email info@diversintl.com; www.diversintl.com. Certification: PADI.
Emperor Divers Rosetta Hotel, Na'ama Bay, Sharm el Sheikh; several centres: tel 20 69 3600 734/fax 20 69 3600 735; email info.sharm@emperordivers.com; www.emperordivers.com. PADI 5-star Gold Palm Resort. Also at Nuweiba Hilton Coral Resort, Nuweiba; tel 20 69 3600 056/fax 20 69 3600 735; email numeiba@emperordivers.com.
Ocean College Dive Centre Ocean Lodge Hotel, Râs Umm Sid, Sharm el Sheikh; tel 20 69 3600 305/fax 20 69 3600 306; email info@ocean-college.com; www.ocean-college.com. Certifications: PADI, TDI, DSAT and BS-AC.
Oonas Dive Club Na'ama Bay, Sharm el Sheikh; tel 20 69 3600 581/fax 20 69 3600 582; email info@oonasdiveclub.com; www.oonasdiveclub.com. PADI 5-star Gold Palm Resort.
Red Sea Diving College, Sultana Building, Na'ama Bay, PO Box 67, Sharm el Sheikh; tel 20 69 3600 145/fax 20 69 3600 144; email info@redseacollege.com;

www.redseacollege.com. PADI 5-star IDC and CDC Center, certifies to Instructor level.
Sinai Divers Ghazala Hotel, Conrad International Resort, Ghazala Garden, Sharm el Sheikh; tel 20 69 3600 697/fax 20 69 3600 158; email info@sinaidivers.com; www.sinaidivers.com. Several PADI 5-star IDC Centers, also operates several live-aboard boats. Certifications: PADI, SSI, CMAS and BS-AC.
TGI Diving Sharm el Sheikh; tel 20 69 3600 681/fax 20 69 3600 134; email info@tgidiving.com; www.tgidiving.com. PADI 5-star IDC Centers – several centres in conjunction with others.

Hospitals

Sharm el Sheikh has a new hospital facility between Na'ama and Sharm Town. The nearest alternative is in el Tur, the regional administrative headquarters on the Gulf of Suez.

Diving Emergencies

There is a good recompression (Hyperbaric) chamber in Sharm el Sheikh, which was developed with the support of USAID.

Hyperbaric Medical Center tel 20 69 3660 922/3/fax 20 69 3661 011; email hyper_med_center@sinainet.com.eg.

Local Highlights

Once a tiny, friendly resort only frequented by divers, Sharm el Sheikh is now a huge, low-cost holiday metropolis with many of the problems this entails. South Sinai's biggest attraction is the desert – **Wadi Kid**, the **coloured canyon**, and the oases of **Ain Khudra** and **Ain Kid** are all within range of a day trip from Sharm.

High in the mountains of central Sinai, the ancient monastery of **St Catherine** can be reached in a few hours from the coastal resorts (see page 71). Many visitors choose to combine their visit to the monastery with an ascent of 2285-m (7495-ft) **Mount Sinai**, revered by Muslims, Jews and Christians as the spot where God delivered the Ten Commandments to Moses.

Shore Diving in Sharm

Despite the large number of boats ferrying divers to and from Sharm el Sheikh dive sites, and the obvious preference of most dive centres for boat-based diving, shore diving is still a viable option for most coastal sites. Egyptian and Israeli divers can be seen every weekend all along the South Sinai coast; in fact, until recently, shore diving was the only way to access many Sharm sites. The nicest thing about diving from shore is that you can make your own schedule, miss the 'rush hour' boat traffic and have the sites virtually to yourself.

Roads are generally excellent in the Sharm area, and four-wheel drive is very seldom necessary. Most shore dives do involve a bit of a scramble down sandy wadis or across rough reef tops, but then that's all part of the fun of shore diving.

The only real problem faced by shore divers is the incredible building boom along the coast – roads change from week to week, and some sites are completely blocked by the new developments.

If you want to try some shore dives for yourself, check with one of the local centres for route and access information.

The entrance to Sharm el Moiya, one of the safest anchorages for small boats in South Sinai.

More than any Red Sea country, Egypt has emerged as the leader in marine conservation. Starting with the creation of the Râs Muhammad National Park in 1983, the Egyptian government has succeeded in integrating conservation and sustainable exploitation into its development policies. By protecting the fragile resources on which so much of Red Sea tourism relies, Egypt has led the way for other Red Sea countries as they develop their own conservation policies.

Park Boundaries

When Râs Muhammad National Park was created, it covered the relatively small area of the Râs Muhammad peninsula and the islands of Tiran and Sanafir. Within the boundaries of the park, diving and traditional fishing activities were closely monitored and a range of controls implemented, resulting in a clear reduction in the damage which had begun to appear on other local reefs. As the park's success became apparent, more territory was brought under its control. The Sha'b Mahmûd reefs to the west and the area from Râs Muhammad to Sharm el Sheikh were an early addition, followed by Râs Nusrâni in 1991 and the northern coast in 1992. With these additions, the park now extends from Sha'b Mahmûd to Râs Abu Galûm, almost halfway along the east Sinai coast.

Environmental Education

Within the park boundaries, the park administration runs a broad-based programme of environmental education, policing and research under the aegis of the Egyptian Environmental Affairs Agency. Some of these activities, such as policy seminars for local dive operators, relate directly to the control and policing of recreational diving in the area. Other parts of the programme focus on the needs of the Bedouin communities in the park. These communities rely on fishing as part of their traditional lifestyle, but the increasing pressures of population and outside activities on local reefs has brought the marine environment to crisis point in many other areas. The park's directors consider it crucial to include the local residents in conservation efforts and policy decisions, rather than simply imposing a set of rules and regulations.

The park administration aims to provide local communities with resources and education so that they can play an active part in conserving the area's limited natural resources. The Bedouin communities, living as close to nature as they do, are enthusiastic participants in the new schemes – particularly so since the park's policies have brought clinics, schools and social schemes to this historically underdeveloped region.

Today, the National Park is a complex, multidepartmental organization, overseeing a range of activities from marine research to the maintenance of a tourist centre and visitors' information service, within the park boundaries. Projects such as a marine-bioculture feasibility study aim to expand the area's usefulness to local communities in the future, while a force of rangers in four-wheel-drive vehicles and powerful motorboats ensure that regulations are observed and the park's natural bounty preserved. There are even reports of a secret diving police force of rangers, who join local dive trips incognito, to ensure that dive centres and individual divers are obeying the park's dive guidelines.

The HEPCA Organization

While Râs Muhammad is the highest-profile success story in Egyptian marine conservation, there are many other programmes throughout the region which are having equally profound effects. Foremost among these is the Hurghada Environmental Protection and Conservation Association, or HEPCA. This organization was founded in 1992 by fifteen local dive centres to try to combat the growing destruction of Hurghada's once-pristine reefs.

The Hurghada area was among the first in Egypt to be heavily developed as a dive destination, and its infrastructure boomed as foreign divers flooded in. But what began as a developer's fairytale soon turned into an ecological horror story, with up to 350 of Hurghada's 500 dive boats throwing anchors on to the reefs each day, Hurghada's coral treasures were being pounded to rubble.

HEPCA's counterattack began with a mooring buoy project to stop anchor-dropping on the most vulnerable reefs. After a massive fund-raising effort, the money was found to import a state-of-the-art submarine anchoring system from the USA, complete with the heavy hydraulic equipment that was needed to set the anchors.

An initial target was set to put 60 permanent moorings in place in the Hurghada area. After some teething problems the mooring buoy project got under way, with HEPCA Technical Advisor Philip Jones bearing the brunt of the installation effort, helped by local divers like Mark Maurice, a SUBEX base leader.

Clocking up long hours underwater, the volunteers wrestled with heavy machinery as they learned the fine art of anchor-setting on the job. By the end of the project they had amassed more decompression time than most divers have logged dive hours, but the buoys were in place and Hurghada's reputation as a marine conservation blackspot was changing.

HEPCA's mooring buoy project attracted widespread interest from the outset. A small, community-based non-governmental organization had tackled a huge problem, and had done so on a shoestring budget, using local expertise and community goodwill to achieve its aims.

An Ongoing Struggle

But HEPCA did not rest on its laurels. Using the original mooring buoy project as a springboard, the organization went on to secure funding and assistance from governmental and international sources. Developing a series of further projects in conjunction with USAID, HEPCA worked up a comprehensive plan to install buoys on as many local reefs as possible. It was discovered that an additional 200 buoys were needed to halt the progressive damage that was gradually destroying the area's marine habitat. Far from balking at this challenge, HEPCA secured funding from USAID to purchase the necessary equipment and materials, and undertook to install and maintain them as part of USAID's Red Sea Coast Ecotourism Initiative.

Thus safeguarded, the offshore reefs and islands will become official Protected Areas, under the same regulations that protect Râs Muhammad National Park to the north. HEPCA has worked with the Egyptian Environmental Affairs Agency to implement this change in status, and has been instrumental in devising strategies to manage and monitor the protected areas.

As part of this project, HEPCA has expanded into the area of community education, recognizing that ecological initiatives can only succeed when they are supported by local residents. Seminars and publications form part of the awareness campaign, which targets not just dive centres and dive boat operators, but also local fishermen, hotels and tour offices, officials in the coastguard and tourist police force, and the community at large. Published materials include multi-language pictorial guides introducing the regulations that apply to the newly protected marine habitat. In addition, slide shows, videos and presentations by international experts and local marine biologists are planned, to increase popular awareness.

A Success Story

Moving from its humble beginnings to an ever-closer interaction with governmental and international conservation groups, HEPCA is an unparalleled success story.

The determination and energy of its members prove that the strongest motivation for ecological protection comes from within the community.

HEPCA stands as a shining example for the development of marine conservation in the Red Sea.

SHARM el SHEIKH TO HURGHADA

The clear blue waters between Sharm el Sheikh and Hurghada hide some of the Red Sea's biggest surprises – stunning reefs and mysterious shipwrecks, the legacy of the maritime trade that has flowed through the region for millennia. Strewn across the Strait of Gûbâl, the gateway to the Suez Canal, the reefs of this region are as rich in history as natural beauty.

This chapter encompasses dive sites in Sha'b Mahmûd and Sha'b Ali, the Strait of Gûbâl and Hurghada, spread across 74km (40 nautical miles) of open sea between the tip of Râs Muhammad and the Egyptian mainland at Hurghada. The sites can be reached from either Sharm el Sheikh or Hurghada. Sharm el Sheikh has been covered in the previous chapter (see page 84 for details).

THE PEOPLE AND THE CULTURE

Like the southern Red Sea coast, Hurghada and its environs were once settled only by the Bedouin who were spread sparsely throughout the entire Eastern Desert. Today it is radically different and the deserted beaches of a few decades ago have become Egypt's biggest beach resort. A large proportion of the shopkeepers and hotel and restaurant workers came originally from the tourist centre of Luxor. As the concentration of tourism there reached saturation point over the last decade, many businesses set up satellites on the coast, and a wave of workers soon followed.

CLIMATE

Tempered by sea breezes from the gulfs of Suez and Aqaba, temperatures are mild in winter and blazing hot in summer, often reaching 40°C (104°F) or more. Rainfall is minimal and limited to the winter months. Beware of the danger of fierce sunlight. You should cover up and use a good sunblock.

DIVE HIGHLIGHTS

One of the real highlights of diving in this region is the well-preserved, accessible shipwrecks that litter the seabed across the entrance to the Gulf of Suez. Many major wrecks lie in easy reach of Sharm el Sheikh or Hurghada. There are 19th-century mail steamers, modern cargo ships and historic spice traders lying on the bottom of the sea, all waiting to be explored.

MARINE LIFE

A combination of local features – isolated reefs, tidal movement and lack of nearby intensive fishing – adds up to perfect conditions for reef and schooling fish. Along with the large range of colourful reef species the area boasts some big pelagics and some massive schools of gregarious species. These reefs also offer some of the best chances in the northern Red Sea to swim with dolphins in the wild. Sharks, even hammerheads, are regularly spotted here and sea turtles are common. Recently, two whale sharks were seen from the Shark Observatory in Râs Muhammad National Park and another was seen off El Aruk Gigi, a shallow site opposite the beach at small Giftûn island, Hurghada.

The range of coral species is astounding, and while the occasionally rough sea conditions in these open waters can cause some damage to the reefs, most of the coral growth is in excellent condition. The area boasts some extensive reef systems, incorporating branching

Acropora, vast fields of cabbage coral, bommies and outcrops of massive species such as *Favites* and *Porites*, and gently waving *Dendronephthya* soft corals.

CONDITIONS

Seasonal temperature variation is quite similar to that found in southern Sinai. Water temperatures range from the upper 20s°C (80s°F) in summer to winter lows as cold as 19–20°C (66–68°F). You may be comfortable enough in just a Lycra skin suit in summer, particularly if you normally dive in cold water. Conversely, in the winter, some locals use drysuits. A 3mm (⅛in) or even a 5mm (⅕in) wetsuit would not be out of order for most of the year.

As autumn progresses to winter, the prevailing winds in the area strengthen; Râs Muhammad is sheltered, but by the time they reach the Strait of Gûbâl they can be pretty powerful. Conditions are rarely so bad that diving is impossible, but the boat ride can get rough, particularly since so many of the sites in this area are on open-sea reefs. If you suffer from seasickness take a good supply of motion-sickness tablets.

ACCESS

The vast majority of the sites in this region lie some distance offshore and, while most can be done as day trips from either Sharm el Sheikh or Hurghada, a much more relaxing and enjoyable way to dive them is as part of a short live-aboard trip. Dive centres in both Sharm and Hurghada also organize 'mini live-aboards' from one night to seven nights.

DIVE OPERATORS AND FACILITIES

Both Sharm and Hurghada are packed with dive centres. There were more than 20 in Sharm and more than 70 in Hurghada at the last count. The majority of centres in both resorts are highly professional, with excellent equipment, facilities and organization and multi-lingual dive staff and instructors trained to the highest international standards.

LOCAL DIVE ETIQUETTE AND CUSTOMS

It is important that every diver does his or her bit to preserve the reef environment. If you dive from Hurghada you might want to dive with a centre belonging to HEPCA, the Hurghada Environmental Protection Association. This voluntary organization is working to preserve the area's reefs from further destruction, and has already raised funds to sink permanent moorings at many of the most popular sites. (See feature on page 86.)

DRIVING IN EGYPT

In the main diving areas of Egypt, the ease and convenience of renting a car makes driving yourself a very tempting option. It gives you easy access to dive spots, no need to lug heavy gear-bags, and the freedom to explore the local area on your own. However, you should be aware of a few of the problems driving in Egypt can raise.

At first glance, it may seem that there are no road rules at all. On closer inspection, you w will see that there are rules, even if they don't make much apparent sense.

Lane usage is mainly observed in the breach: faster vehicles routinely overtake at any time, anywhere, in the face of oncoming traffic or round blind corners. Often, but not always, this is signalled by a blast on the horn or a flash of the lights. You are expected to make space for incoming vehicles.

Headlight usage is one true peculiarity in much of Egypt. Many drivers prefer to drive with their lights turned off at night and will angrily flash their high beams at you if you insist on using your own lights to see where you are going. It is conventional to switch off main lights as you approach oncoming vehicles, and to turn on your nearside indicator to give an idea of where your vehicle ends. You may not be prepared to adopt these conventions, but if you don't, be prepared for irate reactions from other drivers.

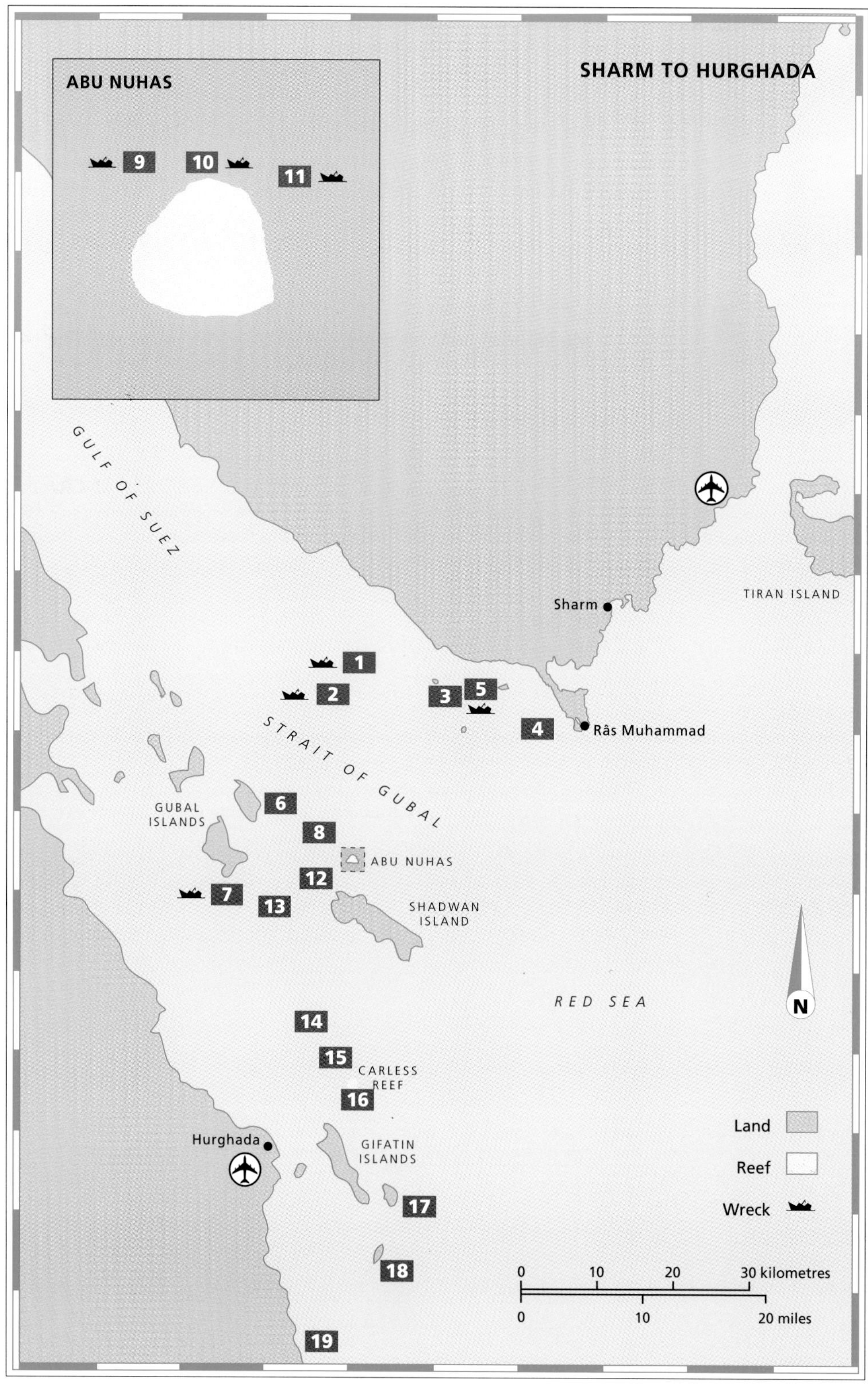
SHARM TO HURGHADA
ABU NUHAS
9
10
11
GULF OF SUEZ
Sharm
TIRAN ISLAND
1
2
3
5
4
Râs Muhammad
STRAIT OF GUBAL
GUBAL ISLANDS
6
8
ABU NUHAS
12
7
13
SHADWAN ISLAND
RED SEA
N
14
15
CARLESS REEF
16
Hurghada
GIFATIN ISLANDS
17
18
19
Land
Reef
Wreck
0
10
20
30 kilometres
0
10
20 miles

1 THISTLEGORM

★★★★★

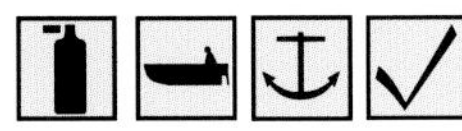

Location: Northeast of Shag Rock, east of the southern end of Sha'b Ali west-northwest of Râs Muhammad.
Access: By day or live-aboard boat from Sharm el Sheikh or Hurghada.
Conditions: Current, waves, wind and swell can all be considerable.
Average depth: 24m (80ft)
Maximum depth: 30m (100ft)
Average visibility: 20m (65ft)

This wreck dive has almost legendary status among Red Sea divers. While the site is suitable for all but the most inexperienced divers in calm conditions, the level of expertise required definitely increases as conditions deteriorate, and they do so regularly. Check for current, wind and wave action, and decide whether the conditions match your skill level.

The *Thistlegorm* lies at 30m (100ft), her largely intact forward section sitting almost upright on the sandy bottom. The aft section was the epicentre of the blast that sunk the *Thistlegorm* and it is is badly damaged. The stern section, its huge propeller clearly visible, boasts crew quarters, the main anti-aircraft gun and a 3.5-in (39-mm) gun on deck. Off the port side of the ship, a railway locomotive lies at 33m (110ft), thrown from its place on deck as the ship sank.

The *Thistlegorm* was an army supply ship and the wreck is like a gigantic, submerged army surplus store. But there are strict penalties for wreck-stripping, so do not help yourself to souvenirs.

Among other attractions, you can visit the captain's bathroom, where tubeworms grow from the silt-filled bathtub like flowers in a window box. The site is fairly well colonized by fish and corals, including lots of big jacks, big schools of snappers, bannerfish and huge groupers. There is quite a bit of soft coral growth throughout.

Dives generally begin at the bow deck, where shot lines will be secured. Descents and ascents should always be made along the line to avoid being swept off by frequently tricky currents.

2 SHAG ROCK

★★★★★★★

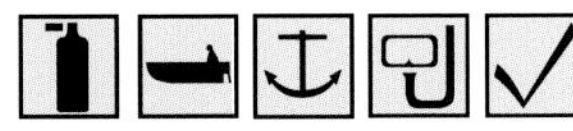

Location: South of the Sha'b Ali reef complex in the Northern Strait of Gûbâl.
Access: By day or live-aboard boat from Sharm el Sheikh or Hurghada.
Conditions: Wind, waves and current can make access impossible.
Average depth: 15m (50ft)
Maximum depth: 25m (80ft)
Average visibility: 20m (65ft)

This barely submerged, egg-shaped reef runs northwest to southeast. The reef top is marked by a light beacon and the wreck of a fishing boat. Surrounded by a sloping reef wall, the reef is made up of a good range of stony and soft corals. There are plenty of branching forms and a few patches of nice soft corals. The site hosts a wide-ranging population of fish with lots of schooling fish and pelagics. The best dive is along the reef's eastern side. To the northeast of Shag Rock, at 27m (90ft) lie the remains of a World War II Dornier Bomber, broken in two but otherwise fairly intact. The location of the wreck of the *Kingston* in the shallows just off the west side of Shag Rock, is a bonus for snorkellers. The stern section is particularly atmospheric, with its looming bulk silhouetted against the light that penetrates the waters.

3 LITTLE PASSAGE (THE SMALL CRACK)

★★★★★★★

Location: Halfway along the Sha'b Mahmûd reef system, northwest of Beacon Rock and the *Dunraven.*
Access: By day or live-aboard boat from Sharm el Sheikh or Hurghada.
Conditions: Tidal currents, wind and waves can all be strong.
Average depth: 15m (50ft)
Maximum depth: 20m+ (65ft+)
Average visibility: 20m (65ft)

This site is a crack or passage in the extensive Sha'b Mahmûd reef, which separates the Sinai coast from the open water of the Strait of Gûbâl. It is one of two navigable passages into the sheltered lagoon behind the reef, and is thus a popular spot with live-aboards anchoring for the night in the lagoon's calm waters.

The main reef at the small crack runs from northwest to southeast, and is a well-formed, steeply sloping coral wall reaching from the surface to 18m (60ft), with a sand slope and scattered coral beyond. The crack bisects this reef and forms a shallow channel to the inner lagoon. This channel is a maximum of 6m (20ft) deep, and averages 2 to 3m (5–10ft), with reef walls of about 2m (5ft) on both sides.

Coral growth throughout is excellent, particularly on the outer reef wall. A mix of stony and soft types can be found, with a very wide range of stony coral species making up the reef walls, and exceptional formations of soft corals. The full range of Red Sea reef fish species can be seen at this site. Pelagics are common, particularly when there is a current running.

Given that most dives will be from a live-aboard anchored in the lagoon, the best plan is usually to take a zodiac through the passage to a point upstream from the passage's outer mouth, then drift with the current along the outer reef and through the passage toward the lagoon. Zodiac pickup in the rougher waters outside the reef can be difficult; this, however, assumes a flood tide, an ebb tide will complicate matters further.

4 THE ALTERNATIVES/STINGRAY STATION

★★★★★★★

Location: Just south of Sha'b el Utâf, west of Râs Muhammad.
Access: By day or live-aboard boat from Sharm el Sheikh or Hurghada.
Conditions: Some strong currents, but site is sheltered from most weather.
Average depth: 18m (60ft)
Maximum depth: 30m+ (100ft+)
Average visibility: 20m (65ft)

This site is named for its relatively sheltered position – in rough weather it serves as an alternative to some of the more exposed sites in the area. The alternatives are, in fact, a chain of shallow patch reefs running from Sha'b Mahmûd eastward toward the Râs Muhammad coast; Stingray Station is only a small part of this extensive chain, near its western end.

The landward side of the reef patches offers maximum depths of 10–15m (35–50ft), while on the seaward side reefs often drop well past 30m (100ft). The reef's isolated heads alternate with numerous sandy wadis and amphitheatres, with numerous large pinnacles and coral heads.

The coral that makes up these reefs is luxuriant, with an especially good range of stony coral species. The soft corals are equally spectacular, with big patches of purple and yellow *Dendronephthya* and *Xeniids* vying for attention. Fish life is abundant and highly concentrated. The numerous sand patches support lots of stingrays – hence the name 'stingray station' – and resident leopard sharks. A bonus is the small whitetip and grey reef sharks which are also sometimes sighted here.

5 DUNRAVEN WRECK

★★★★★★★★

Location: Just south of the light at Beacon Rock, at the southeast end of Sha'b Mahmûd.
Access: By day or live-aboard boat from Sharm el Sheikh or Hurghada.
Conditions: Some strong currents; surface weather can complicate access.
Average depth: 20m (65ft)
Maximum depth: 28m (90ft)
Average visibility: 20m (65ft)

This site is the wreck of a 19th-century steam-sailing vessel that sank in 1876 en route from India to England. It lies about 20m (65ft) off the reef at Beacon Rock, with its stern in about 28m (90ft) of water and its shallowest point near the bow at 15m (50ft). The ship lies bottom-up on the sandy sea floor, its bow pointing westward at a shallow angle to the reef – the hull is broken in two. The ship's propeller is still in place at the stern, and the masts can be seen protruding from under the hull on the seaward side. The wreck is abundantly covered in coral growth, with impressive colonies of soft coral.

The ship's cargo has settled or dispersed, so the interior of the hull is wide open. However, the bow section is narrow and twisty, and penetration is not advised for divers untrained in negotiating tight passages.

After visiting the wreck, swim back along the reef face toward the mooring point. The reef here is an excellent dive in its own right, offering very dense and diverse coral growth and a host of reef fish species. Both stony and soft corals abound, with lots of plate corals and encrusting forms.

Fish life, both on the wreck and on the reef, is exceptional. The highlight of the dive is probably the immense profusion of sweepers inhabiting both bow and stern sections of the wreck, like a shimmering bead curtain drawn across the cavernous interior. The wreck is showing signs of collapse and illegal salvage, so take extra care when penetrating it.

6 BLUFF POINT

★★★★★★

Location: The point sticking out on the east of Gûbâl Saghîra, southwest of Shag Rock, in the Strait of Gûbâl.
Access: By day or live-aboard boat from Sharm el Sheikh or Hurghada.
Conditions: Wind, waves and current can make access difficult.
Average depth: 20m (65ft)
Maximum depth: 30m (100ft)
Average visibility: 20m (65ft)

This site extends like a pointing finger into the Strait of Gûbâl. The reef here is a steep wall, following a meandering path along the coast. It boasts some sheer, cliff-like sections, and is peppered with caves and cavelets. Coral growth is good, with a wide variety of stony and soft corals on the reef face. A particular attraction is the abundant growth of *antipatharian* black coral bushes at depth. A large cave lies just off the lighthouse; south of here, the reef bends inwards, eventually reaching the wreck of a barge, the usual pickup point for dive boats. The section of reef between cave and barge often experiences tricky currents, so stay

Above: *A couple of masked butterflyfish (*Chaetodon semilarvatus*) cruise the reef.*
Below: *The male parrotfish is a mixture of brilliant colours.*

in close to the reef. There are three wrecks north of the point – the *Ulysses*, an oil rig assembly and one that is as yet unknown. Fish and other marine animals abound here – the site is famous for turtles – while Bottlenose Dolphins are also frequent visitors.

7 WRECK OF THE ROSALIE MÖLLER

★★★★

Location: West of the southern Gûbâl Island.
Access: By boat from Sharm el Sheikh or Hurghada.
Conditions: Moderate to strong currents.
Average depth: 40m (130ft)
Maximum depth: 50m (165ft)
Average visibility: 15m (50ft)

The SS *Rosalie Möller*, originally named the SS *Francis*, was built for the Booth Line in 1910. in 1931, she was sold to the Möller Line of Shanghai. Requisitioned for the war effort, she was anchored awaiting clearance into the Suez Canal when she was attacked by Heinkel Bombers.

Today she lies upright on sand, with the bow at 39m (130ft), the rudder at 45m (150ft) and the top of the mast at 17m (55ft). She should only be dived in the best weather due to the currents and the visibility. Fish and coral life is prolific, but because of the depth, divers' bottom time is limited.

8 UMM 'USK

★★★★★★★★

   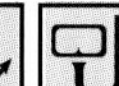 

Location: Between Gûbâl and Shadwân islands, in the southern Strait of Gûbâl.
Access: By day or live-aboard boat from Sharm el Sheikh or Hurghada.
Conditions: Wind, waves and currents can complicate dives here.
Average depth: 18m (60ft)
Maximum depth: 31m (100ft)
Average visibility: 20m (65ft)

This site is a crescent-shaped reef lagoon; the entrance, on the west side of the reef, is partially blocked by a large, elliptical patch reef, which is the site of most dives here. One dive plan covers the outer reef wall of this patch reef and its southern tip; a second plan concentrates on the north end of the reef, the nearby main reef and a smaller satellite reef to the northwest.

The site's profile is varied, with steep reef wall sections, big heads, bommies and undercut, mushroom-like pinnacles. Coral growth is good. Branching forms here are excellent, with many *Acropora* variants in table and spreading formations and several other branched species. Fish life follows the usual local pattern of vibrant reef species, with lots of parrotfish, wrasse, emperors and surgeons, snappers, fusiliers, angelfish and butterflyfish, and nice big groupers. Night dives here will often turn up ghostly squid and cuttlefish, an impressive, other-worldly sight. Another attraction, though not exactly qualifying as fish life, is the frequent appearance of Bottlenose Dolphins in the lagoon.

MINI LIVE-ABOARDS

Live-aboard dive cruises are in many ways the dream of every diver – a chance to visit prime dive sites, avoid the crowds, and relax between dives in the stress-free environment of a well-appointed dive boat. Unfortunately, this luxury comes at a cost, and the prices of full-scale live-aboard dive holidays put them out of the reach of many divers.

There is, however, a way for divers in the Egyptian Red Sea to experience live-aboard diving on a limited budget. Most dive centres in Sharm el Sheikh and Hurghada offer regular overnight trips, on a variety of boats ranging from basic to luxurious, to local sites such as the *Thistlegorm* wreck, Sha'b Ali and 'Abu Nuhâs. These safaris are reasonably priced and offer divers the chance to sample the delights of a full-scale dive charter at a fraction of the cost.

If you are interested in joining a safari, you should check with your dive centre as soon as possible to find out about scheduling and availability. The safaris are very popular and spaces tend to go quickly.

9 GIANNIS D

★★★★★

  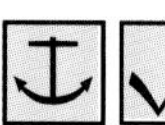

Location: At the northwest corner of Sha'b 'Abu Nuhâs, west of the *Carnatic* and *Chrisoula K* (Sites 10 and 11).
Access: By day or live-aboard boat from Sharm el Sheikh or Hurghada.
Conditions: Very strong wave action on the reef face is common.
Average depth: 18m (60ft)
Maximum depth: 27m (90ft)
Average visibility: 20m (65ft)

This site is one of at least seven victims of 'Abu Nuhâs' notorious northern reef face, navigational errors or deliberate insurance frauds. This Greek-registered freighter was wrecked in 1983 and has become a regular dive attraction. The ship's engine room, in the stern section, is well preserved; the bridge and superstructure, whose shallowest point lies in just 8–9m (25–30ft) of water, offer lots of scope for exploration, while the cavernous interior of the wreck is extremely atmospheric. The wreck has nice soft coral growth plus a few stony corals. Fish include groupers, angelfish, lionfish and a variety of open-water visitors, such as jacks and the occasional barracuda. For atmosphere and ease of diving this is a remarkable site, especially as much of the wreck lies in relatively shallow water.

10 CARNATIC

★★★★★

Location: At the centre of 'Abu Nuhâs' north reef face, between the *Chrisoula K* and the *Giannis D* (Sites 11 and 9).
Access: By day or live-aboard boat from Sharm el Sheikh or Hurghada.
Conditions: Wind, waves and heavy breakers make this site impossible in bad weather.
Average depth: 18m (60ft)
Maximum depth: 25m (80ft)
Average visibility: 20m (65ft)

Sunk in 1869, this wreck, lying in the middle of 'Abu Nuhâs' north face, is one of the most fascinating in the Red Sea.

The ship lies on its port side, more or less parallel with the reef on a sandy bottom. Its deck and masts face away from the reef; the bow lies in 18m (60ft), and the stern in 24m (80ft). The hull is broken into three sections, all of which can be penetrated. The engine and boiler room are of particular interest.

Coral growth on the hull is profuse and much of the ship is completely blanketed in soft coral. Stony corals of many types also colonize both the wreck and the reef, offering a particularly wide range of species. There is a fairly dense population of resident reef fishes, including groupers and lionfish, while jacks and other schooling fish often cruise by in the open water.

11 CHRISOULA K

★★★★★

Location: At the northeast corner of Sha'b 'Abu Nuhâs, just east of Umm 'Usk.
Access: By day or live-aboard boat from Sharm el Sheikh or Hurghada.
Conditions: Strong wind, waves and seasonal weather may make access impossible.
Average depth: 18m (60ft)
Maximum depth: 25m (80ft)
Average visibility: 20m (65ft)

There are possibly the remains of three wrecks here, one of which is likely to be an insurance fraud. The *Chrisoula K* is next to the earlier wreck of the *Marcus*, and further to the east is the wreck of the *Olden*. This site, one of

A calm day is a rare occurrence in the Strait of Gûbâl.

the wrecks for which Abu Nuhâs is famous, lies at the northeastern corner of the reef. This position allows you to combine both the wreck and the more sheltered eastern reef face on one dive, as well as offering calmer conditions for snorkellers.

Sunk in 1981, the wreck lies with its bow section on the reef top, with the rest of the hull sloping down the reef. The bow section was almost completely destroyed in the collision, and the forward sections are a mess, but the state of preservation improves as you travel toward the stern, where the hull and superstructure are virtually unscathed. Much of this area can be penetrated, so bring a flashlight. However, the wreck is not too stable, so penetration is inadvisable in bad weather or very heavy current.

The sloping reef to the south is very steep, cliff-like in places, with a fine array of stony and soft corals and a wide range of cracks, canyons and cavelets. Fish life is equally wide-ranging, with reef species such as grouper, wrasse, snapper and many others competing with pelagic species drawn by the sheer profile and big currents. Jacks are very common here, and barracuda are also a possibility, while sharks can occasionally be seen.

The propeller on the wreck of the Kingston *at Shag Rock (Site 2).*

12 SIYUL KEBIRA

★★★★☆☆☆☆

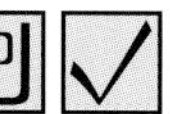

Location: Just south of Umm 'Usk in the southern Strait of Gûbâl.
Access: By day or live-aboard boat from Sharm el Sheikh or Hurghada.
Conditions: Some extremely strong currents.
Average depth: 15m (50ft)
Maximum depth: 22m (70ft)
Average visibility: 20m (65ft)

This site extends east and west around the island of Siyûl Kebîr. The reef has an extremely varied profile, with an undulating reef face split by furrows, sandy 'wadis' and big valleys, hollows and depressions. The reef is composed of very dense coral patches. The north side is especially thickly grown, but is subject to the full force of wind and weather, while the south side is more sheltered, offering good snorkelling possibilities on a series of reef patches.

The site is richly covered by a variety of coral types, both stony and soft. Fish life is equally exuberant. The reef here attracts frequent pelagic visitors and the usual reef species. Leopard and nurse sharks have sometimes been spotted on the sand here.

13 SIYUL SAGHIRA

★★★★☆☆☆

  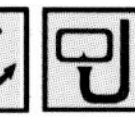 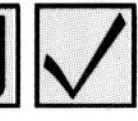

Location: Southwest of Siyûl Kebîra, southern Strait of Gûbâl.
Access: By day or live-aboard boat from Sharm el Sheikh or Hurghada.
Conditions: Current, wind and waves can all be strong.
Average depth: 15m (50ft)
Maximum depth: 25m (80ft)
Average visibility: 20m (65ft)

Despite its name (which means Little Siyûl in Arabic) this is the largest reef in the immediate area at over 4km (2½ miles) long.

The spit is the location of some of the best diving on the reef. Divers often begin their dive on the exposed northern side of the spit, to be propelled by the current along the sloping reef, before turning the corner at the end of the spit and awaiting boat pickup on the sheltered southern side.

To the south, the main body of the reef is an extremely shallow 3m (10ft), offering excellent snorkelling but not quite deep enough for most divers. Coral growth is fairly dense.

The reef spit offers a greater depth range, with good cover down to 20 or 25m (65–80ft). Corals here are luxuriant and tightly packed, with an excellent range of stony and soft varieties. Fish life is also dense and varied and the open water area nearby draws its fair share of pelagic species.

14 UMM QAMAR ISLAND

★★★☆☆☆

  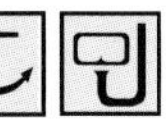 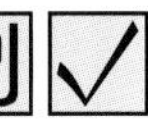

Location: 9km (5½ miles) north of Giftûn Island, between Hurghada and Shadwân.
Access: By day or live-aboard boat from Sharm el Sheikh or Hurghada.
Conditions: Waves and current can affect dives here.
Average depth: 20m (65ft)
Maximum depth: 35m+ (115ft+)
Average visibility: 20m (65ft)

This site lies off the island of Umm Qamar, or Mother of the Moon in English, at the south end of a very large, isolated reef. The favoured area for diving is on the southeast side, where the prevailing north wind and waves are broken by the bulk of the island and the reef. The site has a steeply sloping wall profile, dropping to depths beyond 35m (115ft); the wall is quite sculpted, boasting a number of caves and cavelets, one of which, about halfway along the east coast of the island, is absolutely packed with sweepers.

Coral cover is patchy, but there is a decent range of soft corals in the shallows, and the reef has some good examples of most species, stony and soft. One notable species is the *antipatharian* black bush coral, a relative rarity on most reefs.

Fish life is more interesting than the relatively limited coral, with the reef's isolated position drawing a large number of pelagics in addition to a vibrant community of reef species. Sharks are often spotted, as are barracuda, jacks and trumpetfish.

15 SHA'B UMM QAMAR

★★★★★☆☆☆

 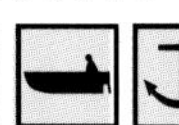 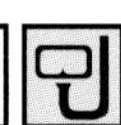 

Location: 2km (1¼ miles) south of Umm Qamar Island.
Access: By day or live-aboard boat from Sharm el Sheikh or Hurghada.
Conditions: Surface weather and swells can make this site impossible to dive.
Average depth: 20m (65ft)
Maximum depth: 35m (115ft)
Average visibility: 20m (65ft)

This is one of the nicest sites in the Hurghada area, packing lots of action into its small confines. There is a small wreck, lying at around 25m (80ft), as well as a very dense population of reef and pelagic fishes. The reef has a sloping wall profile, with a number of caves and crevices. Coral growth is fairly good, with a variety of species present.

Fish life is what the site is about and many of these fish are exceedingly tame and approachable as a result of prolonged fish-feeding. Off the reef, the show continues, with a phenomenal concentration of pelagics and schooling reef species. Sharks are also a possibility, drawn by the reef's vibrant fish population.

16 CARLESS (CARELESS) REEF

★★★★☆☆☆☆

Location: 5km (3 miles) north of Giftûn Island, south of Sha'b Umm Qamar.
Access: By day or live-aboard boat from Sharm el Sheikh or Hurghada.
Conditions: Exposed reef vulnerable to big seas and bad weather.
Average depth: 20m (65ft)
Maximum depth: 40m+ (130ft+)
Average visibility: 20m (65ft)

This isolated reef, lying between Sha'b Umm Qamar and Giftûn Island, is known to divers the world over for its large population of semi-tame moray eels. Weather conditions often make the exposed site difficult or impossible to dive.

The reef centres on two pinnacles, or high peaks,

which brush the surface in an otherwise open sea. The valley between these pinnacles is about 16m (50ft) deep, and offers a wide range of dive possibilities for those not interested in deep diving. A few metres east of the saddle, a steep wall drops well beyond 40m (130ft), with a contoured profile offering many caves and cavelets for the more experienced diver.

Reef composition is diverse, with most coral species, both stony and soft, making a vibrant and interesting coral habitat. As well as the famous eels, there are innumerable species of reef fishes. The reef's isolation, combined with the deep water in which it lies, make it ideal for pelagic-spotting, and sharks are as likely here as at any reef in the area. Jacks, tuna and barracuda are also frequently spotted.

The big draw is, of course, the large population of giant and other morays flourishing here, thanks in part to the numerous dive guides who have almost domesticated them with regular gifts of food. The eels vary in size, but several are at the upper limit of their growth range. They will often remain outside their lairs in the presence of divers.

17 GIFTUN SAGHIR

★★★★★★★

Location: East of Giftûn Kebîr, east-southeast of Hurghada.
Access: By day or live-aboard boat from Sharm el Sheikh or Hurghada.
Conditions: Strong wind, waves and currents all possible.
Average depth: 20m (65ft)
Maximum depth: 40m+ (130ft+)
Average visibility: 20m (65ft)

This spectacular wall dive lies on the eastern side of the smaller of the two Giftûn islands. Boat moorings on the southern side of the island offer some of the best shelter in the area for overnighting or just a lunch break.

The eastern wall drops sheer to great depths; it is very contoured, and its craggy profile features some interesting caves. Some of these lie fairly deep – one arched swim-through at over 45m (150ft) is particularly impressive, but lies too deep for many divers. The reef shallows along the southern coast are less challenging, with depths from 18m (60ft) upward.

The reef is well covered with both stony and soft corals. The steep wall section boasts a phenomenal congregation of gorgonian fans, as well as dense growth of sea whips and *antipatharian* black corals. The reef shallows are particularly rich in friendly smaller reef fish while big impressive pelagics buzz past in the blue waters off the wall.

18 ERG ABU RAMADA

★★★★★★★★

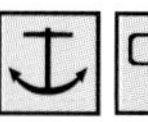

Location: Off southeast Abu Ramada Island, south of the Giftûn Islands and about 12km (7½ miles) southeast of Hurghada.
Access: By day or live-aboard boat from Sharm el Sheikh or Hurghada.
Conditions: Strong currents and big swells possible.
Average depth: 15m (50ft)
Maximum depth: 18m (60ft)
Average visibility: 20m (65ft)

This small site, on a group of coral pinnacles just offshore from Abu Ramada, is an incredibly dense collection of the best in coral growth and reef fishes.

The pinnacles are carpeted in rich layers of coral, with colourful soft corals predominating, along with some gorgonians and a fairly wide range of stony species. The openings and walls of the caves and cavelets are often particularly vibrant, with colonies of *Dendronephthya* and other vividly coloured soft corals.

Fish life here is sensational, with a reef fish population that seems concentrated on this small spot by the favourable conditions. Pelagics such as jacks and barracuda are equally common.

19 SHA'B ABU RAMADA/THE AQUARIUM

★★★★★★★★★★

Location: 3km (2 miles) south of Abu Ramada.
Access: By day or live-aboard boat from Sharm el Sheikh or Hurghada.
Conditions: Some current and wave action possible.
Average depth: 12m (40ft)
Maximum depth: 15m (50ft)
Average visibility: 20m (65ft)

Rising from a flat, sandy seabed around 15m (50ft) deep, this site is even more isolated than Erg Abu Ramada (Site 18). About 2km (1¼ miles) south of Abu Ramada island, the site is relatively shallow and quite flat, with a collection of smaller coral heads around it.

Fish life here is phenomenal, possibly the richest in the area. The smaller reef fishes are well represented and the sand floor hosts stingrays and even nurse or leopard sharks. Jacks, barracuda and small tuna can often be seen in big schools off the reef, and there is always a chance that a grey or whitetip reef shark may cruise by.

Opposite: *Incredible water clarity on the reef.*
Overleaf: *A group of three-spot damselfish (*Pomacentridae sp.*) swirls in the current.*

How to Get There

The sites in this section are accessible from either Sharm el Sheikh or Hurghada. For details of how to get to Sharm el Sheikh see page 84.

By air: Hurghada's international airport receives a huge number of daily scheduled and charter flights. The high volume tourist traffic means that it is one of the cheapest flight destinations in Egypt. There is also a full range of domestic and regional flights for short hops in Egypt and the Middle East.

By ferry: There are regular scheduled ferry services from Sharm el Sheikh. This is a relatively cheap way of seeing both Sharm and Hurghada in one trip, but the crossing can be quite rough, and crossing times often far exceed the advertised four hours.

By road: There is a wide range of buses to or from Hurghada, with air-conditioned services to Cairo, Luxor, Sharm and many other tourist centres, and an even more extensive network of local buses and coaches to smaller destinations. Minibuses and service taxis also ply many of these routes.

Getting around in Hurghada can be very difficult: many visitors simply give up and stay within the walls of their chosen resort. The town's sprawling layout, stretching along more than 20km (12 miles) of coast, means that motor transport is required for most journeys. Taxis are expensive, but there is a good choice of reasonably priced car rental outlets. However, beware of hair-raising Egyptian driving. The cheapest option is the many public minibuses that ply fixed routes along the main drags. There will be plenty of helpful locals to point you in the right direction, and the minibuses are a bargain.

Where to Stay

Hurghada's plentiful accommodation ranges from regally luxurious to backpacker penurious. The former are located on the seafront in either direction from the town centre. Less swanky establishments lie a few metres back from the beach, and the cheapies are to be found in backstreets in the town centre. Most Hurghada dive centres are in the grounds of big hotels. El Gouna is to the north of Hurghada, and there is a private airfield nearby with flights to Cairo and Luxor. Port Safâga is to the south. If your budget stretches to it, you might want to stay in the same complex as the centre you are diving with and avoid the early-morning commute. A few good hotels include:

InterContinental Abu Soma Resort K48 Hurghada Safaga Road, Hurghada; tel 20 65 3260 700/fax 20 65 3260 749; email abu_soma@interconti.com; www.intercontinental.com/ www.ichotelsgroup.com.
Jasmine Village South Coast, Hurghada; tel 20 65 3442 442/fax 20 65 3442 441; email jasmine@tut2000.com.
La Bambola Hotel Hurghada; tel 20 65 3442 086/fax 20 65 3442 085.
Magawish Tourist Village 16km (10miles) south of Hurghada; tel 20 65 3442 620/fax 20 65 3442 255; email info@magawish.com; www.magawish.com.
Mövenpick El Gouna Hotel PO Box 72, Hurghada; tel 20 65 3600 100/fax 20 65 3600 111; email resort@elgouna-movenpick.com; www.moevenpick-hotels.com.
Sea Horse Hotel PO Box 123, Hurghada; tel/fax 20 65 3548 704; email seahorse@red-sea.com; www.redseahorse.com
Sheraton Soma Bay Resort Soma Bay; tel 20 65 3545 845/fax 20 65 3545 885; email reservationssomabayegypt@sheraton.com; www.sheraton-somabay.com/home.html.
Three Corners Rihana Resort El Gouna; tel 20 65 3580 025/fax 20 65 3580 030; email rihana@threecorners.com; www.threecorners.com.

Where to Eat

Hurghada is loaded with pizza parlours and seafood restaurants. All the upmarket hotels and resort complexes have restaurants. In the centre of Hurghada and along the main coastal roads there are innumerable places to choose from, offering felafel, shawarma, roast chicken etc. A few notables include **Felfela's** in Sigala, a branch of the national chain of Egyptian-style restaurants and a very good place to get to grips with local cuisine; the excellent **Chez Pascal**, good for a splurge; and the **Chinese/Korean** restaurant outside the Grand Hotel, with delicious seafood dishes and sizzling Korean barbecues. Downtown, the **Peanuts** bar is possibly the best place in Egypt for a beer.

Dive Facilities

Hurghada is overflowing with dive shops. Any attempt at a full listing would be pointless, as centres regularly shut down or open up. The centres listed are not necessarily the best. A good starting point would be the HEPCA member centres (see following list). These centres are committed to environmentally friendly dive activities, conservation and educational programmes. **Emperor Divers** are regularly voted top (or near top) Red Sea Dive Centre by readers of *English Diver* magazine.

Colona Divers Magawish Resort, Hurghada; tel 20 65 3464 631/fax 20 65 3464 632; email hurghada@colona.com; www.colona.com. Certification: PADI.
The Dive Tribe PO Box 72, El Gouna Mövenpick Resort, El Gouna, Hurghada; tel 20 65 3580 120/fax 20 65 3545 160; email info@divetribe.com; www.divetribe.com. A PADI Gold Palm Resort, 5-star IDC Centre and TDI technical training.
Diving World Hurghada Sheraton Hotel, Hurghada; tel 20 65 3443 582; email hurghada@divingworldredsea.com; www.divingworldredsea.com. Certification: PADI.
Emperor Divers & Red Sea Scuba Schools Hilton resort, and Egypt and Grand Azure, Safâga Road, Hurghada; tel/fax 20 65 3444 854; email info.hurghada@emperordivers.com. Certification: BS-AC; PADI 5-star Gold Palm Resort.
James & Mac Diving Center Giftûn Beach Resort, Hurghada; tel 20 65 3463 003/fax 20 65 3562 141; email info@james-mac.com; www.james-mac.com.
Jasmin Diving Center Jasmine Village, Hurghada; tel/fax 20 65 3460 475; email info@jasmin-diving.com; www.jasmin-diving.com.
Orca Red Sea La Pacha Resort, Hurghada; tel 20 65 3444 150; fax 20 65 3443 705; email kontakt@orcaredsea.de; www.orcaredsea.de. Certifications: CMAS, PADI.
Rudi Direct Red Sea for Tourism and Diving, Shedwan St. 5, Hurghada Harbour, Hurghada; tel 20 65 3442 960/fax 20 65 3443 234; e-mail info@rudi-direct.com; www.rudi-direct.com. Certification: PADI.
SUBEX Hurghada Diving Center PO Box 207, Aldahar, Hurghada; tel 20 65 3548 651/fax 20 65 3547 471; email redsea@subex.org/hurghada@subex.org; www.subex.org. Certifications: CMAS, SSI, PADI.

Hospitals & Diving Emergencies

There is a good recompression (Hyperbaric) chamber at the **El Gouna Hospital**, and smaller ones at **Hurghada Naval Hospital** and **Port Safâga**.

El Gouna Hospital tel 20 69 3549 702/ fax 20 69 3580 020; email info@elgounahospital.com.
Hurghada Naval Hospital tel 20 69 3449 150. **Port Safâga** tel 012 2190383.
Sharm el Sheikh Hyperbaric Medical Centre tel 20 69 3660 922/3/ fax 20 69 3661 011

Local Highlights

Hurghada is a beach resort, and doesn't offer too many activities. The beach hotels offer the usual range of **water sports** – windsurfing, jet-skis etc. **Sindbad Submarine** gives non-divers a taste of the deep, as do **glass-bottomed boats**.

The monasteries of **St Anthony** and **St Paul** are about 200km (124 miles) north of Hurghada, a reasonable day-trip possibility.

The Gulf of Suez, the Red Sea's north-western arm, has been an artery for maritime trade since time immemorial. Early shipping brought trade goods to the Gulf's northern end to be transported by land into mainland Egypt. The precursors of today's Suez Canal linked the Gulf with the Nile from as early as 500BC, thus accelerating trade along sea routes which, by the 15th century AD, reached from the Indian Ocean to the western Mediterranean and beyond.

The completion of the modern canal in 1869 revolutionized maritime trade, enabling the largest freighters to travel directly from the rich trading ports of Asia to European markets, bypassing the long and dangerous trip round Africa's southern cape. This massive increase in shipping travelling through the Red Sea was the start of a trend that continues to this day. The number of shipwrecks strewn across the seabed are evidence of the scale of heavy boat traffic over the years.

Among the densest of the concentrations of wrecks in the Red Sea lies around the Strait of Gûbâl at the mouth of the Gulf of Suez. Here a labyrinth of islands and submerged reefs guards the passage between the open sea and the Gulf's shallow waters. No one knows how many ships have perished in this stretch of water in the long history of Red Sea trade. Even in the century and a quarter since the building of the Suez Canal, untold numbers of vessels have been lost.

The stories of the countless disasters that mark this maritime crossroads make fascinating reading. For divers, these wrecks and their histories are doubly fascinating, since many lie in waters accessible to the sport diver and can be visited from nearby diving centres.

Below are the stories of two of the area's wrecks and directions to enable you to reach them. These two are well known, but there are many others whose location remains undiscovered or is a closely guarded secret. As diving in the region continues to grow, campaigns to locate known wrecks of historical significance are increasing. Over the coming decades names will certainly be added to the list. The thrill and mystery of diving on the area's wrecks remains a lure, whether it be a pioneering dive on a newly discovered ship, or the one-hundredth dive on an old favourite.

The Thistlegorm

Sha'b Ali, a massive reef lying at the northern edge of the Straits of Gûbâl, is the site of one of the Red Sea's most fascinating wrecks, the *Thistlegorm.* It is one of the highlights of diving, not just in the Red Sea but in the whole world. Discovering this wreck's history is almost as fascinating as diving it.

The *Thistlegorm* was a 4898-ton freighter, built in 1940 in the Sunderland shipyards of J. Thompson & Sons. She was one of the massive number of freight vessels requisitioned during the war years to supply the Allied war effort. The *Thistlegorm* was engaged in just such a supply mission when she sank here on 6 October, 1941.

Laden with a mixed cargo of war materials, the *Thistlegorm* had made the long, perilous journey from England round the Cape of Good Hope. She was carrying supplies for the British Western Desert (XIII) Force in North Africa and her cargo included every conceivable type of war material, from rifles to artillery shells, motorcycles to jeeps and trucks, and car tyres to tank tracks. Even uniforms and combat boots were on board.

The *Thistlegorm* was lying at anchor off Sha'b Ali in the early hours of 6 October. By some accounts she was waiting at the entrance to the Gulf until the Canal, closed by German attack, could be reopened. Other accounts say she was engaged in observing the complex approach drills required of shipping entering the Canal zone in wartime.

Whatever the case, she was a sitting target when she was spotted by two German long-range bombers based out of Crete; The bombers commenced their attack at 1:30am and delivered their deadly payload with Teutonic precision, two bombs penetrating the ammunition-packed No. 4 hold, triggering an explosion that tore away the entire stern section of the ship. She sank to the bottom in an upright position, coming to rest on the sandy bottom 28m (95ft) below.

There the *Thistlegorm* lay until 1956, when she was first dived by Jacques Cousteau on his early voyages aboard *Calypso*. Despite this high-profile discovery, her location was subsequently lost. Not until 1991 were her precise bearings fixed and recreational diving begun on this supreme wreck.

The Carnatic

This historic wreck was a P&O mail steamer carrying over 230 passengers and crew to Bombay, along with a consignment of gold worth £40,000 on the market at that time (considerably more at today's prices). In the early hours of 13 September 1869, the vessel was making good time across a calm, flat sea when, due to a miscalculation in navigation, she ran onto the reef at Abu Nuhâs. The weather remained calm as day broke, and after the initial shock subsided the British stiff upper lip asserted itself. Passengers were served meals, as usual, in the plushly appointed dining room.

The Captain decided, fatefully, that given the calm conditions, the passengers should remain on board for a further night. Evacuation was postponed. Life aboard the ship continued as normal until, without warning, the *Carnatic's* hull snapped in two at 10:50am. Twenty-seven passengers and crew were drowned in the ensuing chaos. The survivors were forced to drag the ship's boats across the shallow reef and row to Shadwân Island, where with bonfires and an emergency rocket they managed to attract the attention of another P&O vessel, the *Sumatra*, which carried them to safety.

Not surprisingly, given the value of the ship's cargo, a huge salvage operation was mounted. In this, one of the first commercial salvages using the new compressed-air helmet diving rigs, £32,000 in copper and bullion was raised from the ship's temporary resting place in the shallows. What happened to the remaining gold? No one knows, because in March 1870, the *Carnatic* shifted, settling at the bottom of the reef where you will find her today. There she lay, beyond the reach of the limited diving equipment of the time, until the first scuba divers arrived.

Motorcycles stacked on the back of trucks on the Thistlegorm wreck.

SOUTH EGYPT

As more and more divers discover the diving areas of northern Egypt, attention has turned to the dive sites of the south. The region offers warm, clear waters and lush coral gardens, without a hint of pollution, along hundreds of kilometres of little-developed coastline.

For our purposes, South Egypt is the area along the Red Sea coast from just south of Hurghada all the way to the southern border with Sudan. There were dive operators at Port Safâga before Hurghada was developed for dive tourism, and the offshore reefs further south have been dived by live-aboard boats since the 1970s. Since the early 1990s, a good coastal road has opened up land-based dive operations and the new airport at Marsa 'Alam is almost certain to turn the area into the next Sharm el Sheikh.

THE PEOPLE AND THE CULTURE

Traditionally, the occupants of the southern Egyptian Red Sea coast and the Eastern Desert were almost exclusively Bedouin, descendants of earlier migrations from Sinai and the Arabian peninsula. The inhabitants of the area's few scattered towns and villages were the exception to this rule, coming from a mixed background reflecting the historical trade routes on which their existence relied – Arabs, Indians, East Africans and even the ancient Romans traded along this coast. In 2004, the well-preserved timbers and riggings of ancient pharaonic seafaring ships were found inside two man-made caves at Wadi Gawasis, some 25km (16miles) south of Port Safâga and 50km (31miles) north of Quseir. Today, the balance of population has again shifted, with a new influx of immigrants from the Nile Valley arriving to find work in the emerging fields of industry and tourism.

CLIMATE

Temperatures in July and August can reach 45°C (113°F), while in winter the temperature in the surrounding desert can sometimes drop below freezing at night. Rainfall is minimal but what there is generally falls in December and January.

DIVE HIGHLIGHTS

Diving here is fantastic. Stick a pin in the map almost anywhere on the coast, and you would most likely find a prime dive site of pristine beauty. This is an area of elaborate coral gardens, maze-like labyrinths of caves and canyons, drop-offs and gentle slopes, shallow undersea playgrounds and submarine valleys.

MARINE LIFE

Most of the reef fish species can be seen in huge numbers and display little of the timidity which has become common further north. Huge schools of snappers, surgeonfish, barracuda, fusiliers and jacks are extremely common, while solitary reef fishes are present in numbers usually reserved

CAVE DIVING TECHNIQUES

Reefs in the Quseir area boast a wide range of canyons, caves and tunnel systems. While these can offer an excellent opportunity for exploration, divers should be aware that cave diving is a specialized, potentially dangerous type of diving, and should be treated with great caution. No one should engage in extensive cave diving without proper training and certification, but following these basic rules should make small-scale exploration a bit safer.

- Follow the rule of thirds - never use more than one-third of your air supply while penetrating a cave or tunnel, leaving one-third for the return trip and one-third for emergencies.
- Control your buoyancy and fin gently to avoid stirring up sediment and ruining visibility.
- Do not proceed into a cave or tunnel unless you are sure you have a clear exit route or enough space to turn around and retrace your entry route.
- If you become stuck, relax, breathe slowly, then calmly try to extricate yourself (usually by using your hands to move backwards).
- Never attempt to imitate advanced techniques, such as removing your tank to squeeze through small passages, unless you have been properly trained.

for schooling species in the Red Sea. Groupers reach unbelievable sizes; big moray eels fill nooks and crannies in the reef; colourful angelfish of many species abound; and looming giants, such as Napoleon Wrasse and parrotfish, patrol the waters along the reef's edge. The sandy bottoms along the coast support a variety of rays and some oddities, such as Guitar Sharks and crocodilefish. Other sharks, including Reef Whitetips, Grey Reefs, Hammerheads and even the majestic Whale Shark, have all been seen in these waters.

The area's other marine residents are sea turtles, squid, cuttlefish and octopuses, and this is one of the few places in the world where wild dolphins have been known to play with divers in the water. There are even areas where that most elusive of marine mammals, the dugong, has been seen by divers.

The corals are incredibly diverse and healthy. All the soft and stony species are represented in extensive reefs composed of every conceivable mixture, where big beds of single species, such as *Dendronephthya* forests or fields of *Acropora* tables, alternate with complex jumbles of dozens of species. Huge gorgonian sea fans and castle-like bommies of massive corals feature on many reefs, and carpet anemones and bubble corals can be found throughout the area.

Conditions

Water temperatures range between 29°C (84°F) in the summer to the lower 20s°C (70s°F) in winter. While habitual cold water divers may be content with a Lycra suit or a shortie wet suit, locals wear full suits even in summer, and opt for 7-mm (¼-in) suits with hoods or even drysuits in the winter months. Prevailing winds largely determine dive conditions here, especially as much diving is done from shore or long-range boat, where sheltered access or anchorages are important. Wind-driven waves, particularly in the autumn and winter, can limit access to some sites and divers would be well advised to practise entries through heavy surf.

Visibility is generally very good, with averages over 20m (65ft), and highs far beyond that. As with any tropical sea, however, seasonal fluctuations can bring seriously reduced visibility in the form of plankton blooms or other natural phenomena.

Dive Operators and Facilities

There are many operators working out of Port Safâga, which is easily reached from Hurghada airport. Previously the domain of long-range live-aboard boats, which specialized in the better-known offshore and near-shore reefs, the south Egyptian Red Sea has now been developed, and operators' 'House Reefs' and local shore-dives are also becoming popular.

There is now a small number of high-quality dive operators arranging diving on the most southerly coast, and, as interest in the region increases, this number is bound to rise. In addition, several live-aboards now spend the summer months based out of ports along the most southerly coast, and other boats from the northern ports have added south coast destinations to their itinerary.

Local Dive Etiquette and Customs

Divers are expected to follow a 'hands-off' policy when diving in the region. This means careful attention to buoyancy and constant vigilance to make sure no part of your body, from fin-tip to fingertip, comes into contact with the reef.

Most dive centres and live-aboard operators insist on an initial checkout dive to evaluate divers' skills. The responsible diver will accept this constraint as a courtesy to the operator and a necessary precaution to safeguard the region's exquisite reefs.

The Egyptian Government has increased the Environment Tax from $1 per diver per day to $3 per diver per day from 1 May 2005. This applies only to the mainland of Egypt, not the Sinai.

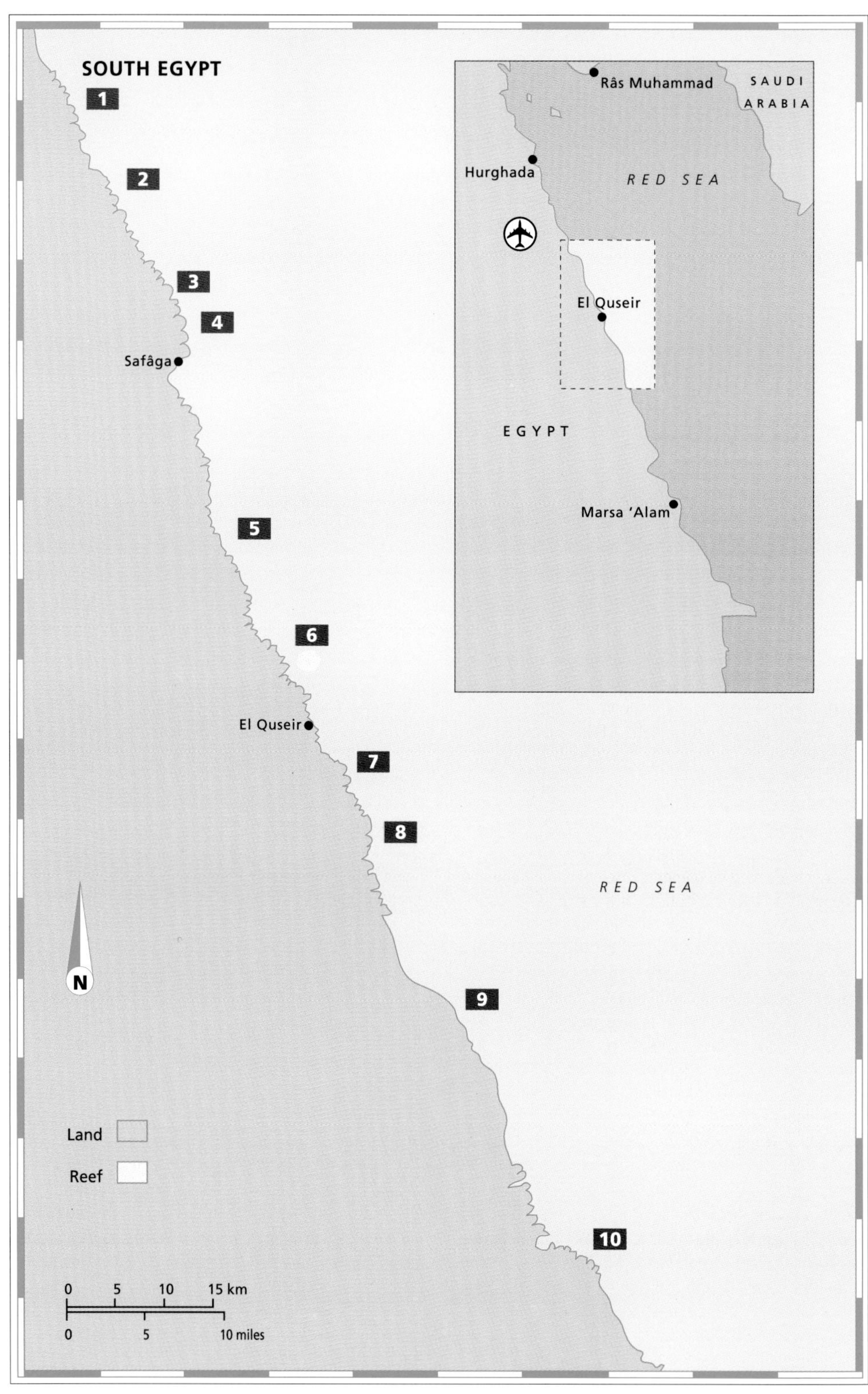
SOUTH EGYPT
1
2
3
4
Safâga
5
6
El Quseir
7
8
RED SEA
9
10
N
Land
Reef
0 5 10 15 km
0 5 10 miles
Râs Muhammad
SAUDI ARABIA
Hurghada
RED SEA
El Quseir
EGYPT
Marsa 'Alam

A wave breaking on a healthy reef of stony corals.

1 GREEN HOLE

★★★★★★★★★

Location: 59km (37 miles) north of Quseir on the Red Sea coast.
Access: By jeep from Quseir, then a reef entry from shore.
Conditions: Some surge is likely in the entry passage even on relatively calm days; runout from falling tide can make exit tricky.
Average depth: 20m (65ft)
Maximum depth: 25m (80ft)
Average visibility: 20m (65ft)

This dive begins with a descent to about 9m (30ft) through a submerged, greenish hole in the reef top. The dive continues from the bottom of the entry hole, past a pair of coral pinnacles with rich growth of soft corals, down a steeply sloping valley or canyon. This canyon drops to depths of 35m (115ft), and is bordered on both sides by a gently sloping reef.

Coral growth is excellent on the reef face and there is a good range of reef fishes to observe, while in the open, eagle rays are frequently sighted and dolphins occasionally come in for a curious look at divers.

The best plan for this dive is to drop down the canyon to your maximum depth, then turn left along the reef face for a leisurely swim until you reach a large coral block at 20–25m (65–80ft). At this point, turn back and begin ascending gradually, and finish off the dive with an exit through the green hole to the reef top. Be aware that visibility can be poor in the hole and the reef top surge area generally, and make sure to maintain a good reserve of air in case you need to deal with currents or strong runout during your exit.

2 MAKLOUF

★★★★★★★★

Location: 48km (30 miles) north of Quseir on the Red Sea coast.
Access: By jeep from Quseir, then a shore entry across the sheltered reef top.
Conditions: As with many Quseir sites, surge and runoff can adversely effect entry conditions, but the site is well sheltered from strong waves.
Average depth: 18m (60ft)
Maximum depth: 40m+ (130ft+)
Average visibility: 20m (65ft)

Entry is through a canyon which descends through the coral mass of the reef top, before broadening into a large sandy area stretching south, dotted with coral heads. This sandy area slopes down to about 40m (130ft), and is interrupted by large coral reef blocks to both north and south.

The southern section is particularly rich in stony corals but soft corals are also well represented. There is an unusual anemone at about 15m (50ft) on an isolated coral block in the middle of the sand.

There are lots of jacks and fusiliers and huge numbers of swarming coral fish, such as fairy basslets, sweepers and damsels on the various coral heads and blocks. Lionfish abound, and the sand hosts populations of crocodilefish and Bluespotted Ribbontail Rays, and the occasional sleeping Whitetip Reef Shark. Eagle Rays are also frequently spotted here. During your exit, take some time to poke around in the many cavelets which lead off the entry/exit canyon. A smaller passage branches to the right as you pass your entry point. This passage ascends to about 1m (3ft), affording the easiest exit from the canyon.

3 KILO 37 NORTH

★★★★★★★

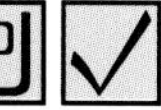

Location: 42km (26 miles) north of Quseir (37km (23 miles) from Subex Dive Centre).
Access: By jeep from Quseir, then a shore entry across a wide reef top.
Conditions: Strong runoff and longshore currents on the reef top can complicate access.
Average depth: 18m (60ft)
Maximum depth: 35m+ (115ft+)
Average visibility: 20m (65ft)

This site is a sloping coastal reef featuring an extensive system of caves and tunnels which honeycomb the reef table. The reef top is over 100m (330ft) wide here. The canyon that marks the beginning of the dive drops from near the reef edge to a depth of about 15m (50ft) before giving way to a sandy slope running to 35m (115ft) or more. On the sand at a depth of 30m (100ft), directly out from the mouth of the canyon, is a group of impressive coral heads.

Turning right from the canyon mouth, the reef is steeply sloping and extremely contoured. It is particularly rich in stony corals, with *Acropora* in table, staghorn and branching forms, massive corals shaped like fairy castles, big patches of cabbage coral, and plenty of plate and encrusting forms.

Fish at the site can include Whitetip Reef Sharks, lots of schooling fusiliers, goatfish and snappers, large numbers of extra-large groupers, many unicorn and surgeonfish, triggerfish, fairy basslets, angelfish, butterflyfish and lots of tiny pipefish on the coral heads.

Note: Before entering the smaller caves which riddle the reef top, divers should understand and adhere to the basic rules for cave diving.

BOOTIES

The Quseir area is unusual in that virtually all the region's diving is done from shore. Access tends to involve a walk across the reef flat, which is generally very rough and spiky. For most divers this is more an inconvenience than a serious problem, but divers using full-foot fins should remember to bring hard-soled booties along even if they normally wear their fins over bare feet. A 100m (328ft) barefoot walk over sharp coral is at best time-consuming and uncomfortable; at worst, it could result in serious cuts, infections and missed dives. So remember, you will need adequate footwear.

4 SAFÂGA 1/KILO 32 NORTH

★★★★★★★★★★

Location: 38km (24 miles) north of Quseir (32km/20 miles north of Subex Dive Centre).
Access: Jeep from Quseir, then slightly tricky shore entry from reef top.
Conditions: If there are waves, the entry through a small slot in the reef may require you to jump past the surf zone before donning fins.
Average depth: 18m (60ft)
Maximum depth: 35m+ (115ft+)
Average visibility: 20m (65ft)

The dive is in a shallow bay north of Quseir, whose northern point gives some shelter from prevailing north wind and waves. The reef walls in the bay contain lots of cavelets and passages in depths of 5–6m (15–20ft). The reef outside the bay slopes down to a sandy bottom at around 25m (80ft). Just outside the bay's north point, a long, submerged finger of reef extends to around 35m (115ft).

Stony corals predominate on the reef, with large heads of brain coral, lots of *Acropora* in tables and branching forms, as well as lacy corals. There is also good distribution of *Dendronephthya* and other soft corals.

The bay is home to a wide range of reef fish. Turtles are also prevalent, and Bottlenose Dolphins frequent this stretch of coast. I dived with a group of five big Bottlenoses here for more than ten minutes.

Divers should take care not to get hooked or entangled in the many fishing lines along the bay's northern edge, which is a popular local fishing spot.

5 BEIT GOHA

★★★★★★★★★★

Location: 20km (12½ miles) north of Quseir, just beyond Coastguard station and abandoned village.
Access: By jeep from Quseir, then shore entry from reef top.
Conditions: Strong winds and wave action can make access to this site impossible for most divers.
Average depth: 10m (35ft)
Maximum depth: 30m (100ft)
Average visibility: 15m (50ft)

This labyrinthine coral garden is named after an Egyptian cartoon character renowned for complete confusion – even the guides get lost here. To both the north and south of the entrance, exquisite coral patches alternate with sand and elaborate canyons and tunnels. The site is generally very shallow, averaging 10m (35ft), but depths of more than 30m (100ft) can be reached on the outer side of the reef.

This site is truly phenomenal for growth and diversity of coral. The mixture, distribution and condition of both

Above: *Schooling fish hover over a healthy reef.*
Below: *A stunning Gorgonian sea whip.*

stony and soft species is excellent, with big bommies, beautiful tables, huge massive forms like melted candle wax, extensive soft coral patches, and branching *Acropora*. Thousands of small anemones litter the bottom.

The extensive coral habitat hosts the expected bounty of reef fish and schooling species, such as unicorns and snappers; while the sand patches are home to bottom-dwellers, such as Guitar Sharks, Whitetip Reef Sharks, Bluespotted Ribbontail Rays and crocodilefish. There are a great many varieties of surgeonfish here, plus groupers, trumpetfish, goatfish and triggers.

The entry/exit canyon at least is clearly marked by a line of makeshift buoys made from Baraka mineral water bottles filled with air and tied to the reef.

6 SIRENA BEACH HOUSE REEF

★★★★☆☆☆☆

Location: The bay at Quseir el Qadima, in front of Subex Dive Centre/Mövenpick Hotel, Quseir.
Access: Shore dive or Zodiac from the Subex jetty.
Conditions: The bay at Quseir el Qadima is open to prevailing north wind and waves, so some degree of surge is always likely.
Average depth: 20m (65ft)
Maximum depth: 50m+ (165ft+)
Average visibility: 20m (65ft)

This site is the house reef for Quseir's Subex Dive Centre, a truly enjoyable dive just a few steps from the local dive shop.

You can enter from the jetty and dive either left or right along either arm of the bay, or you can opt for a Zodiac ride from the jetty to the outer reef, from where you can dive back into the bay for an eventual exit at the jetty. Scattered pinnacles line the reef edge on both sides of the bay, and the topography of the reef mass is extremely varied in both directions, with outcrops, caves, tunnels, chimneys and a huge variety of corals.

The outer reaches of the bay are excellent for schooling fish, with deep water meeting the reef at both corners. Tuna, jacks, fusiliers, mackerel and snappers are all abundant, while on the reef Napoleon and other wrasse, lots of morays, big groupers, lionfish, trumpetfish and goatfish are all part of a very vibrant fish population. On the sand, morays, gobies and shrimps are all present, and in the inshore sand shallows schools of squid are a common sight.

Opposite: *The hawksbill turtle (*Eretmochelys imbricata*) has the characteristic brown and yellow markings of tortoiseshell.*

DUGONGS

The dugong, a massive sea mammal found on sea grass beds throughout the Indo-Pacific region, is one of only four species in the sea-cow family. The other three species, the manatees, are found in mangrove areas and inland waterways, notably in Florida, where they are a common sight. By contrâst, the dugong is shy and retiring, and seldom seen by divers.

Dugongs are said to be most closely related to the elephant family, rather than to other sea mammals such as seals or walruses, or the coincidentally named sea elephant.

Despite a maximum length of over 2.5m (10ft) and a weight of half a tonne, these huge animals move very gracefully in the water, barely breaking the surface when they come up to breathe. Indeed, their movements are so subtle that only the keenest eyes will spot them at the surface.

Once common throughout the Red Sea, often in herds of several hundred individuals, the population has declined drastically in recent years, largely as a result of commercial shark fishing. They are now seldom seen in groups of more than a few individuals, although herds on remote reefs in Saudi Arabia hold some hope for the species' eventual resurgence.

7 EL KAF

★★★☆☆☆

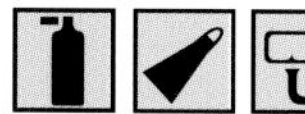

Location: 10km (6 miles) south of Quseir.
Access: By jeep from Quseir, then easy shore entry.
Conditions: Sheltered location with easy access.
Average depth: 18m (60ft)
Maximum depth: 40m+ (130ft+)
Average visibility: 20m (65ft)

Storm damage before the 1998 season left this site reeling; its location at the mouth of a large wadi led to rainwater pushing several tons of desert sand onto the reef. The site is nevertheless still worth a look.

The dive begins with an easy shore entry through a canyon into a narrow sandy bay, bordered on both sides by coral walls. The reef to both sides of the entry canyon is varied, with pinnacles, slopes, shelves and sandy areas. To the south, the reef is split by a series of sandy ravines, small canyons and swimthroughs. At the southern corner of the bay, a semicircular canyon lies in about 6m (20ft), with cavelets, blind alleys and passages leading off it. To the north there are also caves and passages to explore.

Both the reef mass and the more isolated pinnacles and heads show excellent coral cover and development, with some areas more heavily affected by storm damage than others. Large numbers of *Acropora* tables are a high point, as are the carpet-like patches of pale soft corals.

The large fish population includes big groupers, dozens of pufferfish, Bluespotted Ribbontail Rays, crocodilefish, dozens of wrasse species, batfish and trumpetfish. There are schooling fish as well, with snappers, fusiliers, unicorns, sweepers and goatfish.

8 KILO 15 SOUTH

★★★★★☆☆☆☆

  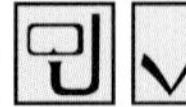

Location: 15km (9 miles) south of Quseir.
Access: By jeep from Quseir, then shore entry.
Conditions: Access is easy, but involves a longish walk. Currents and runoff can affect entry/exit.
Average depth: 20m (65ft)
Maximum depth: 35m (115ft)
Average visibility: 20m (65ft)

This site is accessed through a canyon/tunnel system leading from the reef top to a sand slope at the reef edge. The last few metres of the entry are through a smooth-walled tube from 5–7m (15–25ft); exiting the dive through this tube is generally impossible due to runoff from the reef top, so a second passage just to the south of the entry is used for exits.

The reef follows a moderate sloping profile for some distance, before steepening to vertical walls on both sides. Heading south along the reef, you will encounter a series of pinnacles and coral blocks in 10–15m (35–50ft), before the reef wall begins to curve outwards. At this point, a long coral bar leads out from the main reef; beyond its offshore edge, large table corals are scattered across the bottom from depths of 35m (115ft) or more back to the main reef, which steepens here to form a drop-off or mini-wall.

In this deeper area, chances are excellent for seeing both Whitetip Reef and the rarer Guitar sharks. All the common reef fishes are present in great numbers. Coral growth is good overall, with a predominance of stony species, particularly *acropora*. There are some nice smaller soft corals and a scattering of anemones, but the best of the coral is the fine assortment of table corals off the southern reef.

Bear in mind that the strong runoff from the reef top may make your exit somewhat strenuous. Make sure to maintain a good reserve of air for this eventuality.

9 MANGROVE BAY

★★★☆☆☆

Location: 30km (19 miles) south of Quseir.
Access: By jeep from Quseir, then shore entry.
Conditions: The bay offers excellent protection, but the footing can be treacherous on the short walk across the reef top.
Average depth: 20m (65ft)
Maximum depth: 35m (115ft)
Average visibility: 20m (65ft)

This site is on the south side of a small bay. The north side of the bay is taken up by a large hotel construction project and is occasionally dived by live-aboards which shelter there from the north wind. However, the south side has a reef in a much better state of preservation, with little anchor damage.

The sloping reef is interspersed with sandy ravines and begins midway along the south side of the bay, where a group of small pinnacles sits just off the reef. Follow the deeper section of the reef to the right, to the outside of the bay, then return at a shallower depth to the entry point.

The coral here tends more to stony varieties, with brain and other massive types in evidence. Fish life is diverse and plentiful, with surgeons, unicorns, groupers, emperors, wrasse and basslets in good numbers.

Try to avoid the many holes in the reef top during entry/exit, as it is very easy to put a foot in one and turn an ankle or worse.

10 SHEIKH MAALEK

★★★★★

Location: 50km (31 miles) south of Quseir, opposite a small mosque on the coast road.
Access: By jeep from Quseir, then shore entry.
Conditions: Visibility in the enclosed bay can often be poor.
Average depth: 15m (50ft)
Maximum depth: 20m (65ft)
Average visibility: 15m (50ft)

A labyrinthine site, similar in some ways to Beit Goha (Site 5). Access is through a reef top hole or lagoon. The dive is in a shallow, sandy bay whose mouth is partially blocked by a large coral bar. This enclosed, sandy region, suffers from rather poor visibility. However, as if to compensate for the murky water, the wreck of a small fishing boat lies in the middle of the bay. To the outside of the bay, visibility improves and the mixed, mostly stony corals are healthy. The right/south side has a more varied profile and range of corals, with pinnacles and a very convoluted layout; the left/north side tends more to large, rounded heads and bommies.

Fish life is abundant but the high point is that dolphins and even dugongs have on occasion been sighted here.

The drawbacks here include poor visibility and the need for a long swim to get to the best of the reef.

SURF ENTRY

Along much of the Red Sea coast, shore diving is the only way to access some of the area's prime dive sites. One feature of such shore diving is the need for surf entries across the reef top. This type of entry may seem daunting, but a few simple tips will help you through all but the roughest waves.

- Be prepared – have your mask and regulator in place in case you fall while entering. Fold back fin-straps, ready for quick donning, and practise beforehand so you can don and remove your fins as quickly as possible.
- As you walk into waves, advance only while the water is receding and you can see to check your footing. Stop walking and brace yourself to meet incoming waves, then continue forward during the next backwash.
- If water is knee-deep or deeper, you may be better off donning fins and swimming through the surf zone. In shallow water you will need to advance to the reef edge before donning fins. In some cases it is best to dive head first into deeper water off the reef edge before donning fins. In less strenuous conditions, buddy teams can brace each other while donning fins at the reef edge.
- During entry and exit, work with the waves: swim forward with the force of the water, then hold in place before advancing with the next wave.
- If you fall, use the force of waves to right yourself: brace your feet, turn your back to an oncoming wave and let it push you to your feet, then turn and continue.
- Judge the waves during entry and exit: large waves come in sets, with calmer periods between, during which you should make your entry or exit.

*Whitespotted (Ringed) Pufferfish (*Arothron hispidus*).*

How to Get There

By air: The closest international airport is Hurghada, while Cairo is served by more flights per week. Sharm el Sheikh is another possibility, although it is really too distant unless you also wish to dive in Sinai as well. All the airports are served by a wide selection of direct and non-stop flights.

By road: In Egypt there is a wide range of transport options: crowded, dirt-cheap local buses; air-conditioned luxury coaches; private minibuses; and taxis. Service taxis ply set routes between major towns and cities, departing as soon as there are enough passengers to fill all the seats. They are faster and more comfortable than local buses and travel along the same routes.

Bus and service taxi lines link Safâga and Quseir with Hurghada, Suez, Cairo and other destinations to the north.

Self-drive car rental, with reduced weekly rates, is available from a wide range of companies in Cairo, Hurghada and Sharm el Sheikh. Most companies will rent cars on the strength of a driving licence from your home country, but bringing an international licence (available from your automobile association) is a sensible precaution. You need to be 25 years or older and have a valid credit card.

Where to Stay

Until recently, accommodation in Quseir was limited to either the ultra-luxurious **Mövenpick** to the north of town, or the ultra-basic **Sea Princess** in the centre. Several new options have sprung up since; however, none rival the Mövenpick in either quality or price. The **Fanadir Hotel**, just south of town, is already looking slightly worn, but renovations are promised. Further south, the **Utopia Beach Club** has grown from humble beginnings in a relocated Nile cruiser to a full-blown resort complex. Still further from Quseir, about 30km (20 miles) to the south of town, is the new **Mangrove Bay**, friendly if a little utilitarian.

Fanadir Hotel El Quseir; tel 20 65 331 414/fax 20 65 331 415.
Mangrove Bay Quseir tel 20 2 348 6748/fax 20 2 360 5485; email mangrove@egypt-online.com.
Mövenpick Hotel Sirena El Qadim Bay, El Quseir; tel 20 65 3332 100/fax 20 65 3332 128; email resort@movenpick-quseir.com.eg; www.moevenpick-hotels.com.
Utopia Beach Club tel 20 65 3430 213.

Where to Eat

For fine dining, the **Mövenpick Hotel Sirena** is your best choice, with three different restaurants offering buffet and à la carte dining. By international standards the restaurants are not particularly expensive, and the food quality is as good as you find anywhere in Egypt, with supplies and produce trucked in from Cairo and beyond. At the other end of the spectrum, the cosy, friendly and very authentic **Mata'am Nashad** in town serves roast chicken, fish and local casserole dishes at embarrassingly low prices. Also in town are a collection of **falafel stands** (one of which is run by the man who supplies falafel to the Mövenpick), small snack stands and other cheapies. At the **Subex Dive Centre**, a well-stocked if pricey snack bar serves up sandwiches, grills, snacks and drinks, and boasts an excellent salad bar, a rarity in Egypt and unheard of this far from the tourist centres.

In the evenings, you can either head for the **Top of the Rock** bar at the Mövenpick, or try some of the cafés in town that cater to locals who congregate in the evenings to watch TV. A more pleasant option is the excellent **seafront café** down by the bay, not far from the Sea Princess Hotel, which has no television but does have lovely views and tables right on the beach.

Dive Facilities

By far the best dive base in Quseir is Subex at the Mövenpick Hotel, a superb outfit that could act as a model for other Red Sea dive centres. Dives are arranged from the centre's eco-friendly jetty in Zodiacs, or by jeep along the coast. All equipment is state-of-the-art, and staff are friendly and very professional. The Fanadir, Utopia and Mangrove Bay hotels also have their own dive centres.

Barakuda Diving Lotus Bay, Safâga; tel 20 65 3260 049/fax 20 65 3253 911; email Safaga@Barakuda-Diving.com; www.barakuda-diving.com.
Duck's Dive Center Holiday Inn, Port Safâga or Mangrove Bay Resort, El Quseir; tel 20 65 3260 100/fax 20 65 3260 105; email info@ducks-dive-center.de; www.ducks-dive-center.de.
Sub Aqua Dive Center Utopia Beach Club; tel 20 65 442 473/fax 20 65 430 080; email info@subaqua-divecenter.com; www.subaqua-divecenter.com. Certifications: CMAS, NAUI, PADI.
Subex El Quseir Mövenpick Hotel Sirena, El Qadim Bay, El Quseir; tel 20 65 3332 100/fax 20 65 3332 124; email elquseir@subex.org; www.subex.org. Certfications: CMAS, SSI, PADI.

Hospitals & Dive Emergencies

There is a good recompression (Hyperbaric) chamber at the **El Gouna Hospital**, and smaller ones at **Hurghada Naval Hospital** and **Port Safâga**.

El Gouna Hospital tel 20 69 3549 702/ fax 20 69 3580 020; email info@elgounahospital.com.
Hurghada Naval Hospital tel 20 69 3449 150.
Port Safâga tel 012 2190383.

Local Highlights

The area inland from the Subex Dive Centre is well worth a browse. Here is **Quseir el Qadim**, a medieval Mameluke settlement that grew up on the site of a much earlier Roman trading port – both were eventually abandoned, presumably due to the silting which clogged the bay, moving the coastline and stranding the settlements several hundred metres inland. Recent excavations have uncovered buildings dating from both Islamic and Roman periods of history.

In the centre of **Quseir**, the ruins of a 16th-century Ottoman fort are being resurrected after languishing for years as an unoffical public toilet. In 1998, a British team was brought in to oversee its renovation; great strides have been made despite huge cuts in the budget. The fort will eventually house displays covering the region's history.

Divers performing a boat entry.

OFFSHORE AND THE DEEP SOUTH OF EGYPT

Diving has become a mainstream sport and the Red Sea has changed from an isolated paradise for rugged explorers to a multi-million dollar tourism industry on a massive scale. But the reefs of the deep south still lie beyond the range of dive packages and anyone with the time (and the money) to dive these remote reefs can still see the Red Sea as Hans Hass or Jacques Cousteau first saw it.

CLIMATE

The deep south of Egypt extends down toward Sudan, where summer temperatures often top 50°C (122°F). Winter weather is balmy and even in January you are unlikely to need more than a light jacket or sweatshirt. Surface weather conditions, however, play a big part in dive planning. The seasonal wind changes in autumn bring rough seas and swells big enough to make even the largest live-aboard uncomfortable. Many operators consider these offshore sites undiveable from October onward, so the ideal season for diving is high summer.

DIVE HIGHLIGHTS

The diving here is worth any amount of weather-related discomfort. There are blankets of schooling reef fish pierced by flashing pelagic marauders; coral cliffs that drop out of sight in a riot of scintillating colour; vast expanses of coastal reef virtually untouched by the tarnishing hand of mass tourism, and the serenity of blue skies and even bluer water as you motor across the empty expanse of the open Red Sea.

Some of the big names of Red Sea diving lie in these waters: The Brothers and Dædalus Reefs, isolated towers of pristine coral rising from abyssal depths and shrouded in schools of sharks; and Gezîret Zabargad and Rocky Islet, almost a holy grail of Egyptian offshore diving, with their sheer walls and coral gardens. But there are hundreds of lesser-known reefs that far surpass the best of the northern Red Sea, and they form part of the thrill of exploring the deep south's unknown reefs and seeing sights that few divers will ever see.

MARINE LIFE

The deep south has always had a reputation for sharks, but big schools of snappers, surgeons, bizarre longnosed unicorns, and a host of others are a feature on most reefs. The schooling predators, such as barracuda and trevally, are so common here as to seem quite unremarkable after a while. Dennis the Dugong is still seen regularly around Marsa 'Alam.

On the reef, the colourful profusion of lively fishes almost defies description. Giant groupers swim head to tail with huge Napoleon wrasse. Blue triggerfish appear in their hundreds. Angelfish of every conceivable type play tag with butterflyfish and damsels. Elegant lionfish, prehistoric scorpionfish and eels as thick as telephone poles delight the newcomer. The reefs of the deep south are also brimming with vibrant coral growth, with a density and pristine quality unseen in the north. Waving fields of soft corals and huge, leafy masses of plate coral, *Acropora* tables big enough for a board meeting, giant bommies and lacy seafans are just a few of the delights of the deep south.

Conditions

Water temperatures are high for most of the year: 27°C (81°F) or more in summer and rarely falling as low as 21–22°C (70–72°F) in winter. Like all tropical seas, there is always the chance of plankton or algal blooms that bring sharply reduced visibility, but waters tend to stay clear for most of the year. Average visibility is in the 20m (65ft) range, although it may often be much higher.

Currents and surface swells are often quite strong and, as mentioned above, can make certain sites inaccessible at certain times of the year. On more exposed open sea reefs, such as Rocky Islet or The Brothers, it is not unusual to experience surges from surface swell as deep as 20m (65ft) or more. Some of these sites are challenging, but seldom beyond the range of an experienced open-water diver. The offshore reefs at Port Safâga, that is those outside of Gezîret Safâga (Safâga Island), are exposed to the full force of the wind, so day boats only dive them in good weather.

Access

The only practical means of access to most of the offshore sites is a long-range live-aboard boat. However, for several years, live-aboards were banned from venturing to the offshore sites, and it is only recently that the sites have been opened up again. New mooring buoys have been installed and demanding new regulations set in place, such as the prohibition of night diving, fish feeding or the use of gloves.

Many of the coastal sites could, in theory, be dived from shore. In practical terms, however, you would find it very difficult to manage on your own. The southern Red Sea area is strategically sensitive and you need a whole range of permissions and paperwork to dive here. However, several shore-based operators are now found along the southern coast. During the period that the offshore sites were off-limits, several live-aboards also concentrated on coastal sites such as Sha'b Sharm. Long runs by rigid inflatable boats (RIBs) can be hard on one's back and camera equipment.

The long-distance live-aboard cruises to this area generally operate from Safâga, Hurghada or Sharm el Sheikh, either as part of all-Egyptian itineraries or as part of international dive tours ranging from Israel to Djibouti. Live-aboard boats for the offshore marine park islands must depart from Hurghada or the new Port Ghalib International Marina at Marsa 'Alam.

Big Brother's Lighthouse

The imposing spectacle of Big Brother Island's stone lighthouse is unforgettable. It is the tallest structure for some distance in any direction, piercing the horizon like an admonitory finger. The lighthouse has been warning ships off the rocks since 1880, when it was built by the British, then colonial overlords of most of the western Red Sea coast, as a safeguard for vital Suez Canal shipping routes.

With walls over 120cm (5ft) thick at the base, it is as monumental a building as anything in the Red Sea region. After more than a century, it still looks as if it will outlast most modern constructions. It was originally fitted with an intricate clockwork mechanism to rotate the light. This marvel of imperial technology, made by Chance Bros. of Birmingham, turned a lens mechanism weighing over one tonne by means of a simple suspended counterweight. The lens was no less impressive, magnifying the modest glow of a gas mantle into a beam of light powerful enough to reach distant ships.

The light is still manned, these days by a team of Egyptian military personnel. The British built many lighthouses along the Red Sea, with the larger ones being built in the early 20th century; all are of a very similar construction.

Dive Facilities and Operators

Boats operating on the deep south of Egypt sites range in quality, from the extremely basic to the palatially luxurious. The standard of service is obviously reflected in the price of the trip, and a week on the most opulent of these boats will cost you more than a month of shore-based diving in the north. Even the more basic boats have competent and knowledgeable crew and dive staff, and are generally well equipped and comfortable. The more expensive boats offer air-conditioned splendour and amenities from video movies to en-suite showers, and boast the latest in compressors and fittings.

Local Dive Etiquette and Customs

Bear in mind, as you dive on these pristine sites, that this is what the northern Red Sea dive sites looked like twenty years ago, and that these beautiful reefs could end up as devastated as the worst northern sites within ten years. Each misplaced finstroke or handhold is another nail in the coffin for this delicate ecosystem. Diving here is a privilege and every diver has a responsibility, so please take it seriously. Because too many divers and snorkellers have been bothering the dolphins, the areas where they are common have now been buoyed off.

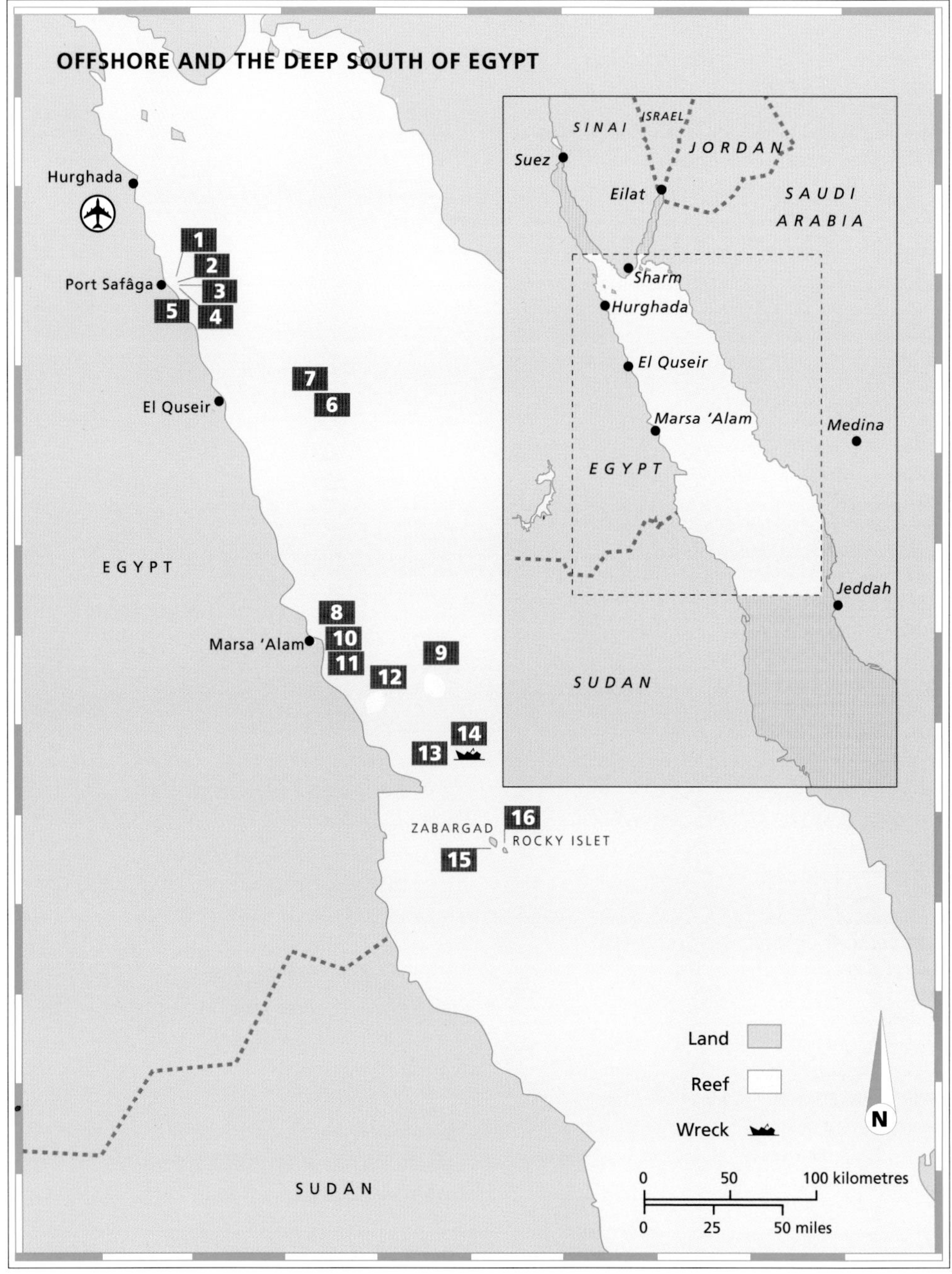

1 PANORAMA REEF

★★★★★★★★★

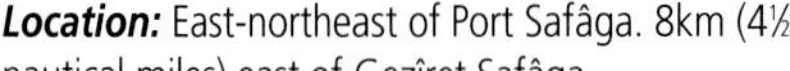

Location: East-northeast of Port Safâga. 8km (4½ nautical miles) east of Gezîret Safâga.
Access: By boat.
Conditions: Choppy with moderate to strong currents.
Average depth: 20m (65ft)
Maximum depth: 50m+ (165ft+)
Average visibility: 30m (100ft)

A highlight of the area, this site is a large circular reef that, when the weather allows, attracts seasoned divers. With walls dropping to over 200m (660ft), there are several good dives around the reef with caves and overhangs. There is everything here: healthy stony corals; *Dendronephthya* soft tree corals and gorgonian sea fans; Black Coral; sharks; turtles; dolphins; groupers; Napoleon Wrasse; barracuda; surgeonfish; angelfish; butterflyfish. In the shallows are anthias, anemones and clownfish.

2 MIDDLE REEF

★★★★★★★★★

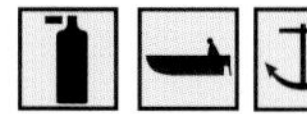

Location: East-southeast of Port Safâga.
Access: By boat.
Conditions: Choppy with moderate to strong currents.
Average depth: 20m (65ft)
Maximum depth: 50m+ (165ft+)
Average visibility: 30m (100ft)

Another reef with brilliant diving. The northern end slopes to 30m (100ft) and then drops into the depths as a wall. The east side shows some anchor damage but, like the very pretty west side, has *Acropora*, *Porites* and lettuce corals, while the south side has caves, tunnels and gullies. The fish life is as profuse as at its neighbouring sites.

3 ABU GAFAN (ABU KAFAN)

★★★★★★★★★

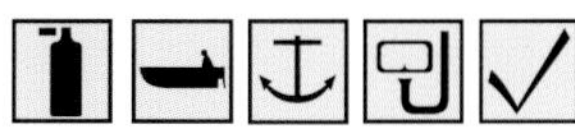

Location: South of Middle Reef (Site 2), east-southeast of Port Safâga.
Access: By boat.
Conditions: Choppy with moderate to strong currents.
Average depth: 20m (65ft)
Maximum depth: 50m+ (165ft+)
Average visibility: 30m (100ft)

Possibly the best diving off Safâga. Abu Gafan is a 300m- (660ft-) long, narrow reef with walls dropping below 100m (330ft) and plateaux at the north and south ends. Great for *Acropora* and *Porites* coral, fire corals, Black Coral, huge gorgonian sea fans, *Dendronephthya* soft tree corals, turtles, barracuda, jacks, groupers, tuna, snappers, Napoleon Wrasse, surgeonfish, fusiliers, angelfish, butterflyfish and Bluespotted Ribbontail Rays.

LIVE-ABOARDS AND REPETITIVE DIVING

The luxury of unlimited diving is what live-aboard holidays are all about – but with this luxury comes added danger, in the form of heavy nitrogen saturation and increased risk of decompression sickness. Add to this the remote nature of most live-aboard itineraries, and the absolute lack of recompression facilities in many areas, and you can see why diver safety needs extra attention on live-aboard cruises.

Diving with your body full of leftover nitrogen from four or five dives a day, you should be planning shallower dives and observing longer safety stops than you would normally. You should be cutting bottom times and avoiding no-decompression limits, and on extended trips, you should consider half-day or even full-day rest breaks. Of course you want to do as much diving as you can, but if you get bent, you will miss a lot more than just a dive or two.

4 SHA'B SHEAR (SHI'B SHEAR)

★★★★★★★★★

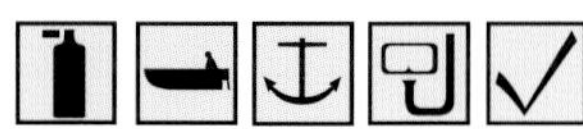

Location: East of Hyndman Reef, southeast of Port Safâga.
Access: By boat.
Conditions: Choppy with moderate to strong currents.
Average depth: 20m (65ft)
Maximum depth: 50m+ (165ft+)
Average visibility: 30m (100ft)

An elongated reef with a shallow lagoon at its south side and coral gardens on its east and west ends. *Acropora* corals, *Porites* corals, fire corals, gorgonian sea fans and *Dendronephthya* soft tree corals abound, while turtles, jacks, groupers, tuna, snappers, triggerfish, rabbitfish, soldierfish, surgeonfish, fusiliers, goatfish, butterflyfish and Bluespotted Ribbontail Rays are common.

5 WRECK OF THE SALEM EXPRESS

★★★★★★★★

Location: Just south of Hyndman Reefs, southwest of Port Safâga.
Access: By boat.
Conditions: Moderate to strong currents.
Average depth: 20m (65ft)
Maximum depth: 30m (100ft)
Average visibility: 30m (100ft)

The *Salem Express* was a welded-steel RoRo (Roll-on Roll-off) ferry built by Forges & Ch. de la Mediterranée in France in 1964. At the time of her sinking on 15

December 1991 she was heading for Port Safâga when, close to midnight, she hit a small reef just south of Hyndman Reefs. Her loading doors burst open and she sank too quickly to give a mayday call. The alarm was only raised when a survivor managed to swim to the mainland. Loaded with Muslim pilgrims returning from Mecca, the official passenger list was less than 700 and the approved death toll was under 200, but she was heavily overloaded and it is believed that the real figure was very much higher.

115m (377ft) long and 17.1m (56ft) wide, this 4770-tonne ship now lies on her starboard side in 30m (100ft) of water with her port side at 12m (40ft). The authorities have closed the ship's interior because of the human remains, but it is easy to swim around the vessel, where there are duffel-bags, suitcases and personal effects scattered everywhere. Lifeboats still hang from their davits, the two funnels have large, raised illustrations depicting the letter 'S' that are already the substrate for red soft tree corals, and the Red Sea's best-known frogfish often puts in an appearance.

Because of the way she is lying, the wreck is best dived in the mornings when she is better lit.

6 THE BROTHERS — BIG BROTHER

★★★★★☆☆☆☆☆

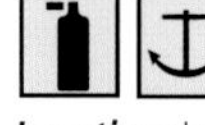
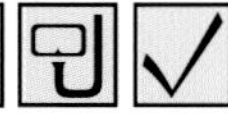

Location: In the central Red Sea, about 59km (32 nautical miles) east-northeast of El Quseir.
Access: By live-aboard.
Conditions: Isolated position makes this site vulnerable to any adverse weather.
Average depth: 25m (80ft)
Maximum depth: 70m+ (230ft+)
Average visibility: 20m (65ft)

The Brothers are a pair of tiny islands – the exposed tips of two massive reef pillars that rise from the depths. They are the only significant reefs in the area, and as such act as a magnet for any pelagic and reef fishes. Washed by the full force of open-sea currents, they support an incredibly dense and diverse coral population, with profuse soft coral growth on all sides.

Big Brother lies about 1km (½ mile) north of its sibling. It is an oblong land mass some 400m (1310ft) long, easily identified by its stone lighthouse. A narrow reef table round the island's shore gives way almost immediately to a sheer vertical wall. Fantastic coral growth begins at the surface and continues unabated into the depths. Gorgonians, sea whips, *antipatharians* and a wealth of soft corals of every conceivable species flourish in the big currents. The stony corals are also well represented. The fish life here is more than impressive, ranging from the tiniest anthias in the shallows to the most impressive sharks in the depths offshore. Big Brother also boasts two wrecks at its northern tip. The 173m (568ft) long SS *Numidia,* which sank in 1901, lies down the northernmost tip starting at 9m (30ft) with the stern at 80m (260ft). The 75m (250ft) SS *Aida*, 100m (330ft) south of the *Numidia*, sank in 1957. The bow section is unrecognizable, but the stern lies in 30–65m (100–210ft) and the rest is scattered over the reef. The strong currents have produced great soft corals on the wrecks while the Brothers attract several species of shark.

7 THE BROTHERS — LITTLE BROTHER

★★★★★☆☆☆☆☆

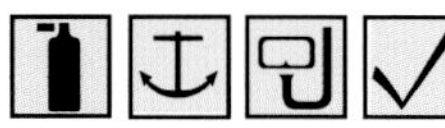

Location: Just southeast of Big Brother, 59km (32 nautical miles) off El Quseir.
Access: By live-aboard.
Conditions: As with Big Brother, exposed to any rough weather.
Average depth: 25m (80ft)
Maximum depth: 70m+ (230ft)
Average visibility: 20m (65ft)

This site is inferior to Big Brother in size only. The soft coral growth here is so rich that the upper 30m (100ft) looks like a psychedelic crocheted cap over the reef and forms the backdrop for some of the most spectacular fish action you are likely to find. Schooling fish are so dense here as to block out the light. In addition to these you will also find any other reef species you can name. Out in the blue, the show goes on with an incredible diversity of pelagics. Like Big Brother, this site attracts numerous sharks: Grey Reefs, Whitetip Reefs, Hammerheads, Tigers, and even the ominous Oceanic Whitetip and majestic Whale Sharks.

8 ELPHINSTONE REEF

★★★★★☆☆☆☆☆

Location: 9km (5 nautical miles) off Marsa Abu Dabbâb on the south Egyptian coast.
Access: By boat.
Conditions: Site offers no shelter in rough seas.
Average depth: 20m (65ft)
Maximum depth: 70m+ (230ft+)
Average visibility: 20m (65ft)

This long, finger-like reef runs from north to south in the open sea. Steep walls drop to the depths on the reef's east and west sides, reaching 70m (230ft) or more, while the north and south ends of the reef are marked by submerged plateaux.

The northern plateau is very shallow, offering some superb snorkelling possibilities, while the southern plateau is much deeper, with a drop-off at 30m (100ft) leading down to the depths where a large underwater arch can be found.

According to legend, the sarcophagus of an unknown Egyptian pharaoh lies beneath the underwater arch, and the outlines of a suspiciously rectangular, coral-encrusted mass can actually be made out in the depths.

Oceanic Whitetip Sharks are common. Inshore at Marsa Abu Dabbâb, the sea-grass beds are visited by Dugongs. Please do not harass them.

9 DÆDALUS REEF

★★★★★★★★★

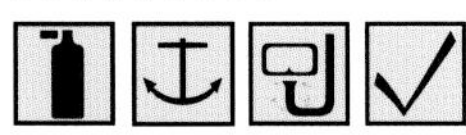

Location: 83km (45 nautical miles) off Marsa 'Alam.
Access: By live-aboard.
Conditions: Weather can make for difficult dive and mooring conditions.
Average depth: 25m (80ft)
Maximum depth: 70m (230ft)
Average visibility: 20m (65ft)

This small, isolated reef lies in the open sea, one-third of the way to Saudi Arabia. Less than 800m (½ mile) across, it is marked by a lighthouse – the only break on the horizon for many miles in any direction. The reef has steep drops on the east, north and south sides, all offering good diving. The southern side offers excellent shelter from the prevailing north winds.

The profile of the reef on the three best sides is very sheer, running from the surface to depths of 70m (230ft) or more. On the west side, there is a drop-off with an 'anemone city' and a section of massive blue coral. To the north, the open water and currents bring the best selection of pelagic fish. Moving down the east coast, another impressive drop-off runs toward the southeast tip of the reef, where there have been repeated sightings of Thresher Sharks, easily recognized by their elongated tails, with which they are said to stun or 'thresh' schools of smaller fish before eating them. The reef is richly developed throughout, with good coral growth from the surface to the depths. Fish life is as dense as you would expect on an isolated reef pinnacle, with the usual reef species complemented by schooling species.

10 KAHRAMANA HOUSE REEF

★★★★★★★★★

 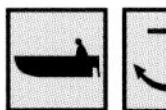   

Location: The fringing reef in the front of the Kahramana Resort Hotel at Blondie Beach, 20km (12½ miles) north of Marsa 'Alam.
Access: By boat or from shore.
Conditions: Calm.
Average depth: 10m (35ft)
Maximum depth: 40m (130ft)
Average visibility: 20m (65ft)

Here the coral slopes down to sand at 30–40m (100–130ft), with *Porites*, brain coral, *Acropora*, gorgonians and *Dendronephthya* soft tree corals. The fish life includes anthias, chromis, sergeant majors, goatfish, Red Sea Bannerfish, sweetlips, fusiliers, Masked Butterflyfish, parrotfish, and more. The invertebrates include Spiny Lobsters, Ghost Crabs, nudibranchs, flatworms, sea stars and sea cucumbers. The site is ideal for night diving.

11 SHA'B MARSA 'ALAM

★★★★★★★★★

Location: The fringing reef in front of the most southerly major town on the coast of Egypt.
Access: By boat or from shore.
Conditions: Calm.
Average depth: 10m (35ft)
Maximum depth: 40m (130ft)
Average visibility: 20m (65ft)

This coastline is just being opened up to divers, with modern hotels being constructed to replace tented campsites either side of Marsa 'Alam. There are almost 100km (62 miles) of divable fringing reef, with a similar underwater topography of coral and coral pinnacles sloping down to sand at 30–40m (100–130ft) as Kharamana House Reef. It is as yet unspoilt by diver pressure, though a few areas are suffering from damage inflicted by Crown-of-Thorns Starfish.

Apart from *Porites*, Brain Coral, *Tubastrea* Coral, and *Arcopora* Table Coral, the area is known for its shoals of goatfish, Red Sea Bannerfish, sweetlips, fusiliers, snappers, jacks and Masked Butterflyfish among a plethora of other reef fish. Invertebrates include Spiny Lobster, Ghost Crabs, flatworms and sea cucumbers.

SHA'B SAMADAI/ DOLPHIN HOUSE REEF

Samadai Reef, which is nicknamed the Dolphin House, is a horseshoe-shaped reef that creates a shallow lagoon where a large pod of Spinner Dolphins like to shelter. Although more shy than Bottlenose Dolphins, they are happy to play in front of snorkellers. However, because they are free, they may be elsewhere during the day when the weather is calm.

Because of diver/snorkeller harassment, the area is now protected from boat traffic by a rope and a line of buoys.

From 1 January 2004, the Governor of the Red Sea and the Environment Protection Agency have levied a fee for all visitors and imposed a rule that no more than 100 divers and 100 snorkellers are allowed into the area per day, with a maximum of 20 people per boat. Visiting times are from 10am–2pm.

12 SHA'B SHARM

★★★★☆☆☆☆

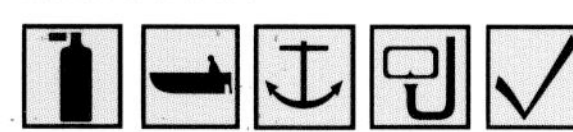

Location: Off the south Egyptian coast, opposite el Sharm.
Access: By boat.
Conditions: Current and waves can make for a difficult dive.
Average depth: 25m (80ft)
Maximum depth: 50m+ (164ft+)
Average visibility: 20m (65ft)

This large, kidney-shaped reef, said to be the top of a volcanic pinnacle, features a steep sloping wall on its east and south sides, with a considerably varied profile. The crescent of reef around the reef's southern tip offers the best diving, with rich coral growth from the surface shallows down. There are numerous undercut sections and reef shelves harbouring dense soft coral growth and a good range of stony corals. There are some good black coral bushes on the wall's deeper sections. Fish life is excellent, with a vast array of huge groupers, schooling barracuda, massive congregations of snappers and unicornfish and some large giant Yellowmargin and Yellowmouth Morays. Currents here can be forceful, and less experienced divers should be wary.

13 SATAYA/DOLPHIN REEF

★★★★☆☆☆☆

Location: 17km (9 nautical miles) north-northwest of Râs Banâs.
Access: By boat.
Conditions: Generally fine, with shelter from most weathers.
Average depth: 18m (60ft)
Maximum depth: 50m+ (165ft+)
Average visibility: 20m (65ft)

A horseshoe-shaped reef lying in open water, its eastern side has a steeply sloping wall profile, giving way to a sandy slope scattered with coral heads and pinnacles toward the reef's southeast corner. The best coral growth occurs in the top 10m (35ft). The southern pinnacles are especially rich, with a wide variety of coral types throughout. The varied stony coral composition of the heads and pinnacles acts as a base for some extremely nice soft coral growth, particularly *Dendronephthya*.

Fish life here is excellent. Schooling fish of all types are seen in large numbers, while reef-dwellers, such as angelfish and butterflyfish, provide flashes of colour. Cuttlefish and shrimps put in an appearance for the invertebrates, and stingrays are common. Sharks of several types can also frequently be spotted here, and there are regular reports of dolphins. The shelter provided by the reef makes this an excellent stop for live-aboards.

14 TUGBOAT WRECK AT ABU GALAWA

★★★★☆☆☆☆

Location: 17km (9 nautical miles) north-northwest of Râs Banâs.
Access: By boat.
Conditions: Moderate to strong currents.
Average depth: 8m (25ft)
Maximum depth: 18m (60ft)
Average visibility: 20m (65ft)

Part of the Fury Shoal group, Abu Galawa has a very old wreck of a tugboat leaning on its south side at the western end. Listing to starboard, the bow of the wreck is on the reef and breaks the surface while the stern is on a sandy bottom. The holds and toilet harbour shoals of sweepers; the propeller is still attached; and the hull is the substrate for prolific stony and soft coral growth including some large *Porites*. The wreck itself has jellyfish, Masked Pufferfish, surgeonfish, angelfish, butterflyfish, chromis, anthias and jacks. There is a sandy bottom on the north side of the reef with all the marine life you would expect of a lagoon, including stingrays.

15 GEZÎRET ZABARGAD

★★★★☆☆☆

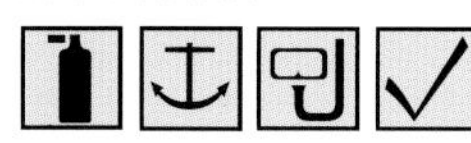

Location: In the open Red Sea, 46km (25 nautical miles) southeast of Râs Banâs.
Access: By live-aboard.
Conditions: Some mild currents, but sheltered from most weathers.
Average depth: 18m (60ft)
Maximum depth: 25m+ (80ft+)
Average visibility: 20m (65ft)

This island was called Topazos in ancient times, and more recently St John's Island. Its Olivine mines were excavated for 3,500 years. Used as an anchorage, the island is a wreck graveyard for three ships. This site lies on the south side of Zabargad Islet, the only large island in this stretch of the Red Sea. It is commonly used as a base for exploring nearby Rocky Islet, and is a popular overnight stop for live-aboards. Zabargad offers an excellent range of reef features in relatively shallow water, so the site is often used for night dives.

A sand slope stretches out from the island's southern shore, covered with an amazing concentration of sculpted stony coral pinnacles, and stepping away down the slope to 25m (80ft) and beyond. Each pinnacle forms a micro-habitat for tiny reef fishes, which spread out like

*The Titan triggerfish (*Balistoides viridescens*).*

a halo round the brilliantly coloured coral. Larger reef fish cruise through the pinnacles, and the sand between them supports stingrays and crocodilefish. Fish life ranges from tiny anthias to huge groupers. Morays are also seen. Plenty of invertebrates, such as cuttlefish, squid, octopus, and nudibranchs are most prominent at night when the site takes on a completely different character. Further south, St John's Reef covers a huge area with many coral heads that are separate dive sites.

16 ROCKY ISLET

★★★★★☆☆☆☆

Location: 5.5km (3 nautical miles) southeast of Gezîret Zabargad.
Access: By boat.
Conditions: Very big surge and moderate to strong currents. An area for advanced divers.
Average depth: 20m (65ft)
Maximum depth: 50m+ (165ft+)
Average visibility: 20m (65ft)

Comparable to the diving at The Brothers and Dædalus, Rocky Islet is a haven for sharks and pelagics. A tiny islet, rising as bare rock from very deep water, it is rarely possible for boats to anchor so Gezîret Zabargad is used for overnight shelter. The northern face is open to the full force of the prevailing wind, so it is normal for divers to be dropped just east of the centre of the north face and then drift or swim around to the calmer waters of the south face. The narrow, sandy shelf that surrounds the islet is widest at its eastern end where, on the southeast corner, it has become the place for divers to observe sharks. In general, Rocky Islet has a jagged vertical profile, but the sheltered south face is broken with canyons and overhangs. These features harbour most Red Sea reef fish, from giant Napoleon Wrasse to tiny anthias, gobies and blennies. The islet attracts shoaling fish, which tend to follow divers as they move from the north or east faces to the south face. As well as having healthy stony, gorgonian and *Dendronephthya* soft tree corals all around, where currents are running, Grey Reef, Whitetip Reef, Silvertip and Hammerhead Sharks are common. The calmer areas have Eagle and Manta Rays, groupers, triggerfish, angelfish, butterflyfish, barracuda, fusiliers, surgeonfish and jacks. Sweetlips, snappers and batfish are common in the spring. Off the reef, technical divers have found a wreck believed to be that of the SS *Maidan*, sunk in 1923.

The lighthouse on Big Brother Island.

How to Get There

Until quite recently, most of this area was only available to divers on live-aboard boats or those diving with a few small outfits operating from the shore around Marsa 'Alam. However, now there is a spate of hotels and resorts being built along the coast road from El Quseir to Marsa Wâdi Lahami, and there is a new airport just north of Marsa 'Alam.

Dive Facilities

As well as inflatable boats, most operators have day boats capable of reaching the near-shore reefs. In good weather, those based furthest north will be able to reach Elphinstone Reef, whie those based furthest south will be able to cover Fury Shoal.

Deep South Diving email info@deep-south-diving.com; www.deep-south-diving.com. Certifications: BSAC, CMAS, PADI, SSI.
El Nabaa Resort Km 101 Quseir/Marsa Alam road; tel 20 12 2353 475/fax 20 195 100 285; email info@elnabaa.com; www.elnabaa.com.
Emperor Divers Sol y Mar Hotel; tel 20 12 7372126; email marsa.alam@emperordivers.com; www.emperordivers.com/marsa_hotel.html.
Kahramana Beach Resort Marsa 'Alam Marsa 'Alam; tel 20 195 100 261/fax 20 195 100 259; email kahramana@link.net; www.kahramanaresort.com. Certification: PADI.
Red Sea Diving Safari Marsa Shagra Safari Camp; tel/fax 20 195 100 262; email info@redsea-divingsafari.com; www.redsea-divingsafari.com. Eco-friendly developments at Marsa Shagra, Marsa and Nakari and Wâdi Lahami.
Wâdi Gimâl Diving Center Shams Alam Beach Resort, Marsa 'Alam; tel 20 8 717 620 7949; email info@shamshotels.com; www.shams-dive.com. Certification: PADI.

Live-Aboards

Few European live-aboard boats now operate in this area; and although Egyptian live-aboard boats have taken their place, only a few of these local operations are capable of challenging the rough weather to reach the offshore reefs such as Dædalus and The Brothers. Various marine park fees and tourist taxes are levied on divers in Egypt. Divers should be patient at the beginning of a live-aboard charter as the boat cannot set sail until the crew have completed all the necessary paperwork and paid all the necessary fees.

The many live-aboard boats available are constantly changing. Some are not up to Western standards, a few are downright dangerous, while others are extravagantly luxurious and consequently expensive. It is wise only to book a place on a boat that has been operating with a good record for some time. The people who know these boats best are the specialist diving tour operators in your home country. Where possible, talk to someone who has been on a boat recently before deciding to book.

Itineraries

These vary, from two-day hops in the northern Red Sea to month-long multi-country extravaganzas. Hunt around to find a boat that meets your needs and your budget. The classified section of your local dive magazine will have up-to-date listings of routes and prices.

Accommodation & Facilities

Despite the many types of vessel operating in the Red Sea, most live-aboards have a few points in common:

Cabin accommodation is the norm – although unless your boat is air-conditioned, you may feel more comfortable sleeping on deck. Cabins will usually be shared, with bunk-style beds, plus there is often one or more cabins with a double bed, generally reserved for couples.

Many boats have private toilets and showers, but shower sparingly as fresh water is a luxury item on board a boat. Rinsing gear is always left until you are ashore, although there is usually a rinse bucket for regulators.

Most boats have separate 'wet areas' for storing the dive gear and changing out of your wet suit. Note that it is taboo to walk into the saloon in full gear, dripping.

Depending on the boat's operator and the passengers, there may be designated smoking and non-smoking areas. It is usually against the rules to smoke in the cabins.

Food and Drink

All boats provide meals and soft drinks. Food ranges from basic rice and stews to nearly Cordon Bleu standard, depending on boats, organizers and crew. Alcohol is generally provided, but must be paid for separately. Tips for the crew and dive master are not compulsory, but they are traditionally given.

Equipment

Live-aboard boats generally have excellent high-capacity compressor facilities and will usually provide at least two tanks per diver to avoid the need for constant refills. Many have their own diving equipment and all can arrange for rentals, but quantity is often limited so if you need to rent gear you should check with your operator well in advance.

Underwater torches are likewise often available for night dives but are also usually limited in number. Bring your own if you have one.

While most boats generally have a good spares kit, and experienced divemasters will usually be able to do basic equipment repairs, you should make sure to bring a comprehensive spares kit of your own. You will, after all, be a long way from the nearest dive shop, and the right 'O'-ring or diaphragm can make the difference between the holiday of a lifetime and sitting on deck watching other people's bubbles for a week.

In the same vein, you should bring enough batteries for all your electronic and camera gear.

Most boats have generators running for several hours a day for charging rechargeables. These are usually 220 volts, so choose your charger accordingly. You should also bring a good stock of alkalines for backup.

Diving Emergencies

There is now a recompression (Hyperbaric) chamber just north of Marsa 'Alam at Ecolodge Shagra Village, tel (0195) 100262/mobile 20 122 461 656.

Important Note

In closing, remember that you are aboard a boat and that the captain and crew have ultimate responsibility for the safety of the boat and its passengers. Weather and other factors often necessitate changes in itinerary or dive plan, and you should accept this with good grace. Bear in mind that the crew is there to give you a good holiday and that its members are not going to cause you inconvenience for no reason. They rely on you for their business and if they have to diverge from the original plan, there must be a good reason for it. Relax and accept their professional advice.

SUDAN

First explored by subaquatic pioneers such as Jacques Cousteau and Hans Hass after World War II, Sudan's coastal and offshore reefs have fascinated the diving world for decades. Yet the country's minimal infrastructure and political instability have combined to make Sudan one of the most difficult parts of the Red Sea region to visit. Despite this enforced isolation, a few dedicated live-aboard operators and dive companies have continued to keep access to Sudanese dive sites open and there is a steady trickle of visitors each year.

Sudan, the largest country on the African continent, lies to the south of Egypt and shares borders with no fewer than nine other African countries, among them Eritrea, Kenya, Ethiopia and Libya. For all its vast size, Sudan has a relatively short coastline along the Red Sea. Both Egypt and Eritrea, its neighbours to the north and south, have longer shorelines, and, in comparison with Saudi Arabia, the Sudanese share of the Red Sea coast is tiny at about 650km (404 miles).

The People and the Culture

The Sudanese population is estimated to be about 26 million, divided among a staggering 300 different tribal and ethnic groups. Seventy per cent of the population is Muslim, about five per cent is Christian, and the remainder subscribes to a variety of animist beliefs. In the coastal northeastern part of the country, the area divers are most likely to visit, the population is mostly Muslim. (An ongoing civil war makes the country's entire southern half a no-go area.) Whatever their religion or ethnic background, the Sudanese are a people of ready smiles and warm, welcoming attitudes.

Climate

Inland summer temperatures soar to 47°C (117°F) or more; while coastal temperatures are somewhat moderated by the sea's proximity, summer highs are in the 40s°C (105°F), and winter temperatures are not much cooler with daytime highs in the mid-30s°C (low-90s°F). There is very little annual rainfall. For most foreign visitors, the only time of year when the

Opposite: *Reef scenes like this take years to develop. Dive carefully, trying not to cause any damage.*
Above: *A manta ray (*Manta birostris*) cruises at the sea surface.*

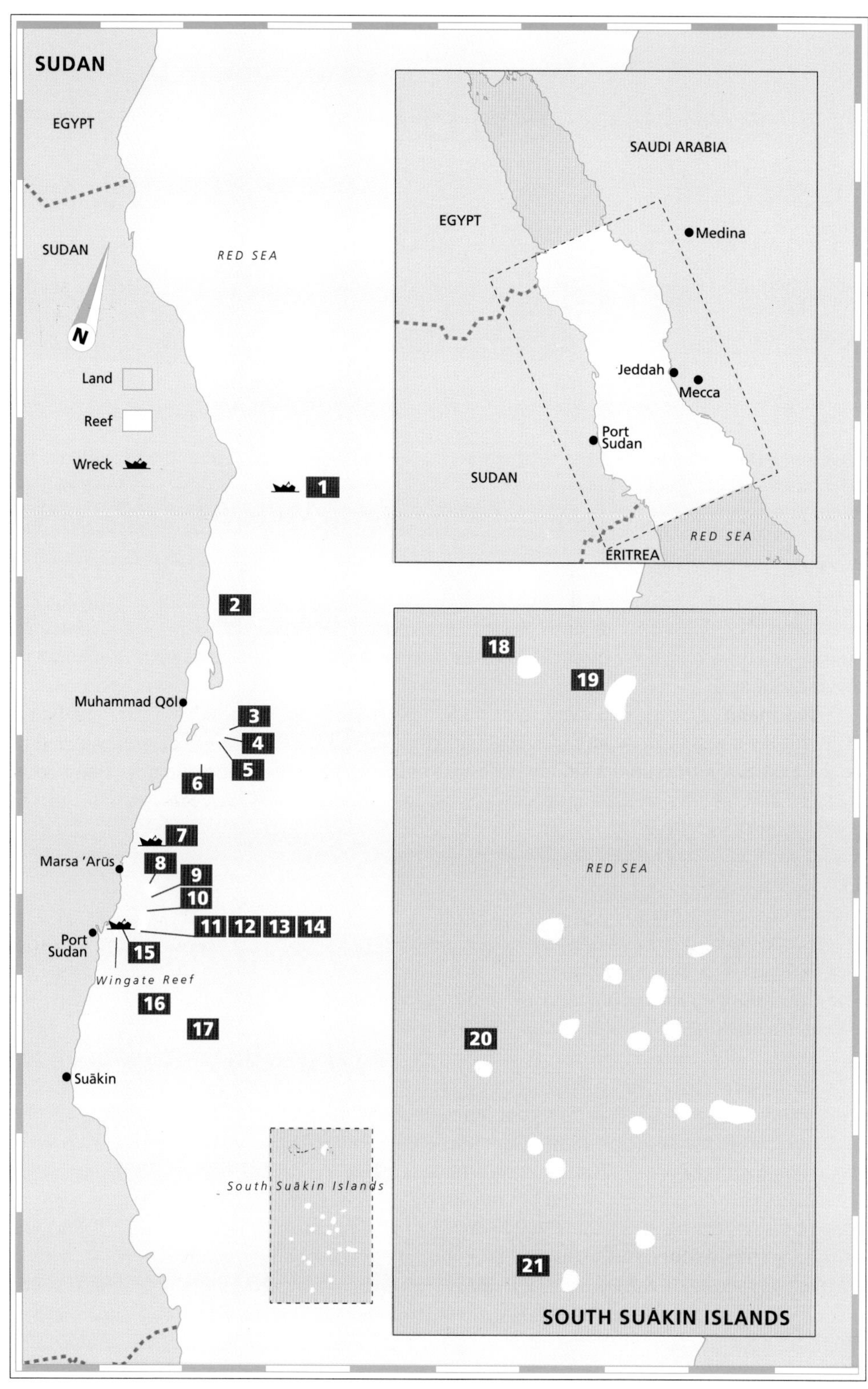
SUDAN
EGYPT
SUDAN
RED SEA
N
Land
Reef
Wreck
1
2
Muhammad Qōl
3
4
5
6
7
Marsa 'Arūs
8
9
10
11 12 13 14
Port Sudan
15
Wingate Reef
16
17
Suākin
South Suākin Islands
SAUDI ARABIA
EGYPT
Medina
Jeddah
Mecca
Port Sudan
SUDAN
RED SEA
ERITREA
18
19
RED SEA
20
21
SOUTH SUĀKIN ISLANDS

climate even approaches comfortable is between November and March.

Dive Highlights

Diving in Sudan is like plunging into the pages of diving history. Here you can explore the remains of Jacques Cousteau's legendary Conshelf II underwater living environment (see page 136), follow the route of his maiden voyage aboard *Calypso*, visit reefs immortalized by Hans Hass in his groundbreaking 1951 film *Adventure in the Red Sea,* and dive on World War II wrecks such as the *Umbria.*

The profuse, perfectly preserved reefs here give new meaning to the term 'coral garden', with schooling fish in untold numbers, the heart-pounding possibility of meeting the sharks for which the area is famed and a dazzling display of every type of tropical reef fish under the sun. Waters are clear and warm and the complexities of arranging a dive trip here mean that you will probably have all this splendour to yourself.

Marine Life

Quantity vies with quality when it comes to fish life in Sudanese waters. Along with a truly phenomenal density of all manner of schooling fish, you will find a huge variety of reef species, including angelfish, bannerfish, moray eels, big groupers, huge parrotfish, butterflyfish, spotted stingrays, Titan Triggerfish, and many more.

Off the reef, barracuda compete for your attention with Grey Reef and Hammerhead Sharks, and Manta Rays. Turtles cruise majestically by, while Nurse and Leopard Sharks wait patiently on the bottom. In many ways, the fish and other marine animals of Sudan's waters are the crowning jewel of the Red Sea. Nowhere else does such profusion and diversity exist.

What makes diving here even more incredible is the fact that Sudan's coral reefs are every bit the equal of the country's amazing fish life. Soft coral forests widely considered to be the Red Sea's finest exist side by side with intricate growths of innumerable stony coral species. The region's reefs, thriving in perfect conditions, are blue-ribbon examples of the bounty nature can produce.

Conditions

The average temperature in the water is around 27–28°C (81–82°F); winter lows drop to the mid-20s°C (mid-70s°F), while summer highs top 30°C (86°F). This is too hot for most marine microorganisms, with the result that summer visibility can be almost unbelievably clear. Visibility is more than acceptable all year round, averaging well over 20m (65ft) and often far better.

Access

The main problem is getting from your home country to Port Sudan, the departure point for diving in the region. Air connections are unreliable, and, if possible, you should try to get a flight via Cairo into Port Sudan, rather than arriving in Khartoum. If you do arrive in Khartoum you could have problems importing camera and video equipment, as well as finding a connecting flight to Port Sudan. There is an uncomfortable bus service where divers are charged for excess baggage even though it is carried on the roof.

Once you are in Port Sudan, your live-aboard's local agent will pick you up, sort out any bonds over camera equipment and deliver you to the boat. Currently all pre-organized diving fom Port Sudan is foreign based. If you arrive on a live-aboard from another country it is imperative that you check in with the authorities and the boat's agent in Port Sudan before you do any diving in Sudanese waters, otherwise the boat will be arrested.

Facilities on the boats vary, but all suffer from the country's shortages. Most spares have to be flown in with the clients, and basic foods and toilet paper are often in short supply – expect fish to be the main food. It is important that the boat begins diving early in the morning and, if possible, you should get written proof from the live-aboard owner as to how many dives you should get in a day if the weather is fine.

All of this may sound daunting, but for the adventurous it is well worth it as the diving north of Port Sudan is equal to the best in the world.

1 ELBA REEF

★★★★★★★★★★

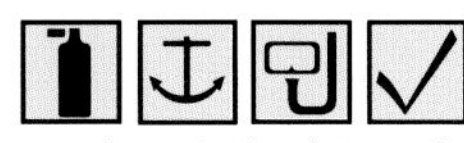

Location: 18.5km (10 nautical miles) east of Marsa Umbeila on the Egypt/Sudan Border
Access: By live-aboard boat from any Red Sea port.
Conditions: Surface weather and current can be tricky.
Average depth: 20m (65ft)
Maximum depth: 70m (230ft)
Average visibility: 20m (65ft)

At the edge of a deep drop-off is the site's main attraction, the wreck of the Italian ship SS *Levanzo*. Little is known about the ship's provenance, but even without historical details the wreck is impressive. The massive hull lies keel-up across the drop-off, its stern section level on the plateau and the bow section stretching into the deep at a steep angle along the drop-off wall. The ship's propeller lies at a shallow 18m (60ft), and the entire upper or stern section can be penetrated. Most of the wreck's deeper section lies beyond the range of all but the most cursory inspections, but it is still a remarkable spectacle.

Further inshore, the reef between 3m (10ft) and 10m (35ft) is covered with a variety of corals, from bommies (large, spherical coral heads) of *Porites*, *Favites* and other massive species to various branching forms in the reef shallows. Fish life is as good as any central Red Sea site, with reef species like grouper often upstaged by pelagic visitors, including frequent sightings of Silvertip Sharks.

2 PFEIFFER REEF

★★★★★★★

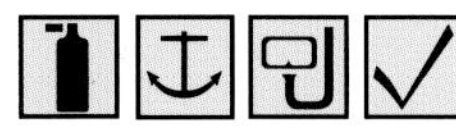

Location: Off the Sudanese coast, about 15km (8 nautical miles) southeast of Marsa Halaka.
Access: By live-aboard boat from any Red Sea port.
Conditions: Currents and rough surface conditions possible.
Average depth: 25m (80ft)
Maximum depth: 60m (200ft)
Average visibility: 20m (65ft)

This site is on the southernmost of a chain of three offshore reefs and the dive is at the south end of this southernmost reef. Although coral growth is not phenomenal, it is certainly the equal of many northern Red Sea sites and snorkellers in particular will enjoy the reef's shallower sections.

The site is arranged around a plateau extending south from the main reef table. A sloping reef leads from the shallows to a plateau at about 40m (130ft), and then drops sharply to 50m (165ft). The upper reef has fair coral coverage but it is the lower drop-off that will interest most divers. Here you will find some of the most exciting shark action in this stretch of the Red Sea.

The range and number of sharks is astounding. You see Hammerheads more than 3m (10ft) long, big Silvertips, Grey Reefs, and many others. It is a rare dive that does not include multiple sightings, so that even snorkellers often interact with the magnificent creatures. Many divers come to the Sudanese Red Sea specifically to see sharks, and this is one site that does not disappoint.

3 ABINGTON REEF

★★★★★★★★★★

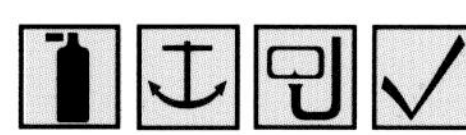

Location: Off the Sudanese coast, 22km (12 nautical miles) southeast of Râs Abu Shagara.
Access: By live-aboard boat from any Red Sea port.
Conditions: Exposed situation can make surface conditions critical.
Average depth: 15m (50ft)
Maximum depth: 30m (100ft)
Average visibility: 20m (65ft)

This is the northernmost of a series of 'Christmas cake' reefs, whose flat tops break the surface between here and Qita el Banna (Site 6) to the south. Abington has sheer drop-offs on three sides, with a sloping plateau on the fourth. It is marked by an unmanned lighthouse which can be seen from some distance.

The reef plateau lies to the southeast of the main reef. It offers some very fine diving. Stony and soft corals sprout in mixed heads all across the slope and there is a wide selection of anemones.

Fish life is up to the generally excellent Sudanese standard, with a broad range of reef species competing with some rather impressive pelagics, including several species of shark and even the odd manta. Shark sightings are common, with inquisitive Silvertips often making close inspections of the reef's human visitors – an experience that can be unnerving for the less experienced diver.

4 ANGAROSH REEF

Location: Just south-southwest of Abington Reef.
Access: By boat.
Conditions: Choppy with moderate to strong currents.
Average depth: 20m (65ft)
Maximum depth: 50m+ (165ft+)
Average visibility: 30m (100ft)

An elongated pinnacle rising from deep water, Angarosh has a sand cay about 2m (6ft) high, but the reef is much larger. There is a long spit running north, but good dives are to be had all around the reef. Sharks can be found around much of the reef, and there are many interesting large indents and caverns with huge marble groupers, lots of Moray Eels, Longjawed Squirrelfish and shoaling reef fish including Bigeye Emperors and Humpback Snappers. As well as Hawksbill Turtles, there are very large 'anemone cities' with hundreds of clownfish.

5 MERLO REEF

★★★★★★★★★★

Location: Just southwest of Angarosh Reef.
Access: By boat.
Conditions: Choppy with moderate to strong currents.
Average depth: 20m (65ft)
Maximum depth: 50m+ (165ft+)
Average visibility: 30m (100ft)

Another pinnacle rising from deep water, Merlo Reef has the wreck of the yacht *Freedom* high and dry to its northwest. There are excellent dive sites all around the reef with good corals, Scalloped Hammerhead Sharks and reef fish including Bumphead Parrotfish and huge marble groupers. The best site is just off the northernmost point, where crossing a 20m- (65ft-) deep gully leads to a shallower reef where divers can stay and watch the shoals (jacks and the occasional Manta Ray can also be found).

6 QITA EL BANNA

★★★★★★★★★★

Location: About 17km (9 nautical miles) south of Shambaya.
Access: By boat.

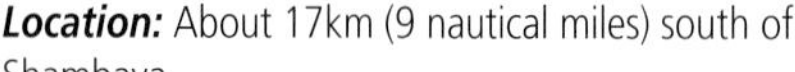

Conditions: Choppy with moderate to strong currents.
Average depth: 20m (65ft)
Maximum depth: 50m+ (165ft+)
Average visibility: 30m (100ft)

Circular and only 200m (650ft) in diameter at the surface, Qita el Banna is another pinnacle that rises steeply from deep water and just breaks the surface with coral heads that seabirds perch on. There are narrow sandy plateaus from 10m (33ft) in the northwest to 20m (65ft) in the southeast, but the main interest is corals, reef fish and sharks along the walls. Huge lone barracuda, shoals of smaller barracuda, cornetfish, Redtooth Triggerfish and Hawksbill Turtles are common, and Oceanic Whitetip Sharks have been spotted.

7 BLUE BELT WRECK (TOYOTA WRECK)

★★★★

Location: Nearly 65km (40 miles) north of Port Sudan, north-northeast of Marsa 'Arus.
Access: By boat.
Conditions: Moderate to strong currents.
Average depth: 20m (65ft)
Maximum depth: 65m (210ft)
Average visibility: 30m (100ft)

The *Blue Belt* went aground on Sha'b Su'adi on 2 December 1977. Two tugs were too enthusiastic when they tried to pull her off and she overturned, sinking on 5 December. A 2545-tonne cargo ship originally built for the Hamburg-Amerika line in 1950, she went through several owners and names before becoming *Blue Belt*. On her final voyage she was carrying many Toyota vehicles, hence her local name.

The wreck now lies upside down with the top of her bow on sand at 15m (50ft), and the rest of the ship at a steep angle descending into the depths at 65m (210ft) on the drop-off. Penetration is difficult due to the ship being upside down. The vehicles that spilled from the deck onto sand at 15m (50 ft) make for an interesting dive, notable for sponge growth. Leaking diesel killed off much of the surrounding coral, but fish life is still prolific.

8 SHA'B RUMI WEST (ROMAN REEF) — THE CONSHELF SITE

★★★★★★★★★★

   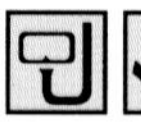

Location: The west side of Sha'b Rumi, 40km (22 nautical miles) north-northeast of Port Sudan; easily reached from Marsa 'Arus.
Access: By boat.
Conditions: Protected diving except during August's south winds.
Average depth: 9m (30ft)
Maximum depth: 70m+ (230ft+)
Average visibility: 20m (65ft)

If there is a holy grail of Sudanese diving, this is probably it – the site of Jacques Cousteau's legendary 1963 Conshelf II experiment, familiar to millions the world over from the award-winning film *Le Monde Sans Soleil* (see page 136). More than any other Sudanese site, this spot captures the imagination.

The reef has two entrances into the inner lagoon on the west side, and the Cousteau site is just outside of the more southerly one. Immediately to the south of the passage, lying in 9m (30ft) of water, is the onion-shaped dome of the submarine garage. The portholes have been removed but the roof is still airtight; in fact, a large bubble has been formed by the exhalations of visiting divers, allowing you to surface to the air trapped in the dome's upper section and chat with your buddy.

Just north of the garage is a tool shed, and north of this are three colourful fish pens, which move around in rough seas and which have a profusion of *Dendronephthya* soft tree corals growing on them. Over the drop-off there is a shark cage, standing upright in 27m (90ft) of water.

Twenty years ago, the fish life at this site was prolific, but the spear-fishing of round-the-world yachtsmen has taken its toll. Similarly, inconsiderate divers have broken off some of the table corals growing on the garage, but the site is still very nostalgic and makes a great night dive.

9 SHA'B RUMI SOUTH POINT

★★★★★

Location: The south end of Sha'b Rumi, 40km (22 nautical miles) north-northeast of Port Sudan, easily reached from Marsa 'Arus.
Access: By boat.
Conditions: Sheltered, but strong currents are normal.
Average depth: 25m (80ft)
Maximum depth: 70m+ (230ft+)
Average visibility: 30m (100ft)

This is perhaps the most famous reef in Sudan. A big draw at Sha'b Rumi is Cousteau's Conshelf site, but despite the lack of historical debris, this southern site is just a better dive for those who prefer marine life.

The site begins with a rich inshore mini-wall, dropping to about 20m (65ft) at the reef's southern edge. To the east and west, sheer walls drop vertically for hundreds of metres, while a flat plateau slopes gently southward from around 20m (65ft) to a depth of 30m (100ft) before dropping off into the depths.

The entire reef is covered in profuse coral. The reef encompasses virtually every Red Sea species. Given the phenomenal richness of this habitat, it is no surprise to find a matching superabundance of reef fish. Take out your fish guide, pick a page at random, and you are almost certain to see the species listed somewhere here.

Off the reef, the fish circus continues, with amazing pelagic displays that can include big barracuda in their hundreds, jacks, tuna, and lots of sharks, particularly the eerie, exotic Hammerheads for which the site is famous.

LIONFISH

Lionfish, the most colourful and among the least toxic of the family *Scorpaenidae*, are represented by up to ten different species in the Indo-Pacific region. The most common of these in the Red Sea, *Pterois miles*, is known variously as the Common Lionfish, Sailfin Lionfish or Turkeyfish, and can be found on virtually every reef.

These majestic, ornately finned creatures, striped in red or brown and white, look more like stately Spanish galleons than lions or turkeys, although you can see parallels with the mane of the one or the fanned tail of the other. The unique display is believed to act as a visual warning to would-be predators, thus making up for the lionfish's lack of speed and agility.

Divers should treat these fish with respect. While lionfish punctures from the venomous spines of the dorsal fins are rarely fatal, they are hideously painful. Photographers especially should beware: every year more than one photo opportunity goes horribly wrong when over-eager shutterbugs try too hard to move their unwilling subject to a more photogenic location.

10 SANGANEB — NORTH POINT

★★★★★★★★★★

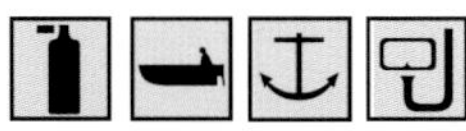

Location: In the Sudanese Red Sea, 30km (16 nautical miles) northeast of Port Sudan.
Access: By live-aboard boat from any Red Sea port.
Conditions: Exposed to the weather; when it is calm the dive has little current in the early morning but strong currents in the afternoon.
Average depth: 20m (65ft)
Maximum depth: 50m+ (165ft+)
Average visibility: 30m (100ft)

Many live-aboards avoid this dive because they cannot anchor, but some hold off the reef for the duration of the dive and others do the journey by inflatable from the inner lagoon. On a good day this is possibly the best dive in the world, with shoals of Hammerhead, Grey Reef and Whitetip Reef Sharks, and huge shoals of barracuda and Manta Rays. A narrow submerged point forms the reef's northern extremity. Here a raised mound or bump rises to 18m (60ft) from the main reef body before giving way to a series of shelves stepping away along a reef spit to the north. To either side, the reef wall drops off to unimaginable depths. The stepped point continues shelving well beyond 60m (195ft), while the upper reef table offers dazzling coral growth in 3m (10ft) or less.

Coral is superb throughout, especially on the upper sections of the reef wall. A wide variety of fish life can be seen, from small reef species in the shallows to massive schools of snappers, surgeons and jacks along the wall and point, and impressive pelagics off the shelving point. These include large solitary barracuda;

Above: *Long-jawed or Sabre Squirrelfish (*Sargocentron spiniferum*).*
Below: *Snappers (*Lutjanus sp.*) are usually found alone or in small groups.*

Hammerhead Sharks and several other shark species. Turtles are also common. There are also the remains of two very old wrecks, both too deep for diving on air.

11 SANGANEB — EAST FACE

  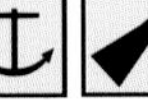  

Location: The east face of Sanganeb, 27–33km (15–18 nautical miles) northeast of Port Sudan.
Access: By boat for from shore.
Conditions: Moderate to strong currents.
Average depth: 20m (65ft)
Maximum depth: 50m+ (165ft+)
Average visibility: 30m (100ft)

Sanganeb's East face is several kilometres long – a sheer wall throughout its length, it drops vertically to 90m (300ft) before shelving off into the depths. It shows signs of at least two large wrecks having been dragged along it by the current. To the north there is a huge anchor at 20m (65ft), and opposite Sanganeb's inner lagoon there are the metallic remains of a wooden wreck at 5–10m (15–35ft) within a curve in the reef that gives shelter from the current. The whole of the face is treated as a series of drift dives, following the prevailing north to south current. The best of reef life is to be found in the shallows – healthy corals, stonefish., Torpedo (Electric) Rays and anthias among others – while a variety of sharks inhabit the deeper waters, and turtles, Manta Rays, Bottlenose Dolphins and Pilot Whales regularly pass by.

12 WRECK OF THE WHITE ELEPHANT (SAIDA III)

★★★★★★★★★

 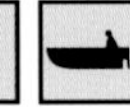  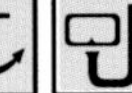 

Location: The anchorage in the outer lagoon of Sanganeb, 26km (14 nautical miles) northeast of Port Sudan.
Access: By boat.
Conditions: Sheltered lagoon.
Average depth: 5m (15ft)
Maximum depth: 10m (30ft)
Average visibility: 20m (65ft)

This wreck of a luxury wooden yacht is convenient for night dives. One of several vessels owned by a western live-aboard operator and smuggler, the boat had multiple name boards such that, when it suited him, the yacht was called either *White Elephant* or *Saida III*. By 1990 the boat had become uninsurable, so with alcohol banned under a new Islamic government, he anchored the yacht at Sanganeb as a floating bar for expatriates. Within months the owner was on another boat that mysteriously disappeared, leaving the yacht to sink slowly.

SCORPIONFISH

The scorpionfish, which include *Scorpaenopsis*, *Scorpaenodes*, *Sebastapistes* and *Rhinopias* spp., are a group of sedentary, carnivorous fishes marked by the venomous spines found along the dorsal fins of all members of the family. While the larger family, *Scorpaenidae*, includes such diverse members as the lionfish and the deadly stonefish, the family *Scorpaenopsis* in the Indo-Pacific is limited to about 20 species, of which at least eight are found in the Red Sea. All exhibit the large heads, spiny bodies and bony cheek-ridges characteristic of the *Scorpaenidae*.

Many scorpionfish are heavily camouflaged, with lumpy, textured skins mimicking their habitat. Most are capable of some degree of colour change, and some species are also equipped with moss-like skin growths. Some members of the group take this decoration even further, using specialized, wormlike tendrils mounted above the jaw to lure prey while the scorpionfish waits motionless.

Scorpionfish venom tends to be less powerful than that of the closely related stonefish, but the scorpionfish are still highly venomous creatures and stings can and do result in fatalities. Divers should treat them with great caution.

13 SANGANEB SOUTHWEST POINT

★★★★★★★★★★

Location: In the Sudanese Red Sea, 26km (14 nautical miles) northeast of Port Sudan.
Access: By boat or from shore.
Conditions: Sheltered from all but the August south winds.
Average depth: 25m (80ft)
Maximum depth: 70m+ (230ft+)
Average visibility: 30m (100ft)

Almost as good as Sanganeb's north point, this site can be dived all of the year apart from some days in August. It can also be dived at night. If it were possible to award twenty stars, this site would get them. This is the epitome of Red Sea diving. It consists of an unbelievably rich tower of brilliant, pristine coral rising through hundreds of metres of clear blue sea. The entire site is blanketed in reef fish, while silvery pelagics, from jacks to huge Hammerheads, spin round the reef in a shimmering orbit.

Topographically, Sanganeb is a huge offshore tower reef rising from a seabed over 800m (2625ft) deep. The dive site is on the reef's southwest tip. A shallow reef top, only a few centimetres deep, is packed with vivid corals. Sheer vertical walls plunge from the reef top to immense depths on almost all sides, while to the southwest, a large reef plateau juts like a tab from the main reef before giving way to the prevailing wall profile. This plateau is the centrepoint for Sanganeb dives. It is carpeted in soft corals interspersed with heads and pinnacles of mixed stony coral. This site is regarded by many divers, with good reason, as possibly the finest coral site in the Red Sea. The reef fish here defy description and you can find examples of almost any coral species you choose to name. But, rich as the reef life may be, it is the action offshore that really distinguishes Sanganeb: a never-ending procession of pelagic life to rival any site in this or any other sea. Sharks, including Whitetip Reefs, Grey Reefs, Silvertips and immense Hammerheads, all appear in bewildering numbers. When the north winds are very strong in winter, shoals of up to nine Manta Rays can be found here. Sanganeb has a manned lighthouse complete with keepers and the Sudanese Military are also now in residence. Both keepers and military personnel will no doubt be glad to see you but remember to treat them with respect. It is their turf and you are here as a visitor.

14 SANGANEB — SOUTH FACE

★★★★★☆☆☆☆☆

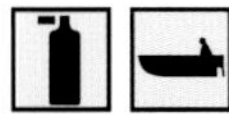   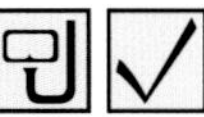

Location: 26km (14 nautical miles) northeast of Port Sudan.
Access: By boat or from shore.
Conditions: Sheltered from all but the August south winds.
Average depth: 20m (65ft)
Maximum depth: 50m+ (165ft+)
Average visibility: 30m (100ft)

This is a long wall stretching either side of the lighthouse's southern jetty. An excellent day dive, it is also rated as one of the world's best night dives with guaranteed sightings of Spanish Dancer Nudibranchs, crabs carrying anemones for disguise, Sea Hares, octopuses, Basket Stars, parrotfish sleeping in their mucus cocoons and, occasionally, Tun Shells. As a day dive it has everything except the large shoals found elsewhere around Sanganeb.

15 UMBRIA WRECK

★★★★★☆☆☆☆☆

Location: To the north of the ships' anchorage, just off Port Sudan.
Access: By boat.
Conditions: Sheltered, can be dived in any weather.
Average depth: 15m (50ft)
Maximum depth: 36m (120ft)
Average visibility: 30m (100ft)

Originally named *Bahia Blanca*, this 10,237-tonne, 155-m (509-ft) combined cargo and passenger vessel was built in Hamburg in 1912. Sold to Italy before World War II and renamed *Umbria*, she was requisitioned for the war.

Recent Additions to the Wrecks at Wingate Reef

The 618-gross-ton freighter SS *Hassanein* (registered in Belize), which appeared to be abandoned in the harbour, was towed out to within 400m (1300ft) of the *Umbria*, where she sank in 22m (72ft) of water on 6 April 2003.

The SS *Jassim*, a 2312-gross-ton RoRo passenger/cargo ferry built in Norway and launched in 1961, sank at the Wingate Reef anchorage on 1 December 2003. 80.5m (265ft) long, 15m (50ft) wide with a draught of 9.5m (31ft), she was owned by Al Ramzani Sea Transport of Qatar and registered in La Paz, Bolivia.

The British authorities seized the ship, but the crew had already sabotaged it so the ship sunk. Hans Hass was, in 1949, the first civilian to dive the *Umbria*. This wreck is one of the Sudanese Red Sea's real treasures and ranks among the finest wreck dives in the world. With a maximum depth of 36m (120ft), she is shallow by most wreck divers' standards, and at her shallowest point she actually breaks the surface. Snorkellers with good breath-hold technique will be able to explore much of the wreck's upper area; scuba divers will also benefit from the extended bottom times possible on the ship's shallower sections. The *Umbria* lies on her port side. The hull is still completely intact, although heavily encrusted. It can be fully explored both internally and externally.

16 NORTH SUAKIN GROUP

★★★★☆☆☆☆

Location: Southeast and east-southeast of Port Sudan.
Access: By boat.
Conditions: Moderate to strong swell and surge.
Average depth: 20m (65ft)
Maximum depth: 50m+ (165ft+)
Average visibility: 20m (65ft)

Popular with Italian live-aboards, North Jumma Shoal, Hindi Gider (Site 17) and Sha'b 'Anbar are among the many low-lying islands and reefs at the northern end of Suakin Group. This group is heavily fished, not too deep and without much sand, so the diving and visibility is not as good as north of Port Sudan. Many of the reefs near to shore have been spoilt by merchant ships stealing coral with crowbars. The reefs tend to have steep slopes rather than walls. Lone Grey Reef, Whitetip Reef, Nurse and Variegated (Leopard) Sharks are common.

17 HINDI GIDER (HIND KADAM)

★★★★★☆☆☆☆☆

Location: 55km (30 nautical miles) east-northeast of Suakin.
Access: By boat.
Conditions: Choppy with moderate to strong currents.
Average depth: 20m (65ft)
Maximum depth: 50m+ (165ft+)
Average visibility: 30m (100ft)
Rather larger than a cay, Hlndi Gider is a small, sandy island with an automatic light on a tower, a Marabout's (Muslim holy man's) Tomb and other graves and some very large osprey nests. When the swell and current allows diving, the north of the reef tumbles into the depths but the eastern and southern parts of the reef are also very good, with pretty coral drop-offs and gardens, lots of reef fish and Scalloped Hammerhead, Silvertip, Grey Reef and Whitetip Reef Sharks.

18 MASAMIRIT

Location: The northernmost of the South Suakin Islands, 174km (94 nautical miles) southeast of Port Sudan.
Access: By live-aboard boat from any Red Sea port.
Conditions: Surface weather and waves can make the site inaccessible.
Average depth: 25m (80ft)
Maximum depth: 50m+ (165ft+)
Average visibility: 20m (65ft)
This is an almost triangular reef marked by an automatic navigational light. The reef's eastern side is an excellent wall, which drops steeply into the deep, but which is broken by a sloping sandy platform or plateau at its northern end. This plateau lies at 25–30m (80–100ft) and is dotted with coral heads. It forms an amazing vantage point for watching the superabundant pelagic life that swarms off the reef. Sudan's sharks are well represented and turtles are also common here. The usual dizzying array of reef fishes lends even more colour to a reef already dazzling with densely growing coral.

Both stony and soft coral species thrive here. They are glowingly healthy throughout and would make the site worth a dive even without the phenomenal fish life.

19 KARAM MASAMIRIT

★★★★★

Location: Just southeast of Masamirit (Site 18).
Access: By live-aboard boat from any Red Sea port.
Conditions: Surface weather and strong currents may affect dive plans.
Average depth: 25m (80ft)
Maximum depth: 50m+ (165ft+)
Average visibility: 20m (65ft)
This site drops sheer from near the surface to unimaginable depths. At the north and south ends, shallower platforms lead down to the drop-off at about 25m (80ft), where the same amazing walls continue. Either of these platforms serve as a balcony seat for the unique shark theatre, and for a good view of the pelagics.

The upper 20m (65ft) of the reef boasts some of the most rich coral growth in the Red Sea.

20 DAHRAT GHAB

★★★★★

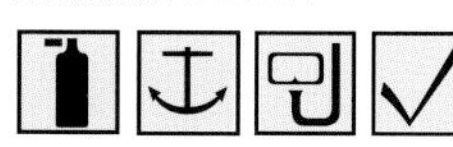

Location: About 28km (15 nautical miles) south-southwest of Masamirit.
Access: By live-aboard boat from any Red Sea port.
Conditions: Big winds, waves and currents all possible.
Average depth: 20m (65ft)
Maximum depth: 50m+ (165ft+)
Average visibility: 20m (65ft)
The entire reef is diveable, but the area off the reef's southern tip is dive paradise. Here, a strange, horseshoe-shaped ridge radiates from the end of the reef, separated from the reef table by a crescent-shaped valley 26m (85ft) in depth. The top of the ridge is at 22m (70ft), and its outer edge gives way to a drop-off, a continuation of the sheer wall that forms the main reef's east and west sides. Every millimetre of this reef is covered in the densest imaginable coral growth, and its finned inhabitants are every bit as spectacular as the reef. Rarities like green turtles and Manta Rays are common.

21 DAHRAT ABID

★★★★★

Location: About 28km (15 nautical miles) south of Masamirit (Site 18).
Access: By live-aboard boat from any Red Sea port.
Conditions: Waves, wind and current can all be strong.
Average depth: 25m (80ft)
Maximum depth: 50m+ (165ft+)
Average visibility: 20m (65ft)
The upper reef supports the wreckage of a wooden fishing boat, while the reef's submerged portion is bordered by sheer walls with platforms at its north and south corners. The reef walls are fissured and intricately contoured, offering scope for snorkelling or shallow scuba exploration. Schooling reef fishes are common, as are true pelagics, such as jacks, tuna and Silvertip Sharks. Coral growth is remarkable throughout, with a blend of stony and soft species on all the wall sections and a particular profusion of soft coral forms on the southern corner.

Sudan

How to Get There

By air: A number of international air carriers offer flights to Khartoum, but connecting flights between here and Port Sudan are unreliable. Occasional international flights to Port Sudan via Cairo operate. Most reliable are the flights from Jeddah, Saudi Arabia, but these are only available to Saudi Arabian nationals or expatriates working in Saudi Arabia.
By road: The border with Egypt at Wadi Halfa is now open again but desert-driving experience is necessary for most of the route. The border on the coast road is closed. Buses travel from Khartoum to Port Sudan, a 16-hour journey with a single driver.
By rail: The rail route from Khartoum to Port Sudan is cheap but very slow and often breaks down; it is not recommended.
By live-aboard: It is not possible for live-aboards to register their intention to dive in Sudanese waters from overseas. Visiting boats must register and pay their tourist-taxes in Port Sudan before diving in Sudanese waters, otherwise they risk arrest.

Where to Stay

Most divers will be rushing straight from the airport to their live-aboard, with little reason to stay in a hotel in either Khartoum or Port Sudan. Should you need a hotel because of missed connections or for any other reason, the following are possibilities:

Khartoum
Acropole Hotel Sharia Babika Badri; tel 249 11 72860/fax 249 11 70898; email acropolekhartoum@yahoo.com. Mid-range.
Araak Hotel PO Box 1957; tel 249 11 74826. Mid-range.
Hilton International Hotel PO Box 1910; tel 249 11 774100/fax 249 11 775793. Top of the range. Outside town, just before the confluence of the Blue and White Niles.
Meridien Hotel Sharia Al Qasr Avenue; tel 249 183 775970/fax 249 183 779087; email info@meridienkh.com; www.meridienkh.com. Top of the range. Located in the town centre.
Sudan Hotel PO Box 1845, Nile Avenue; tel 249 11 80811. Bottom of the range.

Port Sudan
Baasher Palace Hotel tel 3341. A favourite with stranded divers as it has air-conditioning and a reasonable restaurant.
Hilton Hotel PO Box 105, Port Sudan, tel 249 311 39800/fax 249 311 31183; email RM_Port-Sudan@Hilton.com. A new hotel close to the live-aboard's landing jetty.

Where to Eat

The following list of restaurants may be useful to divers passing through.

Khartoum
If you can afford it, the **Hilton**'s buffet is the best value as you can eat as much as you like. For individual meals, the **Hilton** and **Meridien Coffee Shops** are cheaper, but the Meridien is better. There are many small, cheap local restaurants that are all very good if you order local food.

Port Sudan
For both Western and local food, the restaurant at **Baasher Palace Hotel** is good, though the cheaper local restaurants are fine if you don't need air-conditioning.

Dive Facilities

Due to various restrictions and the ban on alcohol under the present government, land-based operations are not successful. Currently almost all tourist diving in Sudan is by live-aboard boat. Vessels have cross-border itineraries out of Egypt. Due to the constantly changing situation, it is best to check recent adverts in French, German, Italian and Swedish diving magazines, as those in British diving magazines and on British websites may contain inaccuracies.

Land-based operator
DeKock Sudan Red Sea Camp Resort A local operator is again trying to operate from Arus (Arous) north of Port Sudan; email Iman at info@sudanredsearesort.com; www.sudanredsearesort.com.

Live-aboard boats
M/Y Le Baron Noir (The Black Baron) email info@lebaronnoir.com; www.lebaronnoir.com
MS Royal Emperor/MS Freedom Tony Backhurst, The Scuba Centre, Smithbrook Kilns, Cranleigh, Surrey, GU6 8JJ, UK; tel 44 1483 271 765/fax 44 1483 272 163; email info@scuba.co.uk; www.scuba.co.uk.
MS Royal Revolution is now advertising cross-border itineraries from Port Ghaleb in Egypt, but some of the information on their website is inaccurate. email: info@royalevolution.com; www.royalevolution.com
M/V Don Questo email info@sudandiving.it; www.sudandiving.it. The Don Questo has a private one-man recompression chamber on board.
M/Y Felicidad II Aurora Branciamore; email maufel@iol.it; www.felicidad.it.
MSY Ishtar Diving World, Bank Chambers, 6 Borough High Street, London SE1 9QQ; tel 44 20 7407 0019/fax 44 20 7378 1108; email info@diving-world.com; www.diving-world.com.

Hospitals

Chronic shortages and understaffing make Sudan one of the worst places in Africa to get ill. Try to contact your embassy for advice on reliable doctors if necessary, and make sure your medical insurance covers you for repatriation.

Diving Emergencies

Do not get bent in Sudan. The nearest chamber is either Eritrea or Egypt, and either one is much too far away to be of any use. Dive extremely cautiously and plan a safety stop on every dive.

Local Highlights

Some 58km (36miles) south of Port Sudan, the ancient island trading town of **Suakin** is slowly sinking into decay. Once the area's major trading port, used by the ancient Egyptians as early as 1000BC, it had fallen into decline when the Ottoman Turks restored it to glory as the centre of the regional slave trade in the 19th century. Many of the island's fabled coral stone buildings date from this period, but the town has once again slipped into obscurity, this time due to the emergence of Port Sudan as the region's main port. The undoubtedly picturesque ruins can be viewed on day trips from Port Sudan.

Sudan would be one of the best countries for tourism if it were not for the civil war. The centre and south are full of interesting, colourful tribes, and the south has all the animals of the African plains. However, if you do not mind roughing it (there isn't any accommodation), the desert north of Khartoum contains several ancient temples and pyramid complexes of the same era as those that are popular in Egypt.

Cousteau's Conshelf Experiment

Jacques Cousteau's and Hans Hass's explorations of the world's oceans are legendary. In fact, the early history of Red Sea diving as we know it would not exist without their boundless enthusiasm.

Although Hass preceded Cousteau by a decade, both of them explored its jewel-like reefs and rich marine life, and both made the films and wrote the books that planted the seeds of today's Red Sea dive-tourism industry by inspiring untold numbers of modern divers. The Red Sea was also to become the location for Cousteau's second experiment in underwater living, Conshelf II.

Cousteau's involvement in researching underwater habitats began in 1962 as the result of a collaboration with an American naval doctor, George Bond. Bond had originated a proposal to build modules for extended underwater living based on the new techniques of saturation diving. He reasoned that with proper support, a group of divers could remain at depth for days or weeks at a time without needing to return to the surface. The advantage of this would be that the many wasted hours of decompression necessary for each separate dive could thus be postponed until the end of the divers' extended stay underwater. One lengthy decompression could then be carried out in the comfort of a bell or chamber, rather than in the water.

Bond had first asked the US Navy to research this theory, but they considered the idea too far-fetched and refused to fund the experiment. Bond turned instead to Cousteau, whose pioneering underwater work was achieving international recognition. Cousteau was intrigued by Bond's ideas and immediately began preparations for constructing a submarine habitat known as Conshelf I. Conshelf I was a submerged, air-filled chamber in which two men lived and worked from 14–21 September 1962. The chamber was submerged off the coast at Frioul, near Marseilles, to a depth of 10m (35ft), although the dive team left the chamber daily for work at up to 20m (65ft).

The success of the Conshelf I experiment paved the way for more ambitious projects. Cousteau decided to design and build a second underwater habitat, capable of housing a five-man team. The divers would live and work at similar depths to the Conshelf I habitat, but for a month instead of just a week. A second, smaller module would also be built (filled with a helium-oxygen atmosphere) to house two divers. This second module was to be sunk to a much greater depth than the main module, with an even deeper working depth of 49m (160ft). Further structures, including an underwater garage for submersible vehicles, would also be built in order to test the capacity for sustained underwater work.

These submarine units were intended to demonstrate the viability of remote, self-contained underwater work stations. A location far from the support of a modern Western port was therefore needed. The Red Sea fulfilled these requirements perfectly and was an obvious choice, but there was another very important factor in selecting it as a venue. Cousteau had failed to secure financial backing through the traditional sources of research funding, so he decided to fund the project himself by producing a feature film based on the experiment. For his film to enjoy commercial success, he needed a location that would lend it colour and excitement. The stunning reefs and marine life of the Red Sea fit the bill perfectly.

So it was that in the spring of 1963 Cousteau was back in the Red Sea with *Calypso*, scouting for a location that would meet the scientific and cinematic needs of the project. After a two-month trip he settled on the reef at Sha'b Rumi, an oval reef lagoon 40km (22 nautical miles) north of Port Sudan.

Cousteau chartered a freighter, the *Rosaldo*, to transport the French-made components of Conshelf II to the site in the Red Sea. The *Rosaldo*, moored in the lagoon, would also act as a base for the project's compressors and electrical generators while *Calypso* ferried the men and equipment to their destination. By April both ships were at Sha'b Rumi and construction began.

The first task was to get the *Rosaldo* to her mooring in the lagoon. A channel had to be dredged through the shallow reef to allow her deep-keeled hull to pass through, but she was eventually settled into place and construction began. The laborious process of transferring the living modules from the *Rosaldo* to the chosen site on Sha'b Rumi's west side was to take several weeks. This was because not only the bulky modules but also their ballast of more than 100 tonnes of lead in 50-kilo (110-lb) weights, had to be transferred manually from *Rosaldo* to *Calypso*, then from *Calypso* to the seabed.

The first unit was occupied by its five-man dive team on 15 June 1963. It rested on the bottom at just over 9m (30ft) and was christened the 'starfish house' because of its arrangement of arm-like sub-cylinders branching off a central chamber. It was equipped with a range of amenities that included sun lamps, a telephone, television and hi-fi systems, and even a talking parrot. While the team in the starfish house carried out their tasks, the second, deeper module was being prepared. It was known as the 'little house' and its two-man team took up residence on 4 July. From the module's base depth of 27m (90ft) the divers explored the limits of the heliox dive mix, eventually reaching working depths of over 100m (330ft), more than double their originally proposed maximum depth.

The two teams gathered a wealth of information during their undersea sojourn. An unexpected discovery was the revelation that while the growth of hair and beards was noticeably slower in the high-pressure atmosphere, cuts and abrasions healed at an extraordinarily rapid rate.

The experiment was successfully concluded on 15 July, when the two teams returned to the surface, tired but healthy. The two living modules were raised and transported back into France, but the submersible garage was left in place for possible future use. It can be visited today, still airtight and housing a large bubble formed by visitors' exhalations.

The scientific success of the project was matched by the commercial success of Cousteau's film. Not only did it meet the costs of the expedition but it was also a huge box-office success.

Most of the stony corals have now fallen from Conshelf II's submersible garage.

ERITREA

When it was part of Ethiopia, Eritrea was one of the Red Sea's oldest diving destinations. This is hardly surprising, since Eritrea has only been an independent country since 1993, when its bitter, thirty-year struggle for independence from Ethiopia came to an end. Since independence, the country has begun the massive task of rebuilding its shattered economy. Unfortunately, peace was shortlived, and recent conflicts with both Ethiopia and Yemen, and the fact that the government has done nothing to encourage dive tourism, means that only the hardiest of divers currently go there.

Eritrea is a funnel-shaped slice of land, sandwiched between the Red Sea coast to the east and Sudan and Ethiopia to the north and west. It covers an area of just 125,000sq km (48,000sq miles), but boasts 1200km (746 miles) of coast. In fact, the southern part of the country is composed of little more than a narrow strip of shoreline stretching down to Djibouti. From sea level at the east coast, the country rises to uplands more than 2000m (6560ft) high, before sloping away into the western lowlands.

The People and the Culture

Eritrea is home to a mix of five major ethnic groups among its 2.5 million or so people. Historically, the population was almost equally divided between Christians and Muslims, with perhaps five per cent following animist religions. Higher levels of displacement among Muslim communities during the war has temporarily tilted the balance in favour of the Christians, but this is expected to change as refugees return home.

The main languages on the coast are Tigrinya and Arabic, but a large proportion of the population has a working knowledge of English, particularly in the cities as education and television were in English under the communist Ethiopian regime. For the most part, English is enough to get by, but knowledge of a few words of either Tigrinya or Arabic will certainly make life easier. The Eritreans are an extremely warm and accommodating people, and will generally go out of their way to help you learn about their language and culture.

Opposite: *A well-earned rest after a day's diving.*

Above: *A Lyretail (Lunartail) grouper (*Variola louti*).*

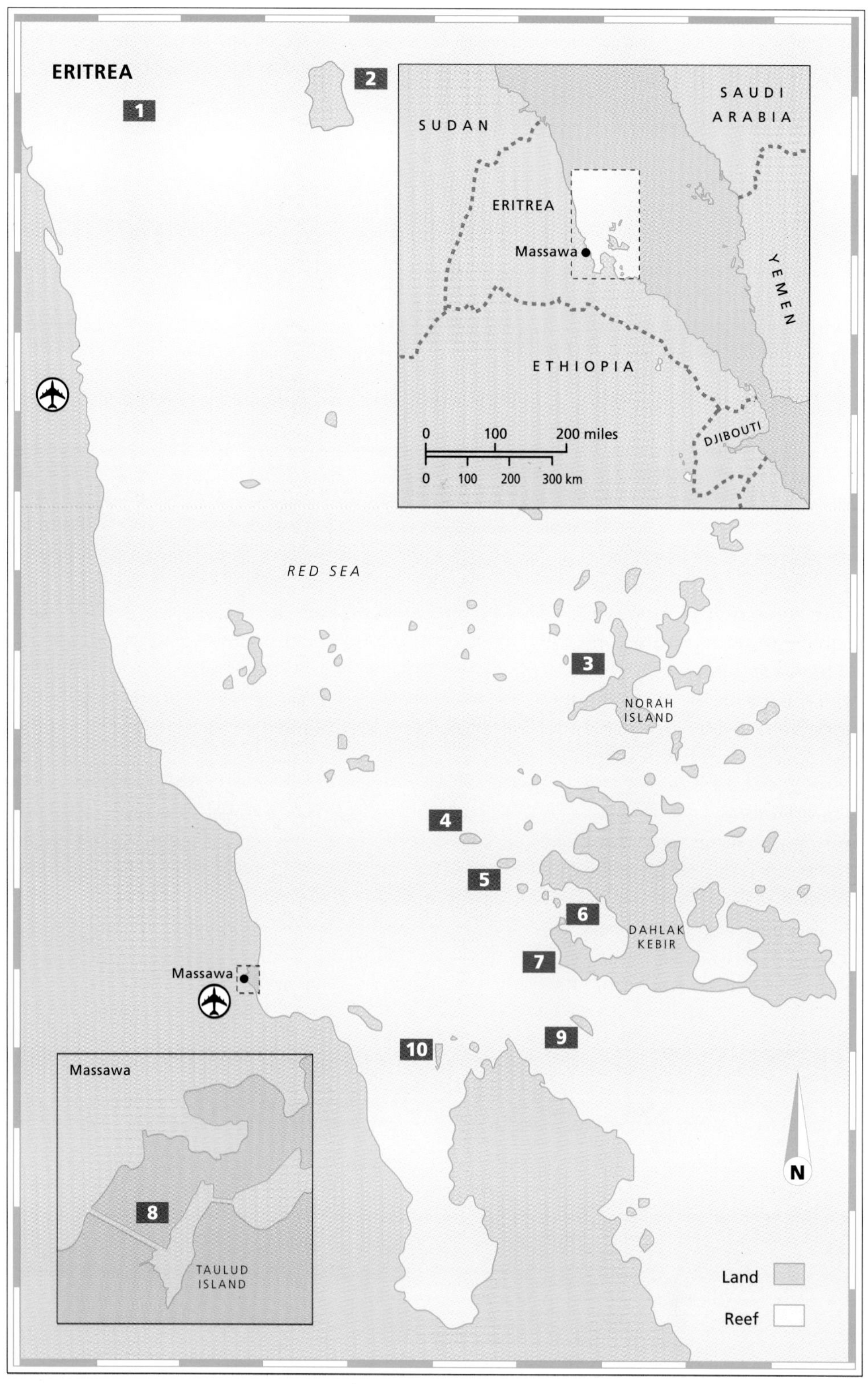
ERITREA
1
2
SUDAN
SAUDI ARABIA
ERITREA
Massawa
YEMEN
ETHIOPIA
0 100 200 miles
0 100 200 300 km
DJIBOUTI
RED SEA
3
NORAH ISLAND
4
5
6
DAHLAK KEBIR
7
Massawa
9
10
Massawa
8
TAULUD ISLAND
N
Land
Reef

CLIMATE

Eritrea's weather covers a wide range of extremes. On the coast, summer temperatures reach a hellish 50°C+ (122°F+), with winter temperatures in the upper 20s°C (80s°F). Highland temperatures on the plateau range from 30°C (86°F) in summer to freezing in the winter months. Rainfall, infrequent on the coast, is most likely in December and January.

DIVE HIGHLIGHTS

Diving here is radically different from elsewhere in the Red Sea, due in part to Eritrea's coast and offshore islands lying on a shallow plateau.

There is also a small number of unusual species to be found in these waters, as well as an unusual balance of the species common elsewhere in the Red Sea. This certainly means that diving here has a substantially different feel to diving in other regions. Divers who take an interest in marine species will find plenty to catch their attention.

MARINE LIFE

The shark life for which Eritrean waters were once famed has taken a serious beating in recent years, but many individuals can still be spotted; Grey Reef and Guitar Sharks in particular. Big turtles, stingrays, cuttlefish, Manta Rays, octopuses and dolphins are also all present in Eritrean coastal waters. Even the rarely encountered dugong frequents the offshore islands, offering the chance of a truly unique diving experience.

Coral growth is not as profuse here as in the northern Red Sea. The shallow water of the Eritrean coastal plateau, with its attendant sediment, summer water temperatures at the extreme upper range for coral survival, and dense algal and planktonic blooms, all combine to limit coral growth. Some scientists believe that the rapid uplift of the undersea plateau, which is rising by several centimetres per year, simply does not allow coral reefs time to form. At any rate, growth tends to be rather sparse and limited to narrow bands of fringing reef of relatively limited depth.

CONDITIONS

In summer, water temperatures above 36°C (97°F) have been reported, and even in winter the water is a comfortable 27–29°C (81–84°F). Exposure protection is not a serious problem. A 3-mm (0.12-in) tropical wet suit or Lycra skin will be enough for most divers.

Visibility is generally very limited, often in the 10–12m (35–40ft) range. This is a direct consequence of the warm water, which encourages abundant planktonic and algal growth, plus sediment stirred up from the shallow bottom by wave and weather.

*Bluespine Unicornfish (*Naso unicornis*).*

ACCESS

Access to the dive sites tends to be expensive. Eritrea lost much of its shipping during the war and sea transport is still at a premium. Luckily, the dive operators normally include transportation in their dive costs, so boat hire negotiations are not the nightmare they once were. This higher transport cost is passed on, however, in the form of rather high diving costs.

DIVE OPERATORS AND FACILITIES

Currently there is only one organization that offers diving for visitors to Eritrea – EriNine Tour Operator and Travel Agency. This is an Eritrean/Italian company based in Asmara and with a representative office in Milan, Italy. It uses the Luul Resort Hotel on the island of Nocra (at the entrance of Ghubbet Mus Nefit, off Dahlak Kebir).

ERITREA/PERMISSIONS

Eritrea, in spite of the short time it has existed as a country, has very strict regulations governing tourist activity on the coast and offshore islands, and has strongly enforced them since the country's earliest days. One foreign dive boat was impounded for two months for visiting Eritrean waters without permission only weeks after independence.

As things now stand, foreign visitors to the offshore islands require a permit from the Ministry of Tourism. Divers must also be accompanied by a local dive guide. There are stiff penalties for failing to observe either of these regulations.

1 DIFNEIN

★★★★★

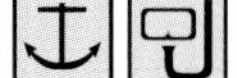

Location: About 110km (68 miles) north of Massawa.
Access: By local or live-aboard boat from Massawa or Luul hotel/dive base on Nocra.
Conditions: Divers should not go ashore because of the possibility of mines.
Average depth: 10m (35ft)
Maximum depth: 15m (50ft)
Average visibility: 18m (60ft)

As in most Dahlak sites the reef is quite shallow, with a maximum depth of only 15m (50ft). The sea floor round the island does reach much greater depths, but unfortunately, everything beyond the foot of the reef is a featureless sand slope. While the dive profile may not benefit from the area's greater maximum depth, there is a marked effect on visibility, which is generally better than sites on the shallower plateau to the south.

The reef, on the island's northeast side, slopes steeply, and is composed of a mix of coral species. As in most sites in the region, massive stony coral species form the bulk of the reef, but there are many other types to be found in small patches around the reef. Coral, however, is not the main attraction here.

Virtually any tropical fish you can think of is here in force. The island's fish population was once a magnet for Italian spearfishermen, and the enforced isolation of the Eritrean war of independence has only increased the sheer density of fish on show here. For the fish lover this site ranks among the region's finest.

ERITREAN FOOD

Eritrean cuisine is something of a discovery for most Westerners. With similarities to both Middle Eastern and Ethiopian food, Eritrea's cooking is also heavily influenced by the Italians who colonized the country for so many years.

- **Injera**, a thin, spongy flatbread made of fermented wheat or sorghum, is the staple of the Eritrean diet. It is traditionally used as Westerners would use a plate, with a generous dollop of spicy meat stew, called **zigini**, in the middle. Diners eat from the same dish, tearing off pieces of bread with the right hand to scoop up the stew.
- **Kitcha** is an unfermented flatbread made of wheat, and is common in Arab-influenced regions.
- **Bani** is European-style bread, usually in small rolls.
- **Fool** or **ful** is mashed beans, usually served with onion and spices, often with yoghurt. It is eaten with any of the breads described above.
- **Shiro** is a tasty lentil stew.
- **Frittata** is a dish of eggs scrambled with onion, peppers and hot spices, usually eaten for breakfast.
- **Arrosto** is roast meat; **capretto** is lamb; **dorho** is chicken; and **asa** is fish.

Coffee, which is a generally excellent legacy of the Italian days, can be ordered in three different styles: **bun** (pronounced 'boon'), is a strong, black espresso; **macchiato** is an espresso with a dash of steamed milk; and **cappuccino** is a real milky coffee in a large cup, usually drunk at breakfast. **Birra** is beer. It is very good quality, made by a brewery that was established by Italians.

Above: *A Giant Reef Ray (*Taeniura melanospilos*).*
Below: *A Bluespotted Ribbontail Ray (*Taeniura lymna*) commonly seen on Red Sea coral reefs.*

2 TWO FATHOM BANK

★★★★★★★

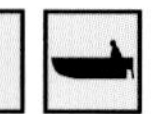

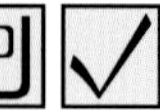

Location: 15km (9 miles) east of Difnein, northern Dahlak archipelago.
Access: By local or live-aboard boat from Massawa.
Conditions: Lack of sheltered anchorage can make access difficult in strong waves and wind.
Average depth: 20m (65ft)
Maximum depth: 30m+ (100ft+)
Average visibility: 20m (65ft)

Two Fathom Bank boasts better than average visibility all year round and is one of the few sites hereabouts where there is something to see at depths greater than 15–20m (50–65ft). The best diving is to be found at the southwestern end of the reef, where coral growth is at its most prolific. Both stony and soft species occur; large formations of massive stony corals are particularly numerous. Fish life is diverse and interesting, with a good cross-section of the usual reef species in evidence.

3 NORAH

★★★★★★★★★★

Location: Off the western shore of Norah Island, about 65km (40 miles) northeast of Massawa.
Access: By local or live-aboard boat from Massawa or Nocra.
Conditions: Very dull sea grass bank will disappoint if the main attraction, dugongs, are absent.
Average depth: 3m (10ft)
Maximum depth: 3m (10ft)
Average visibility: 15m (50ft)

The reef here has no coral, but consists of densely growing sea grass in 2–3m (5–10ft) of water. Occasionally this site is host to dugongs, some of the rarest and most reclusive animals in the sea, and it is the rare meetings with these creatures that can turn an exploration of a boring grass bank into one of the area's most spectacular dive sites. Dugongs are notoriously timid and, unlike their relatives, the manatees, they have never become accustomed to the presence of humans. It is therefore extremely rare for divers to encounter them in the wild.

4 DUR GAAM ISLET

★★★★★★

Location: Just less than half way between Massawa and Nocra.
Access: By boat from Massawa or Nocra.
Conditions: Watch for shallow coral heads on entry.
Average depth: 8m (25ft)

MINES IN ERITREA

The war of liberation that brought modern-day Eritrea into existence has been over since 1991, but the war years have left some unpleasant legacies.

The one of greatest concern to divers is the existence of uncleared, live land-mines on some of the offshore islands. During the war, the strategic importance of the islands meant that a fair number of them were strewn with anti-personnel mines. While the Eritrean government has made every effort to clear the known fields, there remain many uncharted minefields.

The danger posed by the existence of these mines is very great, and you should be careful never to go ashore on offshore islands unless you are absolutely certain that the beaches are free of these devices. Luckily, the dive organization you are most likely to dive with is made up of ex-Eritrean Naval Force divers, who know the location of the danger spots and who will make sure you stay out of harm's way.

If by some chance you do visit the islands without a local dive guide, you should make thorough enquiries about mines before setting foot on the beach.

Maximum depth: 10m (35ft)
Average visibility: 15m (50ft)

This reef has a gently sloping profile for its entire length. Coral tends toward the massive species, such as *Porites*, *Favites* and *Goniopora*, in ornate heads. Some smaller soft coral patches are also present, as are anemones, and there are quite a few nice *Acropora* tables. Coral bleaching has whitened many of these *Acropora* forms. All the common Red Sea reef fish are here, with large numbers of sweetlips, surgeonfish, angelfish and butterflyfish, and an equally big concentration of fusiliers and snappers. Various wrasse, groupers and parrots are in evidence, and shrimp gobies and stingrays inhabit the sand at the reef's base. The Crown-of-Thorns Starfish can be seen at this site, as can its predator, the triton snail.

5 DUR GHELLA ISLET

★★★★★

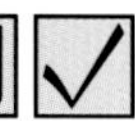

Location: 3km (2 miles) east of Dur Gaam Islet (Site 4).
Access: By local or live-aboard boat from Massawa or Nocra.
Conditions: Waves and wind can limit access.
Average depth: 8m (25ft)
Maximum depth: 12m (40ft)
Average visibility: 15m (50ft)

This is a shallow reef about 50m (165ft) offshore at Dur Ghella Islet, comprising an area of flat reef and a gently sloping reef, both covered with scattered coral heads

Opposite: *The common lionfish,* Pterois miles, *is often seen hovering in caves or near coral heads.*

and reef patches. Inshore, the reef top is 1m (3ft) or less from the surface, with many heads even shallower. At the foot of the reef, a sand slope begins at 12m (40ft).

The reef is composed of mainly massive coral forms interspersed with *Acropora*, *Stylophora* and other branching forms. A major feature of the fish life here is big bumphead parrotfish. Other parrots, surgeons, Yellowbar and Arabian angels, schooling fusiliers, spotted sweetlips, thousands of snappers, groupers and cardinals all make up an exciting reef population.

6 DRY DOCK

★★★★★★

    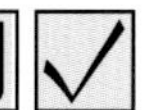

Location: In the north channel between Nocra and Dahlak Kebir, 50km (31 miles) east-northeast of Massawa.
Access: By local or live-aboard boat from Massawa or Nocra.
Conditions: Visibility can be poor; divers should watch for submerged debris during entry.
Average depth: 15m (50ft)
Maximum depth: 21m (70ft)
Average visibility: 15m (50ft)

This deep wreck dive, on a scuttled floating dry dock left behind by the Ethiopian/Russian navies at the end of the Eritrean war of independence, is a real exception to the general pattern of diving in the Dahlak group. The wreck lies just offshore at the eastern end of the Nocra Naval Base in the narrow north channel between Nocra and Dahlak Kebir. It is rectangular, with two large cranes protruding from the water at its corners, while a catwalk runs round much of the circumference just below the surface, in about 4m (15ft) of water. The winches and all of the other parts of the dock's working machinery can be seen on deck at 5–7m (15–25ft).

The wreck is populated by a wide range of reef and other fishes and the sand flats around the wreck are home to stingrays. Despite the relatively short time the dry dock has been submerged, it has been colonized to a remarkable degree by a number of different corals. Chief among these are *Dendronephthya sp.*, whose delicate bushy heads are scattered across the wreck in every imaginable colour, including violet, deep purple, maroon, and exquisite whiteheads.

7 INTIARA (ENTEARA)

★★★★★

Location: About 10km (6 miles) southwest of Nocra/Luul Hotel.
Access: By local or live-aboard boat from Nocra or Massawa.

Conditions: Some slight current is possible. Visibility is sometimes poor.
Average depth: 8m (25ft)
Maximum depth: 12m (40ft)
Average visibility: 12m (40ft)
The gentle undulations and curving layout of this wide reef more or less follow the coastline. The dive is shallow, with coral growth rarely exceeding 10m (35ft), and the bulk of the interesting fish and coral life is compressed into the narrow band between 3–8m (10–25ft). The body of the reef is largely made up of massive stony coral forms, with heads of *Favites*, *Porites*, *Goniopora*, and other corals. There are some table and branching forms, and profuse growths of gently waving soft corals are found in some areas.

The reef is populated by a broad range of reef fishes, with a large number of lined and spotted snappers in evidence, angelfish, checkerboard and other wrasse, lots of spotted groupers, parrotfish, and some large schools of species such as fusiliers and jacks.

8 RESEARCH STATION HOUSE REEF

★★

Location: Offshore at the Marine Resources research station, at the southwest corner of Taulud Island, Massawa.
Access: Shore dive from the research station boat ramp.
Conditions: Generally very poor visibility, but a very easy dive otherwise.
Average depth: 5m (15ft)

NOCRA NAVAL BASE

Opposite the Luul Hotel, one of Eritrea's main diving centres on the island of Nocra, lies the old Nocra naval base, established by the Ethiopian and Soviet governments during the war for independence, and abandoned by them in the war's closing days.

One of their final acts before pulling out was to scuttle any equipment that the Eritreans might have found useful; this spiteful behaviour has left an interesting legacy for divers to explore (see site 6 – Dry-Dock). As well as the large dry dock, there are patrol boats, other ships, and a variety of military hardware, including a Stalin Organ multiple rocket launcher, which has been raised from the sea to sit on the nearby dock,

As well as the more mundane fittings and fixtures, the Russians left behind one particularly idiosyncratic souvenir: a fully appointed officers' sauna, seating twenty... in one of the hottest spots on Earth, where temperatures reach more than 50°C (122°F) in summer.

*Octopus (*Octopus sp.*) are able to squeeze into tiny crevices and are not often seen in daytime.*

Maximum depth: 10m (35ft)
Average visibility: 5m (15ft)
This is not a spectacular dive, but it does have the attraction of being constantly accessible. The entire reef is about 5m (15ft) wide, and ranges in depth between 2 and 7m (5–25ft). Beyond this, a featureless sand slope drops gradually away, with nothing but the occasional stingray to look at. Coral growth on the reef is sparse and rather limited in size, with a predominance of massive stony corals and some small soft coral, all quite silted and patchy. However, the fish population here is dense and approachable, with large numbers of seemingly fearless reef fish to study up close. There is a truly staggering number of yellowbar angelfish on this site, more than you are likely to see in one spot anywhere else in the Red Sea. Other attractions include butterflyfish, parrotfish, a wide variety of wrasse, shrimp gobies and blennies, cuttlefish, octopuses, and stingrays.

9 SCIUMMA (PORT SMYTH)

★★★☆☆☆

Location: 5km (9 miles) south of Dahlak Kebir, about 30km (19 miles) east of Massawa.
Access: By local or live-aboard boat from Nocra, Massawa or Dahlak Kebir.
Conditions: Strong south winds are often encountered in winter.
Average depth: 8m (25ft)
Maximum depth: 15m (50ft)
Average visibility: 15m (50ft)
Located along the southwest side of Shumma, the reef drops down from the shallows to what is by Dahlak standards a reasonably deep 15m (50ft), before bottoming out on sand. The reef wall is well covered in stony corals and there are some soft varieties. Density and diversity are both up to local standards. Fish and other animal life here is good, with a number of unusual species among the more familiar residents. Along with the usual reef dwellers it is not uncommon to see turtles and Snake eels, and the more perpendicular profile seems to attract visitors from the open water, such as jacks, Spanish mackerel and tuna.

10 DISSEI

★★★☆☆☆

Location: About 30km (19 miles) southeast of Massawa.
Access: By local or live-aboard boat from Nocra or Massawa.
Conditions: Visibility can occasionally be very poor here.
Average depth: 15m (50ft)
Maximum depth: 20m (65ft)
Average visibility: 12m (40ft)
This site, on the south side of Dissei Island, is slightly deeper than the general run of Dahlak sites, and thus offers more range for exploration. The reef follows the island's southern coast, and has a flat sloping profile, descending to a maximum depth of 20m (65ft). Coral growth follows the normal Dahlak pattern, with *xeniid* and other soft corals and a perhaps slightly denser than usual concentration of various stony coral species.

Fish life is vibrant, with a full complement of reef species and the occasional school of jacks or the odd ray to liven things up out in the open water. The often limited visibility tends to keep your attention focused on the reef-dwelling species, and there is certainly enough here to keep you occupied.

With a full range of depth possibilities, from shallow snorkelling to scuba at 20m (65ft), and a respectable range of fish and coral life, this site is well worth a visit.

ASMARA AND ALTITUDE

As any trained diver knows, there are special rules that apply to flying after diving, and no certified diver would think of getting on a plane immediately after diving.

Yet many divers would think nothing of doing a dive in the islands in the morning, and then jumping on a bus to Asmara in the afternoon. What they fail to realize is that Asmara, while only 64km (40 miles) southwest of Massawa, is almost 2,400m (7,875ft) above sea level – almost exactly the altitude to which an aircraft cabin is pressurized, and more than high enough to cause decompression sickness in divers who have not planned a long enough surface interval before travelling.

You should therefore make a point of observing no-fly rules when travelling from Massawa to the interior. The best plan of all is to leave a full 24 hours between your last dive and your trip up the hill.

SHARK FISHING

Eritrean waters were once famous for their shark population. Given the effective ban on fishing imposed by the Eritrean war of independence, it could have been assumed that the shark population had increased still further. Certainly in the period immediately following the war, shark sightings were common throughout the Dahlak archipelago.

Unfortunately, recent events have changed this situation. Commercial shark fishing, mostly by Yemeni fishermen (who have been practising this trade for decades), has made serious inroads into the area's shark population. Many divers believe that the remaining sharks have been forced deeper, beyond the range of the nets, but also, sadly, beyond the range of divers.

Clashes between Yemen and Eritrea over the two countries' boundaries may eventually reduce the activity in Eritrean waters, but even so, it will be many years before sharks are once again common in the area.

DJIBOUTI & YEMEN

Yemen has good diving, and was becoming a fully fledged tourist diving destination with both live-aboard boats and land-based operations when Eritrea attacked and confiscated the Hanîsh Islands (along with some of the islands' European diving staff). Following this, several Westerners were murdered on the mainland and some yachts experienced acts of violent piracy off the southern coast, although the perpetrators may not have been Yemeni nationals. The World Court has since ruled that the Hanîsh Islands belong to Yemen. At the time of writing many Western governments were recommending that tourists do not visit Yemen as it is not yet considered to be safe.

DIVE HIGHLIGHTS

Like the Dahlak and Farasan Banks, this part of the Red Sea is not as deep as that found further north in the Sudan, and the bottom is often sandy so the visibility is not so good – 15–20m (20–65ft) is the norm. There is no drop-off or wall diving, but the marine life is profuse and often shows subtle differences from that to the north.

The farthest islands to the north are the Kamaran group, 65km (35 nautical miles) north northwest of the main port of Al Hudaydah (Hodeida). Spread among the shoals the six main low-lying, sandy islands have idyllic looking beaches and are a favourite nesting ground for turtles, but they often suffer from rats due to fishermen cleaning their catches. The shallow fringing reefs and mangroves support a diverse ecosystem and give easy diving.

The Zubair group of islands, located 95km (51 nautical miles) northwest Al Hudaydah (Hodeida), is made up of 10 isolated volcanic islands and rock outcrops including Quoin Rock that offer challenging diving with lots of visiting pelagics when the weather is fine.

Further south, the Zuqar and Hanîsh Groups, 95km (51 nautical miles) west of the coast at Al Khawkhah (Hocha) offer the most variety of diving in Yemeni waters. Made up of 17 main islands, there is good stony and soft coral, large groupers, sharks, shoals of jacks, tuna, barracuda, snapper and sweetlips, and several wrecks.

Furthest south are the narrow, turbulent Straits of the Bab al Mandab (Bab el Mandeb), with currents from the tides sweeping in from the Indian Ocean. The little archipelago of Djibouti's Seven Brothers have many large pelagics and some unusual, large Spanish Dancer type nudibranchs.

Following pages, page 150: *Tree corals, mixed corals and anthias lit up by the bright sun.*
Below: *Silky shark (*Carcharhinus falciformis*).*

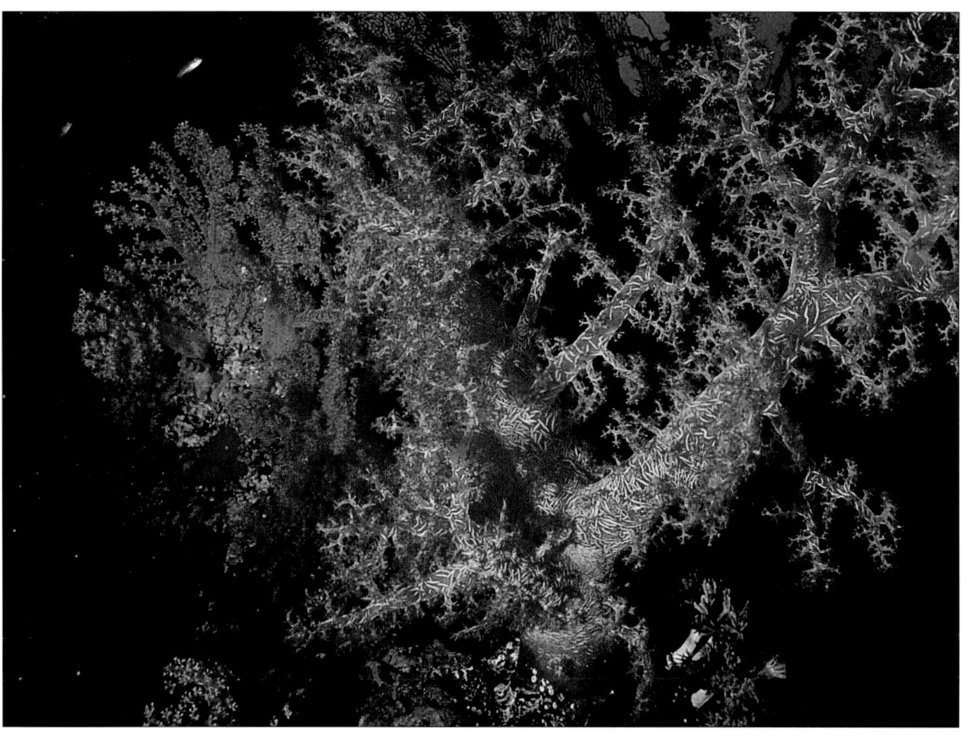

Above: *A blaze of colour in the shape of a* Dendronephthya *soft tree coral.*
Below: *A close-up shot reveals the intricacies of the soft tree coral.*

How to Get There

By air: Eritrea is served by Lufthansa, Saudi (Saudi Arabian Airways), Egypt Air and Sudan Airways, but is currently at loggerheads with Ethiopia, whose airline has the largest network in the region.
By road: The country has an efficient bus system spreading out from Asmara. But, whether by minibus, bus or taxi, the 115km (71 miles) from Asmara to the coast at Massawa takes much longer than expected. Many switchbacks have to be negotiated as the road drops in altitude from 2347m (7700ft) to sea level.

Where to Stay

The main hotels in Eritrea are not graded, but generally provide facilities related to price. In a rough order of quality from high to low, the possibilities include:

Asmara
InterContinental Hotel Asmara PO Box 5455, Warsay Avenue; tel 291 1 150 400/fax 291 1 150 401; email asmara@interconti.com; www.ichotelsgroup.com.
Ambassador Hotel PO Box 73, Asmara; tel 291 1 126 544.
Sun Shine Hotel Emperor Yohannes no. 76, PO Box 3406, Asmara; tel 291 1 127 880/fax 291 1 127 866.
Keren Hotel PO Box 181, Asmara; tel 291 1 120 740.
Emba Soira Hotel PO Box 181, Asmara; tel 291 1 123 222/fax 291 1 122 595; email embasera_hamasien@tse.com.er.
Hamassien Hotel PO Box 181, Asmara; tel 291 1 123411/fax 291 1 122 595.
Nyala Hotel PO Box 867, Asmara; tel 291 1 123 756.
Expo Hotel PO Box 3737, Asmara; tel 291 1 181 967.
Legesse Hotel PO Box 986, Asmara; tel 291 1 125 054.

Massawa
Red Sea Hotel PO Box 180, Massawa; tel 291 5 552 839.
Corallo Hotel Massawa; tel 291 5 552 406.
Gedem Hotel Taulud Island, PO Box 166, Massawa; tel 291 5 552 057.
Gurgusum Beach Hotel PO Box 5354, Massawa; tel 291 1 552 911.
Hamassien Hotel PO Box 225, Massawa; tel 291 1 552 725.
Luna Hotel PO Box 91, Massawa; tel 291 1 552 272.
Dahlak Hotel PO Box 21, Massawa; tel 291 1 552 980.

The most common base for diving is the **Luul Resort Hotel** on the island of Nocra, at the entrance of the Ghubbet Mus Nefit, off Dahlak Kebir. This hotel can be booked through EriNine (see Dive Facilities below).

Where to Eat

All the middle and upper-range hotels in Massawa have restaurants or dining rooms of varying quality and price. In town, the **Eritrean Restaurant** is cheap and excellent, with good pasta, steaks, grilled fish and salads. Another major attraction is the **Salaam** fish restaurant, deep in the old quarter of Massawa. Sitting at rickety tables in the street outside this very basic eatery, you can sample some of the finest grilled fish available in the Red Sea. Prices are extremely reasonable and portions are huge. Cafés are dotted around the old town, with good selections available along the main street near the telecommunications office and near the mosque. As is the case throughout Eritrea, the years of Italian colonialism have left a legacy of excellent espresso coffee.

In the evenings, the terrace outside the **Dahlak Hotel** overlooking the bay is a nice spot for a beer, as is the relaxed terrace bar at the **Corallo**.

Food at the **Luul Hotel** on Nocra is provided on full-board basis – there are no other restaurants or hotels on the island.

In Asmara, the streets are lined with quality cafés and restaurants.

Dive Facilities

The German company Eritrea Divers have given up trying to operate in Eritrea. Dive tourism is organized through:

EriNine Plc PO Box 266, Asmara; tel 291 1 127 300/fax 291 1 127 297; email eri.nine@mail.com; www.erinine.com. The company also has a representative office in Milan, Italy.

Hospitals

The **Italian Hospital** in Asmara is the best medical facility in Eritrea. But bear in mind that due to Asmara's 2347-m (7700-ft) altitude, diving-related emergencies should not be transferred there because of the increased risk of decompression sickness.

Diving Emergencies

There is a **recompression chamber** available, and diving emergencies should be referred to the Eritrean Shipping Lines dive team, or to the Department of Marine Resources research station.

Local Highlights

In the Massawa area the biggest attractions are the excellent **beaches** and the fascinating backstreets of the **old town**, brimming with shops and cafés. There is also a beautiful covered market, and intricate buildings dating from the Turkish period in every state of repair.

The three **tanks**, near the causeway to the mainland, were the spearheads of the final assault on Massawa by the Eritrean People's Liberation Front fighters. They have been left where they stopped as a memorial to the fighters who fell freeing the town. Other reminders are visible everywhere.

Further afield, Eritrea is packed with interest, from the Italianate colonial grandeur of **Asmara** to the hill-station tranquillity of **Keren**. Eritrea may be a small country but it packs a wide range of attractions into its narrow boundaries, from the tribal desert regions of Denkalia to the south; through the historic trade centres of the coastal regions; up into the rugged eastern escarpment; across the upland plateau and into the western lowlands.

Djibouti

Djibouti and the Straits of Beb el Mandab are out of the way, so there is no mass tourism. Known for its big fish, including Whale Sharks for three months of the year, dolphins, turtles and Manta Rays, the best-known area is the Seven Brothers islands. Nearer to Djibouti town are the Musha and Maskali islands located in the Gulf of Tadjura.
Dive Facilities
Dolphin Excursions PO Box 4467; tel 253 350 313/fax 253 350 380; email dolphinexcursions@hotmail.com. Certification: PADI.
Djibouti Divers email: info@djiboutidivers.com; www.djiboutidivers.com

Different Diving

Eritrean diving can be extremely rewarding, but divers who come here looking for the crystal clear waters and coral drop-offs of the northern Red Sea are asking to be disappointed.

In Eritrea, the entire coast lies along a region of geological uplift, resulting in very shallow seas. For divers, the result of this topography is simple: greatly reduced visibility due to sediment and warm-water microorganisms, and a lack of the sustained coral-growth conditions which result in large-scale reef building.

This does not mean that Eritrean diving is bad diving – far from it. It simply means that different standards apply. In this case, the attractions are not spectacular reef walls and endless visibility, but a diverse and fascinating marine population.

The scorpaenidae – Stonefish, Scorpionfish and Lionfish

These reef dwellers are non-aggressive, feeding on small fish and crustaceans. They boast an array of venomous spines along their dorsal fins which can administer a painful sting to anyone foolish or unlucky enough to come into contact with them. Their threat to divers results from their near-perfect camouflage. It is easy to place an unwary hand on one in the belief that it is just another piece of reef – yet another reason to keep your hands off the coral.

The stings, while excruciatingly painful, are rarely fatal to adults. Treatment of stings should begin with the immediate removal of the victim from the water. The affected area should be bathed in very hot water and immediate medical attention sought.

Stingrays

Although possessed of a wicked, venomous spike at the base of their tails, these bottom-dwellers are generally passive. The main threat posed by stingrays is that of a defensive reaction to a carelessly placed hand or foot; stingrays are often concealed beneath a thin layer of sand, indistinguishable from the sea bed. Small rays also hide in caves and crevices, so divers should take care when putting their hands into any small, sheltered openings. The treatment for ray stings is identical to that for *scorpaenidae* stings.

Sharks, Eels and Barracuda

None of these animals is known to be aggressive toward divers. All known injuries are believed to be a result of mistakenly triggered defence or feeding behaviours. Dead fish carried by divers are known to provoke attacks. Barracuda are also said to be attracted by bright, shiny objects such as jewellery.

Divers should keep a respectful distance between themselves and big carnivores, and avoid abrupt movements that could be seen as threatening. Sharks swimming with exaggerated side-to-side movements are displaying warning-off behaviour and should be treated with great caution. Any animal is likely to attack if it feels threatened and this is true of not only barracuda, sharks and eels but also of other fish. Any creature with a mouth will eventually bite if sufficiently provoked. Turtles, triggerfish, parrots and even clownfish have bitten divers on occasions.

Stinging Creatures

There is a variety of tropical sea creatures with the potential to inflict painful burns and rashes on unwary divers. These include jellyfish, fire corals and stinging hydroids. Brushing against any of these with bare skin will result in a painful sting and often in a welted, burning rash that can take days to subside. None of the jellyfish species found in the Red Sea have stings that can be fatal to humans, but the stings from fire coral and stinging hydroids can be very painful. Some tiny, invisible plankton can also sting, so there are advantages to wearing a Lycra suit if you do not require a wet suit. There are a variety of antihistamine sprays, creams and tablets on the market to treat anyone suffering from such stings.

Sea Urchins

These bottom-dwellers are harmless enough unless you happen to step on one or grab one with an unprotected hand. Then their extremely brittle spines can penetrate the skin, usually breaking off in the wound and causing extreme discomfort. If any part of the spine is protruding, it should be delicately removed with tweezers; otherwise, the traditional remedy is to shatter the spine with a sharp blow to the area from a heavy object, such as a book. In many traditional fishing communities, locals also swear by the application of oil heated until it nearly burns the skin.

Coral Cuts

Cuts from coral can become badly infected in a tropical climate. All scrapes should be treated with antibiotic cream and kept dry.

Above: *The Stonefish (*Synanceia varrucosa*) can produce horrendous pain with its venomous spines.*
Below: *Keep well away from the coral – look but do not touch.*

The Marine Environment

THE NATURE OF CORALS AND REEFS

Tropical reefs are built mainly from corals, primitive animals closely related to sea anemones. Most of the coral types that contribute to reef construction are colonial; that is, numerous individuals, called polyps, come together to create what is essentially a single compound organism. The polyps produce calcareous skeletons; when thousands of millions of them are present in a single colony they form large, stony (in fact, limestone) structures, which build up as reefs.

What happens is that, when corals die some of the skeleton remains intact, thus adding to the reef. Cracks and holes then fill with sand and the calcareous remains of other reef plants and animals, and gradually the whole becomes consolidated, with new corals growing on the surface of the mass. Thus, only the outermost layer of the growing reef is alive.

Corals grow slowly, adding about 1–10cm (0.4–4in) growth in a year. After a certain age they begin to reproduce, releasing tiny forms that float freely among the plankton for a few weeks. Eventually they settle, to continue the growth of the reef. The forms corals create as they grow vary enormously according to the species and to the place on the reef where the colony is growing.

Colonies range in size from a few centimetres in diameter to giants several metres across. Some colonies are many hundreds of years old. Some are branched or bushy, others tree-like; some take the form of plates, tables or delicate leafy fronds, and yet others are encrusting, lobed, rounded, or massive.

Microscopic plants called zooxanthellae are of great importance to the growth and health of corals. These are packed in their millions into the living tissues of most reef-building corals (and of various other reef animals, such as giant clams). Although reef corals capture planktonic organisms from the water, a significant amount of their food comes directly from the zooxanthellae. It is for this reason that the most prolific coral growths are in the shallow, well-lit waters that the zooxanthellae prefer.

Types of Reef

In most regions with plentiful coral communities, the calcareous skeletons of coral polyps have built up to form a variety of different types of reef:

- fringing reefs
- patch reefs, banks and shoals
- barrier reefs
- atolls.

Fringing Reefs

Fringing reefs occur in shallow water near to land. Typically they extend to depths of 15–45m (50–150ft), depending on factors such as the profile and depth of the seabed and the clarity of the water.

Patch Reefs, Banks and Shoals

In theory, reefs can develop wherever the underlying rock has at some time been close enough to the surface for corals to become established and grow. Sea levels may have risen considerably since then, or other geological changes may have occurred to lower the depth of the bed beneath the surface. Either way, there are many places where reefs exist as isolated mounds or hillocks on the seabed. Patch reefs vary in size from tens to thousands of metres in diameter. Their tops usually come to within a few metres of the sea surface and some emerge above the surface and are topped by sand cays. Patch reefs that occur further offshore in waters hundreds of metres deep, with their tops 20m (65ft) or more below the surface, are usually called banks or shoals.

Barrier Reefs

Barrier reefs occur along the edges of islands or continental shelves, and they are substantial structures. The main difference between barrier and fringing reefs, apart from their size, is that they are separated from the shore by a wide, deep lagoon. The outer edge of the barrier drops away steeply to the ocean floor beyond. These reefs were formed in shallow waters, and gradually, as sea levels rose, they built progressively upward, so that their living topmost parts were still near the surface of the water.

Atolls

These are structures of ancient origin, having formed millions of years ago. They are ring-shaped reefs enclosing a shallow lagoon and dropping away to deep water on the outside. Atolls began as fringing reefs round volcanic islands. As the base of the reef gradually subsided beneath the water level, the top kept growing.

REEF LIFE

Reef Zones and Habitats

Reefs can be divided into a number of zones reflecting differences in features such as depth, profile, distance from the shore, amount of wave action, and type of seabed. Associated with each zone are characteristic types of marine life.

The Back Reef and Lagoon

The back reef and lagoon fill the area between the shore and the seaward reef. Here the seabed is usually a mix-

Opposite: *Anthias and bubble coral.*

ture of sand, coral rubble, limestone slabs, and living coral colonies. The water depth varies from a few metres to 50m (165ft) or more, and the size of the lagoon can be anywhere from a few hundred to thousands of square metres. The largest and deepest lagoons are those associated with barrier reefs and atolls, and may be dotted with islands and smaller reefs.

Sites within lagoons are obviously more sheltered than those on the seaward reef, and they are also more affected by sedimentation. On lagoon sites you find many attractive seaweeds. Most of the corals are delicate, branching types. Large sand-dwelling anemones are often found, and in places soft corals and false corals are likely to form mats over the seabed. Especially where there is a current you may encounter extensive beds of sea grasses, the only flowering plants to occur in the sea. Among the many animal species that make these pastures their home are the longest sea cucumbers you will find anywhere on the reef.

Although some typical reef fishes are absent from this environment, there is no shortage of interesting species. On the one hand there are roving predators – snappers, wrasse, triggerfish, emperors and others – on the lookout for worms, crustaceans, gastropods, sea urchins and small fish. Then there are the bottom-dwelling fishes that burrow into the sand until they are completely hidden, emerging only when they need to feed.

Most entertaining to watch, if you spot them, are the small gobies that live in association with pistol shrimps. In this partnership the shrimp is the digger and the goby, stationed at the entrance to the burrow, is the sentry. The small fish remains ever on the alert, ready to retreat hurriedly into the burrow at the first sign of disturbance. The shrimp has very poor eyesight, so it keeps its antennae in close touch with the goby in order to pick up the danger signal and, likewise, retire swiftly to the safety of the burrow.

The Reef Flat

Reef flats are formed as their associated reefs push steadily seaward, leaving behind limestone areas that are eroded and planed almost flat by the action of the sea. The reef flat is essentially an intertidal area, but at high tide it can provide interesting areas for snorkelling.

The inner part of the reef flat is the area most sheltered from the waves, and here you may find beautiful pools full of corals and small fish. Among the common sights are micro-atolls of the coral genus Porites. They have a distinctive doughnut (toroidal) shape, with a ring of coral surrounding a small, sandy-bottomed pool, which is a result of low water level and hot sun inhibiting the upward growth of the coral. In deeper water, as on the reef rim, the same coral forms huge, rounded colonies.

Toward the outer edge of the reef flat, where wave action is much more significant, surfaces are often encrusted with calcareous red algae, and elsewhere you will usually find a fine mat of filamentous algae that serves as grazing pasture for fish, sea urchins, gastropods, molluscs and other animals. Some fish are permanent inhabitants of the reef-flat area, retreating to pools if necessary at low tide. Others, like parrotfish and surgeonfish, spend a great deal of their time in deeper water, crowding over to the reef flat with the rising tide.

The Seaward Reef Front

Most divers ignore the shoreward zones of the reef and head straight for sites on the reef front, on the basis that here they are most likely to see spectacular features and impressive displays of marine life. Brightly lit, clean, plankton-rich water provides ideal growing conditions for corals, and the colonies they form help create habitats of considerable complexity. There is infinite variety, from shallow gardens of delicate branching corals to walls festooned with soft corals and sea fans.

The top 20m (65ft) or so of the seaward reef is especially full of life. Here small, brilliantly coloured damselfish and anthias swarm around the coral, darting into open water to feed on plankton. Butterflyfish show their dazzling arrays of spots, stripes and intricate patterns as they probe into crevices or pick at coral polyps. Many have elongated snouts especially adapted for this delicate task. By contrast, you can see parrotfish biting and scraping at the coral and leaving, over time, characteristic white scars.

Open-water species, such as fusiliers, snappers and sharks, cover quite large areas when feeding, and wrasse often forage far and wide over the reef. But many species are more localized and can be highly territorial, on occasions even being prepared to take on a trespassing diver. Clownfishes *(Amphiprion sp.)* and *Premnas biaculeatus* are among the boldest, dashing out from the safety of the anemone tentacles in which they hide, to give chase.

Fish-watching can give endless pleasure and there is much else to see besides. Any bare spaces created on the reef are soon colonized, and in some places the surface is covered with large organisms that may be tens or even hundreds of years old. These sedentary reef-dwellers primarily rely on, aside from the omnipresent algae, water-borne food. Corals and their close relatives – anemones, sea fans and black corals – capture planktonic organisms using their tiny stinging cells. Sea squirts and sponges strain the plankton as seawater passes through specially adapted canals in their body walls. Other organisms have rather different techniques. The Christmas-tree Worm, for example, filters out food with the aid of its beautiful, feathery crown of tentacles.

Apart from the fishes and the sedentary organisms there is a huge array of other life forms to observe on the reef. Tiny crabs live among the coral branches and larger ones wedge themselves into appropriate nooks and crannies, often emerging to feed at night. Spiny lobsters hide in caverns, coming out to hunt under cover of darkness.

Gastropod molluscs are another type of marine creature seldom seen during the day, but they are, in fact, present in very large numbers, especially on the shallower parts of the reef. Many of them are small, but on occasion you might come across one of the larger species, like the giant triton *(Charonia tritonis)*.

Some of the most easily spotted of the mobile invertebrates are the echinoderms. The most primitive of these are the feather stars, sporting long, delicate arms in all colours from bright yellow to green, red and black. The best-known of their relatives, the sea urchins, is the black, spiny variety that lives in shallow reef areas and is a potential hazard to anyone walking on to the reef.

Many of the small, brightly coloured starfish that wander over the reef face feed on the surface film of detritus and microorganisms. Others are carnivorous, browsing on sponges and sea mats, and a few feed on living coral polyps. The damage they cause depends on their size, their appetite and, collectively, their population density. Potentially the most damaging of all is the large predator *Acanthaster planci*, the crown-of-thorns starfish.

Whether brilliantly attractive or frankly plain, whether swiftly darting or sessile, all the life forms you find on the reef are part of its finely balanced ecosystem. You are not. You are an intruder, albeit a friendly one. You are under obligation to cause as little disturbance and destruction as possible among these creatures.

MARINE CONSERVATION

Reefs are valuable to local people as fishing grounds and as sources of other important natural products, including shells. But in the past few decades they have come under increasing pressure from human activities. As a result they are, in places, showing signs of wear and tear.

Corals are slow-growing. If damaged or removed they may require years to recover or to be replaced. In the natural course of events, storm-driven waves create havoc from time to time on coral reefs, especially in the typhoon belt. But some human activities are similarly destructive, especially blast-fishing and the indiscriminate collection of corals to sell as marine curios.

Overfishing is a further deadly hazard to reef environments and has already led to a perilous decline in populations of target species in some areas. Overfishing can also cause grave damage to reefs by altering the balance of local ecosystems. For example, decreasing the populations of herbivorous fish can lead to an explosive increase in the algae on which those species feed, so the corals of the reef may suffer by becoming overgrown.

Some areas are being damaged by pollution, especially where reefs occur close to large centres of human population. Corals and other reef creatures are sensitive to dirty, sediment-laden water, and are at risk of being smothered when silt settles on the bottom. Sewage, nutrients from agricultural fertilizers and other organic materials washed into the sea encourage the growth of algae, sometimes to the extent that the corals of the reef suffer by becoming overgrown.

Although, like other visitors to the reef, divers wish simply to enjoy themselves, and although most divers are conscious of conservation issues and take steps to reduce any damage their presence could cause, tourism and development in general have created many problems for the reefs. Harbours, jetties and sea walls are on occasion built so close to reefs – sometimes even on top of them – that the environment is drastically altered and the populations of reef organisms decline. Visiting boats often damage the corals through inadvertent grounding or careless or insouciant anchoring. And once divers enter the water, they may unintentionally cause damage as they move about on the reef.

Growing awareness of environmental issues has given rise to ecotourism. The main underlying principle of this activity is often summarized as 'take nothing but photographs, leave nothing but footprints'. But even footprints can, like any form of touching, cause damage to creatures living in fragile environments, particularly to corals and the species that live among them. A better way to think of ecotourism is in terms of managing tourism and tourists in such a way as to make the industry ecologically sustainable. The necessary capital investment is minimal, and thereafter, much-needed employment becomes available for the local population. In the long term the profits would exceed those from logging or overfishing.

Although divers, as well as many dive operators and resorts, have been at the forefront in protecting reefs and marine ecosystems, we all need somewhere to eat and sleep. If a small resort is built without a waste-treatment system, the nearby reefs may not be irreparably damaged. But if those same reefs start to attract increasing numbers of divers, and spawn more resorts, strict controls become necessary.

In such discussions of ecotourism we are looking at the larger scale. It is too easy to forget that tourists and divers are not amorphous groups but collections of individuals, with individual responsibilities and capable of making individual decisions. Keeping reefs ecologically sustainable depends as much on each of us as it does on the dive and resort operators. Here are just some of the ways in which you, as a diver, can help preserve the reefs that give you so much:

- Try not to touch living marine organisms with your body or your diving equipment. Be particularly careful to control your fins, since their size and the force of kicking can damage large areas of coral. Don't use deep fin strokes next to the reef, since the surge of water these cause can disturb delicate organisms.
- Learn the skills of buoyancy control. Too much damage is caused by divers descending too rapidly or crashing into corals while trying to adjust their buoyancy. Make sure you are properly weighted, and learn to achieve neutral buoyancy. If you have not dived for a while,

practise somewhere you will not cause damage.

- Avoid kicking up sand. Clouds of sand settling on the reef can smother corals. Snorkellers should be careful not to kick up sand when treading water in shallow reef areas.
- Never stand on corals, however robust they may seem. Living polyps are easily damaged by the slightest touch. Never pose for pictures or stand inside giant basket or barrel sponges.
- If you are out of control and about to collide with the reef, steady yourself with your fingertips on a part of the reef that is already dead or covered in algae. If you need to adjust your diving equipment or mask, try to do so in a sandy area well away from the reef.
- Don't collect or buy shells, corals, starfish or any other marine souvenirs.
- On any excursion, whether with an operator or privately organized, make sure you take your garbage back for proper disposal on land.
- Take great care in underwater caverns and caves. People cause damage when they crowd into caves, so if possible, go in when there are no crowds. Do not stay too long: your air bubbles collect in pockets on the roof of the cave, and delicate creatures living there can `drown' in air.
- If booking a live-aboard dive trip, ask about the company's environmental policy, particularly on the discharge of sewage and anchoring. Do not book boats that cause unnecessary anchor damage, have bad oil leaks, or discharge untreated sewage near reefs.
- Do not participate in spearfishing for sport – it is now banned in many countries. If you are living on a boat and relying on spearfishing for food, make sure you are familiar with all local fish and game regulations, and obtain any necessary licences.
- Do not feed fish. It may seem harmless but it can upset their normal feeding patterns and provoke aggressive behaviour. It can also be unhealthy for them if you give them food that is not part of their normal diet.
- Do not move marine organisms around to photograph or play with them. In particular, do not hitch rides on turtles: it causes them considerable stress.

COMMON FISH

Angelfish *(family Pomacanthidae)*
These beautiful fish, with their minute, brush-like teeth, browse on sponges, algae and corals. Their vibrant colouring varies according to the species, like those of the butterflyfish, and they were once thought part of the same family. However, angelfish are distinguishable by a short spike extending from the gill cover. Angelfish are territorial in habit and tend to occupy the same caves or ledges for a period of time.

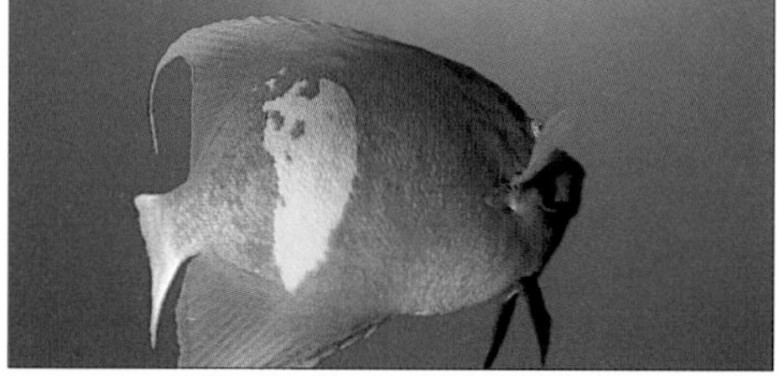
Yellowbar angelfish, 50cm (20in) *Pomacanthus maculosus*

Bigeyes *(family Priacanthidae)*
As their name suggests, these small nocturnal fish have extremely large eyes. Bigeyes are effective predators which hide in protective holes in the coral by day and venture out at night to feed on other small fish, crabs, larvae and the large planktonic animals (the organic life that is found floating at various levels in the sea).

Bigeye, 30cm (12in) *Priacanthus hamrur*

Butterflyfish *(family Chaetodontidae)*
Butterflyfish are among the most colourful of reef inhabitants. They have flat, thin bodies, usually with a stripe near the eye and often with a dark blotch near the tail. This blotch serves to confuse predators, who mistake it for an eye and attack the wrong end of the fish. Butterflyfish can also swim backward to escape danger. Many species live as mated pairs with clearly defined territories, while others school in large numbers.

Masked butterflyfish, 23cm (9in) *Chaetodon semilarvatus*

Damselfish and Clownfish *(family Pomacentridae)*
These fish often farm their own patch of algae, aggressively driving away other herbivores. Found almost everywhere on the reef, they also sometimes form large groups to feed on plankton. Clownfish *(Amphiprion sp.)*, which live among the stinging tentacles of sea anemones, are also members of this family.

Twobar anemonefish, 14cm (5½in) *Amphiprion bicinctus*

Goatfish *(family Mullidae)*
Easily recognized by their chin whiskers – a pair of long barbels which they use to hunt for food – goatfish are often seen moving along sandflats, stirring up small clouds of sand as they feel beneath the surface for prey. They sometimes forage in small groups or large schools. Goatfish are bottom-dwellers, which is the term for fish that feed or lie camouflaged on the ocean floor.

Yellowsaddle goatfish, 10cm (3-4in) *Parupeneus Cyclostomus*

Grouper (*family Serranidae*)
Groupers range from just a few centimetres long to the massive giant grouper, 3.5m (12ft) long. They vary enormously in colour, the most common are grey with darker spots. They move slowly, but attack their prey with remarkable speed. All groupers are carnivorous, feeding on invertebrates and other fish. Like wrasse and parrotfish, some start out as females and become males later, while other are hermaphroditic.

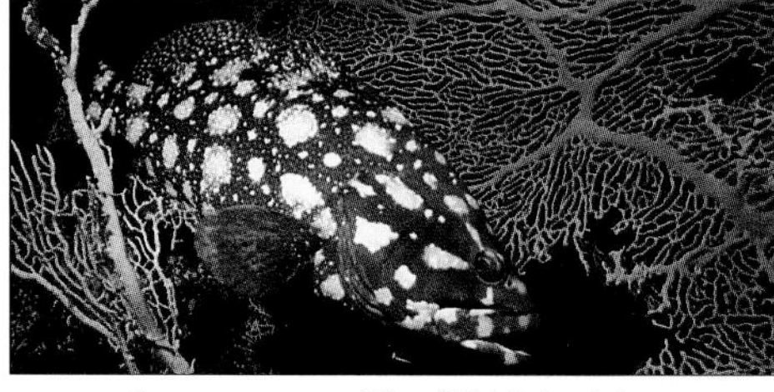
Summana grouper, 52cm (20in) *Epinephelus summana*

Jack and Trevally (*family Carangidae*)
Jacks and trevallies are streamlined, fast-swimming predators, ranging in size from small to very large. They are usually found in the open water, but are occasional visitors to the reef since they follow the current as they feed. Cruising the outer slopes, they dash in with lightning speed to snatch unwary reef fish. They can be seen singly, schooling or in small groups.

Orangespotted trevally, 53cm (20in) *Carangoides bajad*

Moray Eel (*family Muraenidae*)
These ancient species of fish have gained their undeserved reputation for ferocity largely because as they breathe, they open and close their mouth to reveal their numerous sharp teeth. Although they are generally not aggressive, the larger species can inflict serious and painful wounds. Moray eels anchor the rear portion of their bodies in a selected coral crevice and stay hidden during the day, emerging at night to feed on shrimps, octopuses and mussels. They do not have fins or scales.

Giant moray eel, up to 2.4m (8in) *Gymnothorax javanicus*

Parrotfish (*family Scaridae*)
So called because of their sharp, parrot-like beaks and bright colours, the parrotfishes are among the most important herbivores on the reef. Many change colour and sex as they grow, the terminal-phase males developing striking coloration by comparison with the drabness of the initial-phase males and females. Many build transparent cocoons of mucus to sleep in at night, the mucus acting as a scent barrier against predators.

Male Bicolor parrotfish, 80cm (32in) *Cetoscarus bicolor*

Stingray (*family Dasyatididae*)
An attractive ray, easily recognized by its bright blue spots on a greenish-yellow body. Commonly found under ledges, the Bluespotted Ribbontail Ray is a shy, timid fish which tends to bury itself in the sand when divers approach. However, it can deliver a nasty sting from its tail, driving a spine into the victim; the shaft can break off, leaving the tip in the wound.

Bluespotted Ribbontail Ray, 2.4m (95in), *Taeniura lymma*

Pufferfish *(family Tetraodontidae)*
These small to medium-size omnivores feed on algae, worms, molluscs, and crustaceans. Pufferfish are found all the way down the reef to depths of about 30m (100ft). They are slow-moving, but when threatened they inflate themselves into big, round balls by sucking water into the abdomen, so that it becomes almost impossible for predators to swallow them. Many species are prickly and are even more difficult to attack when inflated.

Whitespotted (Ringed) pufferfish, 30cm (12in) *Arothron hispidus*

Snapper *(family Lutjanidae)*
Snappers are important carnivores on the reef, feeding mostly at night. Many are inshore-dwellers, although the yellowtail snapper is a mid-water fish, and the commercially exploited red snapper dwells at all depths. Snappers are becoming much rarer on the reefs because they are long-lived and slow-growing, which means that once populations are drastically reduced by fishing, they take a long time to replenish their numbers.

Red (Twinspot) snapper, 90cm (35in) *Lutjanus bohar*

Soldierfish and Squirrelfish *(family Holocentridae)*
Both soldierfish and squirrelfish are nocturnal species and are often confused with each other. Soldierfish have a rounder, bulkier body and are more evenly coloured than squirrelfish. The red or reddish-orange coloration and large eyes are common also among other nocturnal fish, such as bigeyes. Dozing under rocks or corals by day, they emerge by night to feed. They have serrated, spiny scales and sharp, defensive fins.

Sabre squirrelfish, up to 45cm (18in) *Sargocentron Spiniferum*

Triggerfish *(family Balistidae)*
Medium-to-large fish with flattened bodies and often striking markings. Most species are distinctinctly coloured and easily recognizable. They have powerful teeth and feed on crustaceans and echinoderms on the mid-reef. When a triggerfish is threatened it squeezes itself into a crevice and erects its first dorsal spine, locking it into place with a second, smaller spine, which stays wedged until the trigger is released.

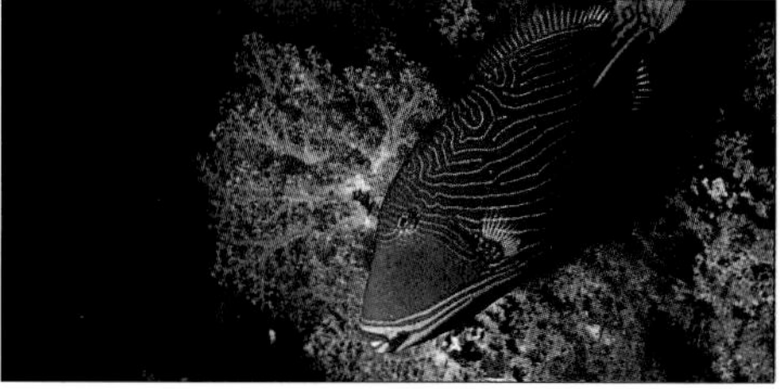

Orangestriped triggerfish, 30cm (12in) *Balistapus undulatus*

Wrasse and Hogfish *(family Labridae)*
Wrasse vary enormously in size, from the tiny cleaner wrasse *(Labroides sp.)* to the giant humphead wrasse *(Cheilinus undulatus)*, which can reach nearly 2m (6½ft) in length. Wrasse are usually brightly coloured and go through various colour and sex changes as they mature. Their distinctive buck teeth are well adapted to pulling molluscs from rocks or picking off crustaceans. Most live in shallow reef areas, although some (for example, the hogfishes) are frequently found at greater depths.

Giant humphead wrasse, up to 2m (61/2ft) *Cheilinus undulatus*

UNDERWATER PHOTOGRAPHY

Underwater still photography requires technical competence and dedication, and can work out expensive, although with digital cameras you can discard any failures without having to pay for them.

You cannot change films or prime lenses in this environment, so it's best to have a clear idea of what you wish to photograph before taking the plunge. Another possibility is to have a zoom lens on a housed camera. If the water is calm you can carry two camera outfits, one for wide-angle and another for close-up or macro. In strong currents, a non-reflex camera will be smaller and therefore easier to handle.

There are several waterproof non-reflex cameras (both film and digital) that do not need waterproof housings, but the best lenses at this level are on the Nikonos V, which has a Through-The-Lens (TTL) automatic exposure system and dedicated flash guns (strobes) made by Nikon and other manufacturers. This camera is now discontinued, but there are still plenty around because they are so popular. However, the lack of reflex focusing makes it difficult to compose pictures and it is easy to cut off part of a subject.

The huge increases in the technical advances of land cameras are the main reason for the demise of the Nikonos. Land cameras are used underwater in specialist metal or Plexiglas waterproof housings. Metal housings are strong, reliable, work well at depth and will last a long time if properly maintained. They are heavy to carry, especially when travelling by air, but have buoyancy in water.

Plexiglas housings are cheaper but more fragile, and require careful handling. Some models compress at depth, making the control rods miss the camera controls. These control rods can be adjusted to work at depths, but then do not function properly near to the surface. Most underwater photographs are taken near the surface, so this drawback is not serious. These housings are lightweight to carry on land, but often too buoyant in the water, where you have to attach extra weights.

Underwater cameras, housings, flash guns and cables have 'O'-ring seals to keep the water out: these and their mating surfaces or grooves must be kept scrupulously clean. 'O'-rings should be lightly greased with special grease (usually silicone) to prevent flooding.

When not in use, store any user-removable 'O'-rings off the unit to avoid flattening. User-removable 'O'-rings on cameras and flash synchronization cables are best replaced every 12 months. Non-user removable 'O'-rings on the Nikonos should be serviced every 12–18 months; those on housings usually last the life of the housing.

Housings without controls, which are designed for auto-everything cameras, require fast films to obtain reasonable shutter speeds and lens apertures in the low ambient light underwater.

When balancing flash with daylight, cameras with faster flash synchronization speeds (1/125 or 1/250 of a second) give sharper results by avoiding the double images associated with fast-moving fish.

Masks hold your eyes away from the viewfinder, so buy the smallest volume mask you can wear. Cameras fitted with optical action finders or eyepiece magnifiers are useful in housings, but this is not so important with autofocus systems.

Light refraction through your mask and through the camera lens causes objects to appear one-third closer and larger than in air. Reflex focusing or visually estimated distances remain correct, but if you measure distances by ruler, these must be reduced by one-third when setting the lens focus if it is inscribed in 'in-air' distances.

If you are using a waterproof housing with a flat port (window) in front of the lens, refraction increases the focal length of the lens and decreases its sharpness due to the individual colours of light being refracted at different angles and speeds (chromatic aberration). This is most pronounced with wide-angle lenses, which should be corrected by using a convex dome port. Dome ports require lenses to be able to focus on a virtual image at around 30cm (1ft), so you may have to fit supplementary positive dioptre lenses to some camera lenses.

When the sun is at a low angle, or in choppy seas, much of the light fails to enter the water. It is best to photograph two hours either side of the sun's highest point. Water acts as a cyan (blue/green) filter, cutting back red, so colour film will have a blue/green cast. For available-light photography, different filters are sold to correct this in either temperate or tropical waters, but they reduce the already limited amount of light available. Flash will put back the colour and increase sharpness.

Modern flash guns (strobes) have automatic exposure systems. Underwater, large flash guns have good wide-angle performance usable up to 1.5m (5ft). Smaller flash guns have a narrow angle and only work up to 1m (3ft); diffusers widen the angle covered but you lose at least one F-stop in output. Most land flash guns are more advanced than underwater flash guns, and can be housed for underwater use (see page 163).

Flash guns used on or near to the camera will light up suspended matter in the water like white stars in a black sky (back scatter). The closer these particles are to the camera, the larger they will appear. The solution is to keep the flash as far as possible above and to one side of the camera. Two narrow-angle flash guns – one on each side of the camera and each pointing slightly outwards but with their light output overlapping in the centre – often produce a better result than a single wide-angle flash gun. However, the result will be flat, as two flash guns of the same power will not give the modelling light that photo-graphers rely on to distinguish features by shadowing.

When photographing divers, remember that the eyes within the mask must be lit and in focus. Flash guns with a colour temperature of 4500degs Kelvin will give more accurate skin tones and colour by replacing some of the red that the water has filtered out.

In a multiple flash set-up the prime flash gun will meter by TTL if this is available, and (unless it has TTL-Slave) any other flash gun connected will give its pre-programmed output so this should be set low to achieve modelling light. TTL-Slave flash guns should have a lower output than the main flash, for the same reason.

Multiple-segment matrix flash exists with some land cameras in housings that are connected to housed matrix-metering flash guns. With other TTL systems, although the ambient light metering may be multiple segment matrix, the flash metering is by a single segment in the centre of the frame. This means that flash on smaller off-centre foreground subjects may not be correctly metered with these systems (see the section on flash with digital cameras).

Although objects appear closer to both your eye and the camera lens underwater, the flash must strike the subject directly to illuminate it. Narrow-angle flash guns must therefore be aimed behind the apparent subject, to hit the real subject. Built-in aiming/focusing lights, or a torch strapped to the flash, will aid both this problem and focusing during night photography. Built-in aiming/focusing lights are best powered by separate batteries, or the main flash battery will not last for a complete dive.

The easiest way to balance flash with the ambient available light is to use TTL flash with the camera on aperture priority metering. Take a meter reading of the mid-water background that agrees with your chosen flash synchronization speed, set your flash to TTL and it will correctly light the subject.

With manual exposure, using an aperture half a stop higher than the meter recommends will give a darker background and make the subject stand out. At distances of less than 1m (3ft), most automatic flash guns overexpose – so allow for this.

DIGITAL CAMERAS AND THEIR USE UNDERWATER

Digital cameras are gradually taking over from film cameras, because without the cost of film they appear to work out cheaper. They particularly appeal to underwater photographers because they can get a lot more shots onto a memory card than they could onto a film. Users can discard any failures and can keep on photographing a subject until they get it right, as long as it does not move.

However, electronics give more problems in a saltwater environment: you have to carry a portable computer or several memory cards to download the images and if used professionally (i.e. heavily), the camera's service life is only about three years, so the saving in film costs is soon negated.

Digital cameras often produce images that lack the punch, contrast or sparkle delivered by a film-based model. The results can be wishy-washy and lack detail in the highlights: you may have to 'up' the colour depth and contrast with image manipulation software.

Image files are stored in various formats: uncompressed as TIFFs (Tagged Image File Format) or compressed as JPEGs (Joint Photographic Experts Group), which can reduce the file size by 8 or 10 to 1 if required. Some modern cameras allow storage as RAW (the raw data as it comes directly off the sensor). There is no standard for this – it uses the proprietary software of the camera manufacturer – but it has the best quality.

PHOTOGRAPHIC TIPS

Point-and-shoot does not work – get closer than arm's length and make sure the subject fills more than half of the frame. Wide-angle close-up shots have impact.

Limit people shots to head and shoulders, unless you have very wide-angle lenses. For smaller creatures use macro lenses, close-up kits or extension tubes with framers.

Wherever possible do not aim the camera down, but aim it horizontally or, better still, upwards; otherwise the background in the picture will be dark.

Digital & optical zoom

Digital zoom is electronic enlargement of the image coupled with cropping to emulate 'zooming in' closer with the lens. In reality, all that is being done is enlargement of the pixels. An optical zoom 'brings the subject closer' optically before recording the image on the sensor – giving better resolution and a higher-quality result.

Image capture, noise, temperature, ISO (International Standards Organization) speeds and white balance

Noise is the visible effect of electronic interference, and usually appears as coloured lines across the image. Two of the major causes are temperature and ISO sensitivity where, in both cases, high equals worse and low equals better. Try not to let the camera get hot, and try to use slower ISO speeds such as 100.

All digital cameras, including video cameras, have an automatic white-balance setting that enables the camera to calculate the correct colour balance for the image. Some have pre-set values for different types of lighting, either by colour temperature on professional models or such settings as sunny, cloudy, incandescent or fluorescent lighting on amateur models. For underwater use some divers use the 'cloudy' setting, or you may have to experiment with 'manual', using a white plastic card as the subject. Some divers use the RAW image format for the freedom of adjusting the white balance setting after the dive.

Flash with digital cameras

Most but not all digital cameras are incompatible with normal TTL flash guns, as they cannot read the flash reflected off film. This is addressed with either a light sensor on the camera body to judge proper exposure or with special flash guns for different digital cameras, many of which send out several pre-flashes and read their intensity when they are reflected back from the subject (DTTL). You can still use manual flash, shoot the picture, review the picture, make any necessary adjustments and reshoot the picture, but this takes time and the subject may have moved. You can delete any shots that were not correctly exposed. One answer to TTL flash problems for underwater photography is to house a land flash gun that is dedicated to your digital camera. The problem with this method is that the land flash guns will not cover the field of view of very wide-angle lenses, though they are fine for close shots. A second is that independent manufacturers of wide-angle under-water flash guns now have models featuring special electronic circuitry for use with the newest digital cameras, yet they are still compatible with the popular film cameras used underwater, including the Nikonos. A third solution is that the Fuji S2 Pro digital camera will work with all standard Nikonos-compatible underwater flash guns. Due to this and the fact that it is based on the Nikon F80/N80 camera body and utilizes Nikkor lenses, this camera has become popular for use in a waterproof housing.

Shutter lag

Most cheaper digital cameras suffer from a time lag between pressing the shutter release and the shutter actually firing, as the camera has to change mode and write to memory or the storage media. Therefore, if you are aiming for an expression on a face or a moving fish, it can be lost by the time the shutter fires. More expensive cameras speed things up by saving to a buffer.

Dust on sensors

Where digital cameras have interchangeable lenses, tiny bits of dust and lint are attracted to the sensor due to static charge on the sensor. Keep the sensor clean of dust.

Image storage

At higher definition settings, underwater photographers will need a large-capacity memory card to hold a reasonable number of images before they have to return to the surface to download them.

Another problem is storage and accessibility. Those who store negatives or transparencies in transparent viewpacks can view 36 frames of film by eye and know what is there very quickly. Viewing them on a computer is nowhere near as fast, and if you are not sure where a particular image is stored, finding it can be a slow business. There is also a problem with hard disk storage space: a 40Gb hard drive is soon full and one has to resort to saving images onto CDs.

Digital cameras and their batteries

Some digital cameras consume their battery power very quickly. There are two types of camera: those that accept standard AA-size batteries and those that use a rechargeable proprietary battery.

AA-compatible cameras usually ship with disposable alkaline batteries. These make acceptable emergency backups, but rechargeable Nickel Metal Hydride (NiMH) batteries offer much better performance and longer life.

UNDERWATER VIDEOGRAPHY

Underwater video is much easier than still photography, and the fact that the subject moves often covers mistakes. Most underwater videographers just set the camera on automatic, place it in a waterproof housing and go. Macro subjects may require extra lighting, but other shots can be taken with available light and if necessary improved electronically afterwards. Back scatter is less of a problem and the results can be played back on site and reshot if necessary, or the tape or disc can wiped clean and reused.

More expensive or professional cameras have more controls, and professional cameras have three chips: three CCD or CMOS sensors each receiving the image through a coloured filter: one filter is red, one green and one blue.

When purchasing a waterproof housing you have the choice of electronic or manual controls. Electronic controls can be easier to use, and with fewer holes in the housing there is less chance of leakage. Some divers prefer manual controls because if something goes awry with electronic controls when you are stranded on a live-aboard boat out-to-sea, the whole housing can become unusable.

Most videographers are happy with videoing for their own pleasure. There are underwater colour-correction filters for use without lights, but if you want more professional results you will require proper lights. You must work out a story-line and follow it, keep the camera steady, use the zoom sparingly, build sequences and keep each shot short unless the subject is particularly interesting. Ideally, for most subjects you would begin with a wide-angle shot to set the scene, then take a medium shot and then move in for a close shot. When visibility is poor, video macro subjects. When videoing a night scene, your normal lights will make it look as though it was shot during the day unless you have lights that can be dimmed.

Most video cameras have dedicated battery packs, so carry at least one spare and keep it charged.

Health and Safety for Divers

The information on first aid and safety in this part of the book is intended as a guide only. It is based on currently accepted health and safety guidelines, but it is merely a summary and is no substitute for a comprehensive manual on the subject – or, even better, for first aid training. We strongly advise you to buy a recognized manual on diving safety and medicine before setting off on a diving trip, to read it through during the journey, and to carry it with you to refer to during the trip. It would also be sensible to take a short course in first aid.

We urge anyone in need of advice on emergency treatment to see a doctor as soon as possible.

WHAT TO DO IN AN EMERGENCY

- Divers who have suffered any injury or symptom of an injury, no matter how minor, related to diving, should consult a doctor – preferably a specialist in diving medicine – as soon as possible after the symptom or injury occurs.
- No matter how confident you are in making a diagnosis, remember that you are an amateur diver and an unqualified medical practitioner.
- If you are the victim of a diving injury, do not let fear of ridicule prevent you from revealing your symptoms. Apparently minor symptoms can mask, or even develop into, a life-threatening illness. It is better to be honest

with yourself and live to dive another day.

- Always err on the conservative side when treating an illness or an injury. If you find that the condition is only minor you – and the doctor – will both be relieved.

FIRST AID

The basic principles of first aid are to:

- do no harm
- sustain life
- prevent deterioration
- promote recovery.

If you have to treat an ill or injured person:

- First try to secure the safety of yourself and the ill or injured person by getting the two of you out of the threatening environment: the water.
- Think before you act: do not do anything that will further endanger either of you.
- Then follow a simple sequence of patient assessment and management:
  1 Assess whether you are dealing with a life-threatening condition.
  2 If so, try to define which one.
  3 Then try to manage the condition

Assessing the ABCs:

Learn the basic checks – the ABCs:
A: for AIRWAY (with care of the neck)
B : for BREATHING
C: for CIRCULATION
D: for DECREASED level of consciousness
E: for EXPOSURE (a patient must be exposed enough for a proper examination to be made)

- **Airway (with attention to the neck):** check whether the patient has a neck injury. Are the mouth and nose free from obstruction? Noisy breathing is a sign of airway obstruction.
- **Breathing:** look at the chest to see if it is rising and falling. Listen for air movement at the nose and mouth. Feel for the movement of air against your cheek.
- **Circulation:** feel for a pulse (the carotid artery) next to the windpipe.
- **Decreased level of consciousness:** does the patient respond in any of the following ways?
  A - Awake, aware, spontaneous speech.
  V - Verbal stimuli: does he or she answer to 'Wake up'?
  P - Painful stimuli: does he or she respond to a pinch?
  U - Unresponsive.
- **Exposure:** preserve the dignity of the patient as much as you can, but remove clothes as necessary to carry out your treatment.

Now, send for help

If, after your assessment, you think the condition of the patient is serious, you must send or call for help from the nearest emergency services (ambulance, paramedics). Tell whoever you send for help to come back and let you know whether help is on the way.

Recovery position

If the patient is unconscious but breathing normally there is a risk that he or he she may vomit and choke on the vomit. It is therefore critical that the patient be turned on one side into the recovery position. This is illustrated in all first aid manuals.

If you suspect injury to the spine or neck, immobilize the patient in a straight line before you turn him or her on one side.

If the patient is unconscious, does not seem to be breathing, and you cannot feel a pulse, do not try to turn him or her into the recovery position.

Do **NOT** give fluids to unconscious or semi-conscious divers.

If you cannot feel a pulse

If your patient has no pulse you will have to carry out CPR (cardiopulmonary resuscitation). This consists of techniques to:

- ventilate the patient's lungs (expired air resuscitation)
- pump the patient's heart (external cardiac compression).

CPR (cardiopulmonary resuscitation)

Airway

Open the patient's airway by gently extending the head (head tilt) and lifting the chin with two fingers (chin lift). This lifts the patient's tongue away from the back of the throat and opens the airway. If the patient is unconscious and you think something may be blocking the airway, sweep your finger across the back of the tongue from one side to the other. If you find anything, remove it. Do not try this if the patient is conscious or semi-conscious because he or she may bite your finger or vomit.

Breathing: EAR (expired air resuscitation)

If the patient is not breathing you need to give the 'kiss of life', or expired air resuscitation (EAR) – you breathe into his or her lungs. The percentage of oxygen in the air you expire is enough to keep your patient alive.

1 Pinch the patient's nose to close the nostrils.
2 Place your open mouth fully over the patient's mouth, making as good a seal as possible.
3 Exhale into the mouth hard enough to make the chest rise and fall. Give two breaths, each over 1 second.
4 If the patient's chest fails to rise, try adjusting the position of the airway.
5 Check the patient's pulse. If you cannot feel one, follow the instructions under 'Circulation' below. If you can, continue breathing for the patient once every five seconds, checking the pulse after every ten breaths.

- If the patient begins breathing, turn him or her into the recovery position (see above).

Circulation

If, after giving expired air resuscitation, you cannot feel a pulse, you should try external cardiac compression:

1 Kneel next to the patient's chest.

2 Place your hands in the centre of the chest, rather than spend time positioning them using other methods.
3 Place the heel of your left hand just above your two fingers in the centre of the breast bone.
4 Place the heel of your right hand on your left hand.
5 Straighten your elbows.
6 Place your shoulders perpendicularly above the patient's breast bone.
7 Compress the breast bone 4–5cm (1½–2in) to a rhythm of 'one, two, three . . .'
8 Carry out 30 compressions.

Continue giving cycles of 2 breaths and 30 compressions, checking for a pulse after every 5 cycles. Carry on using a ratio of compressions to rescue breaths of 30:2 for all casualties.

Check before you dive that you and your buddy are both trained in CPR. If not, get some training – it could mean the difference between life and death for either of you or for someone else.

TRAVELLING MEDICINE

Many doctors decline to issue drugs, particularly antibiotics, to people who want them 'just in case'; but a diving holiday can be ruined by an otherwise trivial ear or sinus infection, especially in a remote area or on a live-aboard boat, where the nearest doctor or pharmacy is a long and difficult journey away.

Many travelling divers therefore carry with them medical kits that could lead the uninitiated to think they were hypochondriacs. Nasal sprays, eardrops, antihistamine creams, anti-diarrhoea medicines, antibiotics, seasickness remedies ... Forearmed, such divers can take immediate action as soon as they realize something is wrong. At the very least, this may minimize their loss of diving time.

Remember that most decongestants and seasickness remedies can make you drowsy and should not be taken before diving.

DIVING DISEASES AND ILLNESSES

Acute decompression illness

Acute decompression illness is any illness arising from the decompression of a diver, that is, by the diver moving from an area of high ambient pressure to an area of low pressure. There are two types of acute decompression illness:

- decompression sickness (the bends)
- barotrauma with arterial gas embolism

It is not important for the diver or first aider to be able to differentiate between the two conditions because both are serious, life-threatening illnesses, and both require the same emergency treatment. The important thing is to be able to recognize acute decompression illness and to initiate emergency treatment. The box on page 167 outlines the signs and symptoms to look out for.

The bends (decompression sickness)

Decompression sickness or the bends occurs when a diver has not been adequately decompressed. Exposure to higher ambient pressure underwater causes nitrogen to dissolve in increasing amounts in the body tissues. If this pressure is released gradually during correct and adequate decompression procedures, the nitrogen escapes naturally into the blood and is exhaled through the lungs. If the release of pressure is too rapid, the nitrogen cannot escape quickly enough and bubbles of nitrogen gas form in the tissues. The symptoms and signs of the disease are related to the tissues in which the bubbles form and it is described by the tissues affected, for example, joint bend.

Symptoms and signs include:

- nausea and vomiting
- dizziness
- malaise
- weakness
- pains in the joints
- paralysis
- numbness
- itching of skin
- incontinence.

Barotrauma with arterial gas embolism

Barotrauma is the damage that occurs when the tissue surrounding a gaseous space is injured following a change in the volume of air in that space. An arterial gas embolism is a gas bubble that moves in a blood vessel; this usually leads to the obstruction of that blood vessel or a vessel further downstream.

Barotrauma can occur in any tissue surrounding a gas-filled space. Common sites and types of barotrauma are:

- ears (middle ear squeeze) → burst ear drum
- sinuses (sinus squeeze) → sinus pain/nose bleeds
- lungs (lung squeeze) → burst lung
- face (mask squeeze) → swollen, bloodshot eyes
- teeth (tooth squeeze) → toothache.

Burst lung is the most serious of these since it can result in arterial gas embolism. It occurs following a rapid ascent during which the diver does not exhale adequately. The rising pressure of expanding air in the lungs bursts the delicate alveoli – air sacs in the lungs – and forces air into the blood vessels that carry blood back to the heart and, ultimately, the brain. In the brain these air bubbles block blood vessels and obstruct the supply of blood and oxygen to the brain. This causes brain damage.

The symptoms and signs of lung barotrauma and arterial gas embolism include:

- shortness of breath
- chest pain
- unconsciousness.

Treatment of acute decompression Illness:

- ABCs and CPR (see pages 165-6) as necessary
- position the patient in the recovery position (see page 165) with no tilt or raising of the legs
- give 100 per cent oxygen by mask or demand valve
- keep the patient warm
- remove to the nearest hospital as soon as possible – the hospital or emergency services will arrange for recompression treatment.

ROUGH AND READY NONSPECIALIST TESTS FOR THE BENDS

A Does the diver know:
who he or she is?
where he or she is?
what the time is?

B Can the diver see and count the number of fingers you hold up?
Place your hand 50cm (20in) in front of the diver's face and ask him/her to follow your hand with his/her eyes as you move it from side to side and up and down. Be sure that both eyes follow in each direction, and look out for any rapid oscillation or jerky movements of the eyeballs.

C Ask the diver to smile, and check that both sides of the face bear the same expression. Run the back of a finger across each side of the diver's forehead, cheeks and chin, and confirm that the diver feels it.

D Check that the diver can hear you whisper when the eyes are closed.

E Ask the diver to shrug his/her shoulders. Both sides should move equally.

F Ask the diver to swallow. Check the Adam's apple moves up and down.

G Ask the diver to stick out the tongue at the centre of the mouth – deviation to either side indicates a problem.

H Check there is equal muscle strength on both sides of the body. You do this by pulling/pushing each of the diver's arms and legs away from and back towards the body, asking him/her to resist you.

I Run your finger lightly across the diver's shoulders, down the back, across the chest and abdomen, and along the arms and legs, both upper and lower and inside and out, and check the diver can feel this all the time.

J On firm ground (not on a boat) check the diver can walk in a straight line and, with eyes closed, stand upright with his/her feet together and arms outstretched.

If the results of any of these checks do not appear normal, the diver may be suffering from the bends, so take appropriate action (see previous page).

Carbon dioxide and carbon monoxide poisoning

Carbon dioxide poisoning can occur as a result of skip breathing (diver holds breath on SCUBA), heavy exercise on SCUBA or malfunctioning rebreather systems. Carbon monoxide poisoning occurs as a result of exhaust gases being pumped into cylinders or hookah systems due to the compressor air intake being downwind of exhaust fumes.

Symptoms and signs of carbon monoxide poisoning include:

- blue colour of the skin
- shortness of breath
- loss of consciousness

Treatment of carbon monoxide poisoning:

- get the patient to a safe environment
- ABCs and CPR (see pages 165-6) as necessary
- 100 per cent oxygen through a mask or demand valve
- get the patient to hospital

Head injury

Any head injury should be treated as serious.

Treatment:

- the diver must surface and do no more diving until a doctor has been consulted
- disinfect the wound
- if the diver is unconscious, contact the emergency services
- if breathing and/or pulse have stopped, administer CPR (see page 165)
- if the diver is breathing and has a pulse, check for bleeding and other injuries, and treat for shock (see page 168)
- if the wounds permit, put the injured person into the recovery position and, if possible, give 100 per cent oxygen
- keep the patient warm and comfortable and monitor pulse and respiration constantly

Hyperthermia (raised body temperature)

A rise in body temperature results from a combination of overheating, normally due to exercise, and inadequate fluid intake. A person with hyperthermia will progress through heat exhaustion to heat stroke, with eventual collapse. Heat stroke is an emergency: if the diver is not cooled and rehydrated he or she will die.

Treatment:

- move the diver as quickly as possible into a cooler place and remove all clothes
- call the emergency services
- sponge the diver's body with a damp cloth and fan him or her manually or with an electric fan
- if the patient is unconscious, put him or her into the recovery position (see page 165) and monitor the ABCs as necessary
- if the patient is conscious you can give him or her a cold drink.

Hypothermia (low body temperature)

Normal internal body temperature is just under 37°C (98.4°F). If for any reason it falls much below this – usually, in diving, because of inadequate protective clothing – progressively more serious symptoms may follow, and the person will eventually die if the condition is not treated rapidly. A drop of 1C° (2F°) causes shivering and discomfort. A 2C° (3F°) drop induces the body's self-heating mechanisms to react: blood flow to the hands and feet is reduced and shivering becomes extreme. A 3C° (5F°) drop results in memory loss, confusion, disorientation, irregular heartbeat and breathing and eventually death.

Treatment:

- move the diver as quickly as possible into a sheltered and warm place; *or:*
- prevent further heat loss: use an exposure bag; surround the diver with buddies' bodies; cover his or her

head and neck with a woolly hat, warm towels or anything else suitable
- if you have managed to get the diver into sheltered warmth, remove wet clothing, dress your patient in warm, dry clothing and wrap him or her in an exposure bag or blanket; however, if you are still in the open, the diver is best left in existing garments
- if the diver is conscious and coherent administer a warm shower or bath and a warm, sweet drink
- if the diver is unconscious, check the ABCs (see page 165), call the emergency services, make the patient as warm as possible, and treat for shock (see below).

Near-drowning

Near-drowning is a medical condition in which a diver has inhaled some water – water in the lungs interferes with the normal transport of oxygen from the lungs into the bloodstream. A person in a near-drowning condition may be conscious or unconscious.

Near-drowning victims sometimes develop secondary drowning, a condition in which fluid oozing into the lungs causes the diver to drown in internal secretions, so all near-drowning patients must be monitored in a hospital.
Treatment:
- get the diver out of the water and check the ABCs (see page 165); depending on your findings, begin EAR or CPR (see pages 165–6) as appropriate
- if possible, administer oxygen by mask or demand valve
- call the emergency services and get the diver to a hospital for observation, even if he/she appears to have recovered from the experience

Nitrogen narcosis

Air contains about 80 per cent nitrogen. Breathing the standard diving mixture under compression can lead to symptoms very much like those of drunkenness (nitrogen narcosis is popularly known as 'rapture of the deep'). Some divers experience nitrogen narcosis at depths of 30–40m (100–130ft). Down to a depth of about 60m (200ft) – which is beyond the legal maximum depth for sport-diving in the UK and the USA – the symptoms are not always serious; but below about 80m (260ft) a diver is likely to lose consciousness. Symptoms can occur very suddenly. Nitrogen narcosis is not a serious condition, but a diver suffering from it may do something dangerous.
Treatment: the only treatment for this condition is to get the diver to ascend immediately to shallower waters.

Shock

Shock is a medical condition and not just the emotional trauma of a frightening experience. Medical shock results from poor blood and oxygen delivery to the tissues. As a result of oxygen and blood deprivation the tissues cannot carry out their functions. There are many causes; the most common is loss of blood.

Treatment:
This is directed at restoring blood and oxygen delivery to the tissues:
- check the ABCs (see page 165)
- give 100 per cent oxygen
- control any external bleeding by pressing hard on the wound and/or pressure points (the location of the pressure points is illustrated in first-aid manuals); raise the injured limb or other part of the body
- use a tourniquet only as a last resort and only on the arms and legs
- if the diver is conscious, lay him/her on the back with the legs raised and the head to one side; if unconscious, turn him or her on the left side in the recovery position (see page 165).

MARINE-RELATED AILMENTS

Sunburn, coral cuts, fire-coral stings, swimmers' ear, seasickness and bites from various insects are perhaps the most common divers' complaints – but there are more serious marine-related illnesses you should know about.

Cuts and abrasions

Divers should wear appropriate abrasive protection for the undersea environment. Hands, knees, elbows and feet are the areas most commonly affected. The danger with abrasions is that they become infected, so all wounds must be thoroughly washed and rinsed with freshwater and an antiseptic as soon as possible after the injury. Infection may progress to a stage where antibiotics are necessary. If the site of an apparently minor injury becomes inflamed, and the inflammation spreads, consult a doctor immediately – you may need antibiotics to prevent the infection spreading to the bloodstream.

Swimmers' ear

Swimmers' ear is an infection of the external ear canal caused by constantly wet ears. The condition is often a combined fungal and bacterial infection. To prevent it, always dry your ears thoroughly after diving. If you know you are susceptible to the condition, insert drops to dry out the ear after diving. If an infection occurs, the best treatment is to stop diving or swimming for a few days and apply ear drops such as:
- 5 per cent acetic acid in isopropyl alcohol; *or*
- aluminium acetate/acetic acid solution

Sea or motion sickness

Motion sickness can be an annoying complication on a diving holiday involving boat dives. If you suffer from motion sickness, discuss the problem with a doctor before your holiday – or at least before boarding the boat. But bear in mind that many medicines formulated to prevent travel sickness contain antihistamines, which make you drowsy and will impair your ability to think quickly while you are diving.

FIRST-AID KIT

Your first-aid kit should be waterproof, compartmentalized and sealable, and, as a minimum, should contain:

- a full first-aid manual – the information in this appendix is for general guidance only
- contact numbers for the emergency services
- coins for telephone
- pencil and notebook
- tweezers
- scissors
- 6 large standard sterile dressings
- 1 large Elastoplast/Band-Aid fabric dressing strip
- 2 triangular bandages
- 3 medium-size safety pins
- 1 pack sterile cotton wool
- 2 50mm (2in) crepe bandages
- eyedrops
- antiseptic fluid/cream
- bottle of vinegar
- sachets of rehydration salts
- seasickness tablets
- decongestants
- painkillers
- anti-AIDS pack (syringes/needles/drip needle)

Biting insects

To regions notorious for biting insects take a good insect repellent, and antihistamine cream to relieve the effects.

Sunburn

Take plenty of precautions against sunburn, which can cause skin cancer. Pay particular attention to the head, the nose and the backs of the legs. Always use high-protection factor creams, and cover up as much as possible.

Tropical diseases

Visit the doctor before your trip to make sure you have the appropriate vaccinations for the regions you intend to visit.

Fish that bite

- **Barracuda** These very rarely bite divers, although they have been known to bite in turbid or murky, shallow water, where sunlight flashing on a knife blade, a camera lens or jewellery has confused the fish into thinking they are attacking their normal prey.
  Treatment: clean the wounds thoroughly and use antiseptic or antibiotic cream. Bad bites will also need antibiotic and anti-tetanus treatment.

- **Moray eels** Probably more divers are bitten by morays than by all other sea creatures added together – usually through putting their hands into holes to collect shells or lobsters, remove anchors, or hide baitfish. Once it bites, a moray often refuses to let go, so you may have to persuade it to by gripping it behind the head and exerting pressure with your finger and thumb until it opens its jaw. You can make the wound worse by tearing your flesh if you pull the fish off.
  Treatment: thorough cleaning and usually stitching. The bites always go septic, so have antibiotics and anti-tetanus available.

- **Sharks** Sharks rarely attack divers, but should always be treated with great respect. Their attacks are usually connected with speared or hooked fish, fish or meat set up as bait, lobsters rattling when picked up, or certain types of vibration, such as that produced by helicopters. The decomposition products of dead fish (even several days old) seem much more attractive to most sharks than fresh blood. Grey reef sharks can be territorial. They often warn of an attack by arching their backs and pointing their pectoral fins downward. Other sharks often give warning by bumping into you first. If you are frightened, a shark will detect this from the vibrations given off by your body. Calmly back up to the reef or boat and get out of the water.
  Treatment: a person who has been bitten by a shark usually has severe injuries and is suffering from shock. If possible, stop any bleeding by applying pressure. The patient will need to be stabilized with blood or plasma transfusions before being moved to hospital. Even minor wounds are likely to become infected, so the diver will need antibiotic and anti-tetanus treatment.

- **Triggerfish** Large triggerfish – usually males guarding eggs in 'nests' – are aggressive and will attack divers who get too close. Their teeth can go through rubber fins and draw blood through a 4mm (1/6in) wet suit.
  Treatment: clean the wound and treat it with antiseptic cream.

Venomous sea creatures

Many venomous sea creatures are bottom dwellers – they hide among coral or rest on or burrow into sand. If you need to move along the sea bottom, shuffle along, so that you push such creatures out of the way and minimize the risk of stepping directly onto sharp venomous spines, many of which can pierce rubber fins. Antivenins require specialist medical supervision, do not work for all species, and need refrigerated storage, so they are rarely available when they are needed. Most of the venoms are proteins of high molecular weight that break down under heat.
General treatment: tie a broad bandage at a point between the limb and the body and tighten it. Remember to release it every 15 minutes. Immerse the limb in hot water (perhaps the cooling water from an outboard motor if no other supply is available) at 50°C (120°F) for two hours, until the pain stops. Several injections around the wound of local anaesthetic (such as procaine hydrochloride), if available, will ease the pain. Young or weak people may need CPR (see pages 165–6). Remember that venoms may still be active in fish that have been dead for 48 hours.

- **Cone shells** Live cone shells should never be handled without gloves: the animal has a mobile, tubelike organ that shoots a poison dart. This causes numbness at first, followed by local muscular paralysis, which may extend to respiratory paralysis and heart failure.
  Treatment: tie a bandage between the wound and the body, tighten it, and release it every 15 minutes. CPR (see pages 165–6) may be necessary.

- **Fire coral** Corals of the genus *Millepora* are not true corals but members of the class Hydrozoa – i.e., they are more closely related to the stinging hydroids. Many people react violently from the slightest brush with them – producing blisters sometimes as large as 15cm (6in) across, which can last for as long as several weeks.
  Treatment: bathe the affected part in methylated spirit or vinegar (acetic acid). Local anaesthetic may be required to ease the pain, though antihistamine cream is usually enough.

- **Fireworms** These white-haired worms display bristles when touched. These easily break off in the skin, causing a burning feeling and intense irritation.
  Treatment: bathe the affected part in methylated spirit, vinegar (acetic acid) or hot water.

- **Jellyfish** Most jellyfish sting, but few are dangerous. When seasonal changes are favourable you can encounter the Portuguese man-of-war (*Physalia physalis*). These creatures are highly toxic and continued exposure to the stinging cells may require hospital treatment. Sea wasps (*Carybdea alata*) can be found in shallow warm water at night and are attracted to light. These creatures often swarm and stings can be severe, causing muscle cramps, nausea and breathing difficulties. Whenever the conditions are favourable for thimble jellyfish (*Linuche unguiculata*), there is always the chance of much smaller and almost invisible micro-organisms in the water column. Wear protection such as a wet suit or a Lycra skin suit.
  Treatment: in the event of a sting, pour acetic acid (vinegar) over both animal and wounds and then to remove the animal with forceps or gloves. CPR (see pages 165–6) may be required.

- **Scorpionfish** These are not considered dangerous in Caribbean waters, but care should always be taken of the spines on top of their dorsal fin.
  Treatment: inadvertent stinging can be treated by bathing the affected body part in very hot water.

- **Sea urchins** The spines of some sea urchins are poisonous and all sea urchin spines can puncture the skin, even through gloves, and break off, leaving painful wounds that often go septic.
  Treatment: for bad cases bathe the affected part of the body in very hot water. This softens the spines, making it easier for the body to reject them. Soothing creams or a magnesium sulphate compress will reduce the pain, as will the application of the flesh of papaya fruit. Septic wounds need to be treated with antibiotics.

- **Stinging hydroids** Stinging hydroids often go unnoticed on wrecks, old anchor ropes and chains until you put your hand on them, when their nematocysts are fired into your skin. The wounds are not serious but they are very painful, and large blisters can be raised on sensitive skin, which can last for some time.
  Treatment: bathe the affected part in methylated spirit or vinegar (acetic acid). Local anaesthetic may be required to ease the pain, though antihistamine cream is usually enough.

- **Stinging plankton** You cannot see stinging plankton, and so cannot take evasive measures. If there are reports of any in the area, keep as much of your body covered as you can.
  Treatment: bathe the affected part in methylated spirit or vinegar (acetic acid). Local anaesthetic may be required to ease the pain, though antihistamine cream is usually enough.

- **Stingrays** Stingrays vary in size from a few centimetres to several metres across. The sting consists of one or more spines on top of the tail; although these point backward they can sting in any direction. The rays thrash out and sting when they are trodden on or caught. Wounds may be large and severely lacerated. Large stingrays have barbs that can pierce the heart. It is essential to control bleeding by leaving them in position until the victim reaches specialist medical help.
  Treatment: clean the wound and remove any spines. Bathe or immerse in very hot water and apply a local anaesthetic if one is available; follow up with antibiotics and anti-tetanus.

Cuts

Underwater cuts and scrapes, especially those caused by coral, barnacles and sharp metal, will usually, if they are not cleaned out and treated quickly, go septic; absorption of the resulting poisons into the body can cause more serious medical conditions.

After every dive, clean and disinfect any wounds, no matter how small. Larger wounds will often refuse to heal unless you stay out of seawater for a couple of days. Surgeonfish have sharp fins on each side of the caudal peduncle; they use these when lashing out at other fish with a sweep of the tail, and they occasionally use them to defend their territory against a trespassing diver. Their 'scalpels' may be covered in toxic mucus, so wounds must be cleaned and treated with antibiotic cream.

As a preventive measure against cuts in general, the golden rule on the reef is: do not touch. Be sure to learn good buoyancy control so that you can avoid touching anything unnecessarily – never forget for an instant that every area of the coral you touch will inevitably be killed.

Brosnahan, Tom, et al.: *Middle East on a Shoestring;* (1994), Lonely Planet Publications, London, UK

Johnson, R.H.: *Sharks of Tropical and Temperate Seas* (1992), Les Editions du Pacifique, Singapore

Lieske, Ewald and Robert Myers: *Coral Reef Fishes* (1994), Collins, London, UK

Paice, Edward: *Guide to Eritrea* (1994), Bradt, Chalfont-St.-Peter, UK

Randall, Dr. John: *Red Sea Reef Fishes* (1983), Immell Publishing Ltd., London, UK

Richardson, Dan and Karen O'Brien: *Egypt, The Rough Guide* (1993), Rough Guides Ltd., London, UK

Simonis, Damien and Hugh Finlay: *Jordan & Syria, A Travel Survival Kit* (1993), Lonely Planet Publications, London, UK

Vine, Dr. Peter: *Red Sea Invertebrates* (1986), Immel Publishing Ltd., London, UK

Vine, Dr. Peter and Hagen Schmid: *Red Sea Explorers* (1987), Immel Publishing Ltd., London, UK

Wayne, Scott and Damien Simonis: *Egypt & The Sudan, A Travel Survival Kit;* (1994), Lonely Planet Publications, London, UK

Woods, Dr. Elizabeth: *Corals of the World:* (1983), T.F.H. Publications, Neptune City, New Jersey, USA

Index